WEST-E History

027

Teacher Certification Exam

By: Sharon Wynne, M.S.
Southern Connecticut State University

"And, while there's no reason yet to panic, I think it's only prudent that we make preparations to panic."

XAMonline, INC.

Boston

XAMonline, Inc.
25 First St. Suite 106
Cambridge, MA 02141
Toll Free 1-800-509-4128
Email: info@xamonline.com
Web www.xamonline.com
Fax: 1-781-662-9268

Library of Congress Cataloging-in-Publication Data

Wynne, Sharon A.
    History: Teacher Certification / Sharon A. Wynne. 1ˢᵗ ed.
    ISBN 978-1-60787-141-5
    1. History 027   2. Study Guides.   3. WEST
    4. Teachers' Certification & Licensure.   5. Careers

Contributing Editor: Robin E. Connors, Ph.D.

Disclaimer:
The opinions expressed in this publication are the sole works of XAMonline and were created independently from the National Education Association, Educational Testing Service, or any State Department of Education, National Evaluation Systems or other testing affiliates.

Between the time of publication and printing, state specific standards as well as testing formats and website information may change that is not included in part or in whole within this product. Sample test questions are developed by XAMonline and reflect similar content as on real tests; however, they are not former tests. XAMonline assembles content that aligns with state standards but makes no claims nor guarantees teacher candidates a passing score. Numerical scores are determined by testing companies such as NES or ETS and then are compared with individual state standards. A passing score varies from state to state.

Printed in the United States of America

WEST-E History 027
ISBN: 978-1-60787-141-5

TABLE OF CONTENTS

DOMAIN II   WORLD HISTORY

DOMAIN III   SOCIAL STUDIES CONCEPTS AND SKILLS

Great Study and Testing Tips!

What to study in order to prepare for the subject assessments is the focus of this study guide but equally important is *how* you study.

You can increase your chances of truly mastering the information by taking some simple yet effective steps.

Study Tips:

1. <u>Some foods aid the learning process</u>.

Foods such as milk, nuts, seeds, rice, and oats help your study efforts by releasing natural memory enhancers called CCKs (*cholecystokinin*) composed of *tryptophan*, *choline* and *phenylalanine*. All of these chemicals enhance the neurotransmitters associated with memory.

Before studying, try a light, protein-rich meal of eggs, turkey or fish. All of these foods release memory-enhancing chemicals. The better the connections in your brain, the more you comprehend. Likewise, before you take a test, stick to a light snack of energy-boosting and relaxing foods. A glass of milk, a piece of fruit, or some peanuts all contain CCKs and help you to relax and focus on the subject at hand.

2. <u>Learn to take great notes</u>.
We learn best when information is organized. When it has a logical structure and we can see relationships between pieces of information helps us assimilate new information.

If your notes are scrawled all over the paper, it fragments the flow of the information. Instead, strive for clarity. Newspapers, for example, use a standard format to achieve clarity. Your notes can be much clearer through use of proper formatting. A very effective format is called the *"Cornell Method."*

> Take a sheet of loose-leaf lined notebook paper and draw a line all the way down the paper about 1-2" from the left-hand edge.

> Draw another line across the width of the paper about 1-2" up from the bottom. Repeat this process on the reverse side of the page.

Look at the highly effective result. You have ample room for notes, a left hand margin for special emphasis items or inserting supplementary data from the textbook, a large area at the bottom for a brief summary, and a little rectangular space for just about anything you want.

3. <u>Get the concept and then the details.</u>

Too often we focus on the details and don't grasp an understanding of the concept. However, if you simply memorize only dates, places, or names, you may well miss the whole point of the subject.

A key way to understand things is to put them in your own words. If you are working from a textbook, automatically summarize each paragraph in your mind. If you are outlining text, don't simply copy the author's words.

Rephrase them in your own words. You remember your own thoughts and words much better than someone else's, and will subconsciously tend to associate the important details to the core concepts.

4. <u>Ask why.</u>

Pull apart written material paragraph by paragraph – and don't forget the captions under the illustrations.

If you train your mind to think in a series of questions and answers, not only will you learn more, but you will also have less test anxiety because you are used to answering questions.

Example: If the heading is "Stream Erosion", flip it around to read "Why do streams erode?" Then answer the questions.

5. <u>Read for reinforcement and future needs.</u>

Even if you only have 10 minutes, put your notes or a book in your hand. Your mind is similar to a computer; you have to input data in order to have it processed. *By reading, you are creating the neural connections for future retrieval.* The more times you read something, the more you reinforce the learning of ideas.

Even if you don't fully understand something on the first pass, *your mind stores much of the material for later recall.*

6. <u>Relax to learn: in other words, go into exile.</u>

Our bodies respond to an inner clock called biorhythms. Burning the midnight oil works well for some people, but not others.

If possible, set aside a particular place to study that is free of distractions. Shut off the television, cell phone and pager, and exile your friends and family during your study period.

If you really are bothered by silence, try background music. Light classical music at a low volume has been shown to aid in concentration over other types of music. Music that evokes pleasant emotions without lyrics is highly suggested. Try just about anything by Mozart. It can relax you.

7. <u>Use arrows not highlighters.</u>

At best, it's difficult to read a page full of yellow, pink, blue, and green streaks. Try staring at a neon sign for a while and you'll soon see that the horde of colors obscures the message.

A quick note, a brief dash of color, an underline or an arrow pointing to a particular passage is much clearer than a cascade of highlighted words.

8. <u>Budget your study time.</u>

Although you shouldn't ignore any of the material, ***allocate your available study time in the same ratio that topics may appear on the test.*** In other words, focus on the areas that are most likely to be included in the test.

Testing Tips:

1. Get smart by playing dumb. Don't read anything into the question.

Don't make an assumption that the test writer is looking for something other than what is asked. Stick to the question as written and don't read anything into it.

2. Read the question and all the choices *twice* before answering the question.

You may miss something by not carefully reading, and then re-reading both the question and the answers.

If you really don't have a clue as to the right answer, leave it blank on the first time through. Go on to the other questions, as they may provide a clue as to how to answer the skipped questions.

If later on, you still can't answer the skipped ones . . . *Guess.* The only penalty for guessing is that you *might* get it wrong. One thing is certain; if you don't put anything down, you will get it wrong!

3. Turn the question into a statement.

Look at the way the questions are worded. The syntax of the question usually provides a clue. Does it seem more familiar as a statement rather than as a question? Does it sound strange?

By turning a question into a statement, you may be able to spot if an answer sounds right, and it may also trigger memories of material you have read.

4. Look for hidden clues.

It's actually very difficult to compose multiple-foil (choice) questions without giving away part of the answer in the options presented.

In most multiple-choice questions, you can often readily eliminate one or two of the potential answers. This leaves you with only two real possibilities and automatically your odds go to fifty-fifty with very little work.

5. <u>Trust your instincts</u>.

For every fact you have read, you subconsciously retain something of that knowledge. On questions that you aren't really certain about, go with your basic instincts. **Your first impression on how to answer a question is usually correct.**

6. <u>Mark your answers directly on the test booklet</u>.

Don't bother trying to fill in the optical scan sheet on the first pass through the test. *Just be very careful not to miss-mark your answers when you eventually transcribe them to the scan sheet.*

7. <u>Watch the clock</u>!

You have a set amount of time to answer the questions. Don't get bogged down trying to answer a single question at the expense of 10 questions you can answer more readily.

DOMAIN I   **U.S. HISTORY**

COMPETENCY 0001   **UNDERSTAND MAJOR DEVELOPMENTS IN EARLY U.S. HISTORY FROM PRE-CONTACT PERIOD TO 1791**

Skill 1.1   Key political, economic, and cultural features of Native American societies

In North America, the landscape was much more hospitable to settlement and exploration than the lands of South America. The North American continent, especially in what is now the United States, had only a few mountain ranges and a handful of wide rivers but nothing near the dense jungles and staggeringly high mountains that South America did. The area that is now Canada was cold but otherwise conducive to settlement. As a result, the Native Americans in North American were more spread out and their cultures more diverse than their South American counterparts.

Native American tribes lived throughout what we now call the United States in varying degrees of togetherness. They adopted different customs, pursued different avenues of agriculture and food gathering, and made slightly different weapons. They fought among themselves and with other peoples. To varying degrees, they had established cultures long before Columbus or any other European explorer arrived on the scene.

The Woods Peoples occupied the area from the Atlantic to the Western plains and prairies. They cultivated corn and tobacco, fished and hunted.

The Plains Peoples, who populated the area from the Mississippi River to the Rocky Mountains, were largely wandering and warlike, hunting buffalo and other game for food. After the arrival of Europeans and the re-introduction of the horse they became great horsemen.

The Southwestern Tribes of New Mexico and Arizona included Pueblos, who lived in villages constructed of *adobe* (sun-dried brick), cliff dwellers, and nomadic tribes. These tribes had the most advanced civilizations.

The California Tribes were separated from the influence of other tribes by the mountains. They lived primarily on acorns, seeds and fish, and were probably the least advanced civilizations.

The Northwest Coast Peoples of Washington, British Columbia and Southern Alaska were not acquainted with farming, but built large wooden houses and traveled in huge cedar canoes.

The Plateau Peoples who lived between the plains and the Pacific Coast lived in underground houses or brush huts and subsisted primarily on fish.

Perhaps the most famous of the Native American tribes is the **Algonquian**. We know so much about this tribe because they were one of the first to interact with the newly arrived English settlers in Plymouth, Massachusetts and elsewhere. The Algonquian lived in wigwams and wore clothing made from animal skins. They were proficient hunters, gatherers, and trappers who also knew quite a bit about farming. Beginning with a brave man named Squanto, they shared this agricultural knowledge with the English settlers, including how to plant and cultivate corn, pumpkins, and squash. Other famous Algonquians included Pocahontas and her father, Powhatan, both of whom are immortalized in English literature, and Tecumseh and Black Hawk, known foremost for their fierce fighting ability. To the overall Native American culture, they contributed wampum and dream catchers.

Another group of tribes who lived in the Northeast were the **Iroquois**, who were fierce fighters but also forward thinkers. They lived in long houses and wore clothes made of buckskin. They, too, were expert farmers, growing the "Three Sisters" (corn, squash, and beans). Five of the Iroquois tribes formed a Confederacy that was a shared form of government. The Iroquois also formed the False Face Society, a group of medicine men who shared their medical knowledge with others but kept their identities secret while doing so. These masks are one of the enduring symbols of the Native American era.

Living in the Southeast were the **Seminole** and **Creek**, a huge collection of people who lived in chickees (open, bark-covered houses) and wore clothes made from plant fibers. They were expert planters and hunters and were proficient at paddling dugout canoes, which they made. The bead necklaces they created were some of the most beautiful on the continent. They are best known, however, for their struggle against Spanish and English settlers, especially led by the great Osceola.

The **Cherokee** also lived in the Southeast. They were one of the most advanced tribes, living in domed houses and wearing deerskin and rabbit fur. Accomplished hunters, farmers, and fishermen, the Cherokee were known the continent over for their intricate and beautiful basketry and clay pottery. They also played a game called lacrosse, which survives to this day in countries around the world.

In the middle of the continent lived the Plains tribes, such as the **Sioux, Cheyenne, Blackfeet, Comanche, and Pawnee**. These peoples lived in teepees and wore buffalo skins and feather headdresses. (It is this image of the Native American that has made its way into most American movies depicting the period.) They hunted wild animals on the Plains, especially the buffalo. They were well known for their many ceremonies, including the Sun Dance, and for the peace pipes that they smoked.

Dotting the deserts of the Southwest were a handful of tribes, including the famous **Pueblo**, who lived in houses that bear their tribe's name, wore clothes made of wool and woven cotton, farmed crops in the middle of desert land, created exquisite pottery and Kachina dolls, and had one of the most complex religions of all the tribes. They are perhaps best known for the challenging vista-based villages that they constructed from the sheer faces of cliffs and rocks and for their *adobes*, mud-brick buildings that housed their living and meeting quarters. The Pueblos chose their own chiefs. This was perhaps one of the oldest representative governments in the world.

Another well-known southwestern tribe was the **Apache**, with their famous leader **Geronimo**. The Apache lived in homes called wickiups, which were made of bark, grass, and branches. They wore cotton clothing and were excellent hunters and gatherers. Adept at basketry, the Apache believed that everything in Nature had special powers and that they were honored just to be part of it all.

The **Navajo**, also residents of the Southwest, lived in hogans (round homes built with forked sticks) and wore clothes of rabbit skins. Their major contribution to the overall culture of the continent was in sand painting, weapon-making, silversmithing, and weaving. Some of the most beautiful woven rugs ever were crafted by Navajo hands.

Living in the far Northwest were the **Inuit**, who lived in tents made from animal skins or, in some cases, igloos. They wore clothes made of animal skins, usually seals or caribou. They were excellent fishermen and hunters and crafted efficient kayaks and umiaks to take them through waterways and harpoons with which to hunt animals. The Inuit are perhaps best known for the great carvings that they left behind. Among these are ivory figures and tall totem poles.

For many Native Americans, much of life was concerned with finding and growing food. The people were great farmers and hunters. They grew such crops as **maize**, or corn, and potatoes and squash and pumpkins and beans; and they hunted all manner of animals for food and other supplies such as oil and hides, including deer, bears, and buffalo. Despite the preponderance of crop-growing areas, many Native Americans, however, did not domesticate animals except for dogs. They might have killed pigs and chickens for food, and a few tribes actually amassed horses, such as the Nez Perce in the Northwest.

Tribes who lived in North America had large concentrations of people and houses, but they didn't have the kind of large civilization centers like the cities of elsewhere in the world. These people didn't have an exact system of writing, either. However, many tribes were quite developed in their technologies involving tools, the processing of food and animal products, and various crafts.

Though not greatly differing from each other in degree of civilization, the native peoples north of Mexico varied widely in customs, housing, dress, and religion. Among the native peoples of North America there were at least 200 languages and 1500 dialects. Each of the hundreds of tribes was somewhat influenced by its neighbors. Communication between tribes that spoke different languages was conducted primarily through an elaborate system of sign language.

While customs varied from tribe to tribe, one consistent cultural element was the smoking of the calumet, a stone pipe, at the beginning and end of a war. In Native American communities, no individual owned land.. Wealth was sometimes an honor, but generosity was more highly valued. Agriculture was quite advanced and irrigation was practiced in some locations. Most tribes practiced unique styles of basket work, pottery and weaving, either in terms of shape or decoration.

Religion was an intimate as well as a tribal matter for nearly all Indians, with beliefs in higher powers extending to Spirits in the sky and elsewhere in Nature. Native Americans had none of the one-god-only mentality that developed in Europe and the Middle East, nor did they have the wars associated with the conflict that those monotheistic religions had with one another. The native peoples of America, like other peoples of the same stage of development, believed that all objects, both animate and inanimate, were endowed with certain spiritual powers. They were intensely religious, and lived every aspect of their lives as their religion prescribed. They believed a soul inhabited every living thing. Certain birds and animals were considered more powerful and intelligent than humans and capable of influence for good or evil.

Most of the tribes were divided into clans of close blood relations, whose **totem** was a particular animal from which they were often believed to have descended. The sun and the four principal directions were often objects of worship. The **shaman**, a sort of priest, was often the medicine-man of a tribe. Sickness was often supposed to be the result of displeasing some spirit and was treated with incantations and prayer. Many of the traditional stories resemble those of other peoples in providing answers to primordial questions and guidance for life. Honesty was a primary virtue, and promises were always honored no matter what the personal cost.

Some communities did not have any formal government; others developed complex systems for determining social structures and leadership. Each individual was responsible for governing himself or herself, particularly with regard to the rights of other members of the community. The chiefs generally carried out the will of the tribe. Boundaries of tribal territories were determined by treaties with neighbors. There was an organized confederation among certain tribes, often called a nation. The Iroquois confederation, for example, was often referred to as The Five Nations (later The Six Nations).

Skill 1.2   European exploration, immigration and settlement of North America

Columbus' first trans-Atlantic voyage was an attempt to prove the idea that Asia could be reached by sailing west. And to a certain extent, this idea was true. It could be done but only after figuring how to go around or across or through the landmass in between. Long after Spain dispatched explorers and her famed conquistadors to gather the wealth for the Spanish monarchs and their coffers, the British were still searching valiantly for the **Northwest Passage**, an open-water route across North America, from the Atlantic to the Pacific, to the wealth of Asia. Not until after the Lewis and Clark Expedition, when Captains Meriwether Lewis and William Clark proved conclusively that there simply was no Northwest Passage, did this idea cease to hold sway.

However, lack of an open-water passage did not deter exploration and settlement. **Spain, France,** and **England** - along with some participation by the **Dutch** - led the way in expanding Western European civilization in the New World. These three nations had strong monarchial governments and were struggling for dominance and power in Europe. With the defeat of Spain's mighty Armada in 1588, England became undisputed ruler of the seas. Spain lost its power and influence in Europe and it was left to France and England to carry on the rivalry, leading to eventual British control in Asia as well.

Spain's influence extended across Florida, along the Gulf Coast of Texas all the way west to California and south to the tip of South America. French control centered from New Orleans north to what is now northern Canada including the entire Mississippi Valley, the St. Lawrence Valley, the Great Lakes, and the land that was part of the Louisiana Territory. England settled the eastern seaboard of North America, including parts of Canada and the US from Maine to Georgia. Each of the three nations controlled various islands of the West Indies. The Dutch had New Amsterdam for a period but later ceded it into British hands.

One interesting aspect of all of this was that each of these nations, especially England, laid claim to land that extended partly or all the way across the continent, regardless of the fact that the others claimed the same land. The wars for dominance and control of power and influence in Europe would undoubtedly and eventually extend to the Americas, especially North America.

The importance of the Age of Exploration was not only the discovery and colonization of the New World, but also a new hemisphere as a refuge from poverty, persecution, and a place to start a new and better life. It led to the development of better maps and charts and new, more accurate navigational instruments. It led to an increased knowledge, great wealth, and new and different foods and items not previously known in Europe. It was also proof that Asia could be reached by sea and that the earth was round. Ships and sailors would not sail off the edge of a flat earth and disappear forever into nothingness.

The part of North America claimed by **France** was called New France and consisted of the land west of the Appalachian Mountains. This area of claims and settlement included the St. Lawrence Valley, the Great Lakes, the Mississippi Valley, and the entire region of land westward to the Rockies. They established the permanent settlements of Montreal and New Orleans, thus giving them control of the two major gateways into the heart of North America, the vast, rich interior. The St. Lawrence River, the Great Lakes, and the Mississippi River along with its tributaries made it possible for the French explorers and traders to roam at will, virtually unhindered in exploring, trapping, trading, and furthering the interests of France.

Most of the French settlements were in Canada along the St. Lawrence River. Only scattered forts and trading posts were found in the upper Mississippi Valley and Great Lakes region. The rulers of France originally intended New France to have vast estates owned by nobles and worked by peasants with the peasants living on the estates in compact farming villages - the New World version of the Old World's medieval system of feudalism. However, it didn't work out that way. Each of the nobles wanted his estate to be on the river for ease of transportation. The peasants working the estates wanted the prime waterfront location, also. The result of all this real estate squabbling was that New France's settled areas wound up mostly as a string of farmhouses stretching from Quebec to Montreal along the St. Lawrence and Richelieu Rivers.

In the non-settled areas in the interior were the **French fur traders.** They made friends with the friendly tribes of Indians, spending the winters with them getting the furs needed for trade. In the spring, they would return to Montreal in time to take advantage of trading their furs for the products brought by the cargo ships from France, which usually arrived at about the same time. Most of the wealth for New France and its "Mother Country" was from the fur trade, which provided a livelihood for many, many people. Manufacturers and workmen back in France, ship-owners and merchants, as well as the fur traders and their Indian allies all benefited. However, the freedom of roaming and trapping in the interior was a strong enticement for the younger, stronger men and resulted in the French not strengthening the areas settled along the St. Lawrence.

Into the eighteenth century, French rivalry with the **British** grew stronger. New France was united under a single government and enjoyed the support of many Indian allies. The French traders were very diligent in not destroying the forests and driving away game upon which the Indians depended for life. It was difficult for the French to defend all of their settlements as they were scattered over half of the continent. However, by the early 1750s, in Western Europe, France was the most powerful nation. Its armies were superior to all others and its navy was giving the British stiff competition for control of the seas. The stage was set for confrontation in both Europe and America.

Spanish settlement had its beginnings in the Caribbean with the establishment of colonies on Hispaniola at Santo Domingo which became the capital of the West Indies, Puerto Rico, and Cuba. There were a number of reasons for Spanish involvement in the Americas, among them:

- the spirit of adventure
- the desire for land
- expansion of Spanish power, influence, and empire
- the desire for great wealth
- expansion of Roman Catholic influence and conversion of native peoples

The first permanent settlement in what is now the United States was in 1565 at **St. Augustine**, Florida. A later permanent settlement in the southwestern United States was in 1609 at Santa Fe, New Mexico. At the peak of Spanish power, the area in the United States claimed, settled, and controlled by Spain included Florida and all land west of the Mississippi River.

Of course, France and England also laid claim to the same areas. Nonetheless, ranches and missions were built and the Indians who came in contact with the Spaniards were introduced to animals, plants, and seeds from the Old World that they had never seen before. Animals brought in included horses, cattle, donkeys, pigs, sheep, goats, and poultry. Barrels were cut in half and filled with earth to transport and transplant trees bearing apples, oranges, limes, cherries, pears walnuts, olives, lemons, figs, apricots and almonds. Even sugar cane and flowers made it to America along with bags bringing seeds of wheat, barley, rye, flax, lentils, rice, and peas.

All Spanish colonies belonged to the King of Spain. He was considered **an absolute monarch** with complete or absolute power who claimed rule by divine right, the belief being that God had given him the right to rule and he answered only to God for his actions. His word was final, was the law. The people had no voice in government. The land, the people, the wealth all belonged to him to use as he pleased. He appointed personal representatives, or **viceroys**, to rule for him in his colonies. They ruled in his name with complete authority. Since the majority of them were friends and advisers, they were richly rewarded with land grants, gold and silver, privileges of trading, and the right to operate the gold and silver mines.

For the needed labor in the mines and on the plantations, Indians were used first as slaves. However, they either rapidly died out due to a lack of immunity from European diseases or escaped into nearby jungles or mountains. As a result, African slaves were brought in, especially to the islands of the West Indies. Some historians state that Latin American slavery was less harsh than in the later English colonies in North America.

Three reasons for that statement are given:

1. The following of a slave code based on ancient Roman laws
2. The efforts of the Roman Catholic Church to protect and defend slaves because of efforts to convert them;
3. The lack of prejudice due to racial mixtures in Spain, which was once controlled by dark-skinned Moors from North Africa.

Regardless, slavery was still slavery and was very harsh - cruelly denying dignity and human worth.

Spain's control over its New World colonies lasted more than 300 years, longer than England or France. To this day, Spanish influence remains in the names of places, art, architecture, music, literature, law, and cuisine. The Spanish settlements in North America were not commercial enterprises but were for protection and defense of the trading and wealth from their colonies in Mexico and South America. The treasure and wealth found in Spanish New World colonies went back to Spain to be used to buy whatever goods and products were needed instead of setting up industries to make what was needed. As the amount of gold and silver was depleted, Spain could not pay for the goods needed and was unable to produce goods for themselves.

Also, at the same time, Spanish treasure ships at sea were being seized by English and Dutch "pirates" taking the wealth to fill the coffers of their own countries. On land, Russian seal-hunters came down the Pacific coast; the English moved into Florida and west into and beyond the Appalachians; and French traders and trappers made their way from Louisiana and other parts of New France into Spanish territory. Facing encroachment on all sides, and without self-sustaining economic development and colonial trade, the Spanish settlements in the U.S. never really prospered.

The **English** colonies were divided generally into the three regions of New England, Middle Atlantic, and Southern. The culture of each was distinct and affected attitudes, ideas towards politics, religion, and economic activities. The geography of each region also contributed to its unique characteristics.

The **New England colonies** consisted of Massachusetts, Rhode Island, Connecticut, and New Hampshire. Life in these colonies was centered on the towns. Farming was done was by each family on its own plot of land, but a short summer growing season and limited amount of good soil gave rise to other economic activities such as manufacturing, fishing, shipbuilding, and trade. The vast majority of the settlers shared similar origins, coming from England and Scotland. Towns were carefully planned and laid out the same way. The form of government was the town meeting where all adult males met to make the laws. The legislative body, the General Court, consisted of an upper and lower house.

The **Middle or Middle Atlantic colonies** included New York, New Jersey, Pennsylvania, Delaware, and Maryland. New York and New Jersey were at one time the Dutch colony of New Netherland, and Delaware at one time was New Sweden. From their beginnings these five colonies were considered "melting pots" with settlers from many different nations and backgrounds. The main economic activity was farming, with the settlers scattered over the countryside cultivating rather large farms. The Indians were not as much of a threat as in New England so there was less need to settle in small farming villages. The soil was very fertile, the land was gently rolling, and a milder climate provided a longer growing season.

These farms produced a large surplus of food, not only for the colonists themselves but also for sale. This colonial region became known as the "breadbasket" of the New World. The New York and Philadelphia seaports were constantly filled with ships being loaded with meat, flour, and other foodstuffs for the West Indies and England.

There were other economic activities such as shipbuilding, iron mines, and factories producing paper, glass, and textiles. The legislative body in Pennsylvania was unicameral or consisting of one house. In the other four colonies, the legislative body had two houses. Also units of local government were in counties and towns.

The **Southern colonies** were Virginia, North and South Carolina, and Georgia. Virginia was the first permanent successful English colony and Georgia was the last. The year 1619 was a very important year in the history of Virginia and the United States with three very significant events. First, sixty women were sent to Virginia to marry and establish families; second, twenty Africans, the first of thousands, arrived; and third, most importantly, the Virginia colonists were granted the right to self-government and they began by electing their own representatives to the House of Burgesses, their own legislative body.

The major economic activity in this region was farming. Here, too, the soil was very fertile and the climate was very mild with an even longer growing season. The large plantations eventually requiring large numbers of slaves were found in the coastal or tidewater areas. Although the wealthy slave-owning planters set the pattern of life in this region, most of the people lived inland away from coastal areas. They were small farmers and very few, if any, owned slaves. Products from farms and plantations included rice, tobacco, indigo, cotton, some corn and wheat. Other economic activities included lumber and naval stores (tar, pitch, rosin, and turpentine) from the pine forests and fur trade on the frontier.

The settlers in these four colonies came from diverse backgrounds and cultures. Virginia was colonized mostly by people from England while Georgia was started as a haven for debtors from English prisons. Pioneers from Virginia settled in North Carolina while South Carolina welcomed people from England and Scotland, French Protestants, Germans, and emigrants from islands in the West Indies.. Cities such as Savannah and Charleston were important seaports and trading centers.

In the colonies, the daily life of the colonists differed greatly between the coastal settlements and the inland or interior. The Southern planters and the people living in the coastal cities and towns had a way of life similar to that of towns in England. That influence was seen and heard in the way people dressed and talked, in the architectural styles of houses and public buildings, and in the social divisions or levels of society. Both the planters and city dwellers enjoyed an active social life and had strong emotional ties to England.

On the other hand, life inland on the frontier had marked differences. All facets of daily living - clothing, food, housing, economic and social activities - were all connected to what was needed to sustain life and survive in the wilderness. Everything was produced practically by the settlers themselves. They were self-sufficient and extremely individualistic and independent. There were little, if any, levels of society or class distinctions as they considered themselves to be equal to all others, regardless of station in life. The roots of equality, independence, individual rights and freedoms were extremely strong and well developed. People were not judged by their fancy dress, expensive house, eloquent language, or titles following their names.

The colonies had from 1607 to 1763 to develop, refine, practice, experiment, and experience life in a rugged, uncivilized land. The Mother Country had virtually left them on their own to take care of themselves. So when in 1763 Britain decided she needed to regulate and "mother" the "little ones;" to her surprise, she had a losing fight on her hands.

Skill 1.3 Characteristics of and regional divisions among England's North American colonies

The thirteen British colonies that would become the first independent American states were divided into three primary regions: New England, including the colonies of New Hampshire, Massachusetts, Rhode Island and Connecticut, the middle colonies of New York, Pennsylvania, New Jersey, and Delaware, and the southern colonies of Maryland, Virginia, North Carolina, South Carolina and Georgia.

These three regions developed different economic resources that were closely connected to the differing geography among the colonies. The relatively difficult growing conditions in the New England led to a reliance on fishing and shipbuilding, supplemented by subsistence farming. The large rivers and excellent harbors of the middle colonies allowed them to flourish as market centers, while agriculture took hold in the interior. In the south, rich soil provided a basis for large, self-sufficient farm plantations

Before setting foot on land in 1620, the **Pilgrims** aboard the Mayflower agreed to a form of self-government by signing the Mayflower Compact. The Compact served as the basis for governing the Plymouth colony for many years, and set an example of small, town-based government that would proliferate throughout New England. The present day New England town meeting is an extension of this tradition. This republican ideal was later to clash with the policies of British colonial government.

Slavery was present in the New World from the beginning, with the first slaves arriving in Virginia in 1619. Beginning in about 1700, the "**triangular trade**" began. Cotton, sugar and tobacco were shipped to Britain, which then distilled rum and created textiles for export to Africa. In Africa, these goods were traded for slaves, which were then carried back to the Americas and traded for more raw materials. The slave trade, which was engaged in by both northern and southern colonies, contributed directly to the success of the new colonies, providing labor and trade opportunities.

As the American colonies moved toward independence, regional differences came into focus. In a democracy that awarded wealthy landowners more access, the southern plantation owners were at an advantage; however the political and economic centers were in the north. The US Constitution and Bill of Rights attempted to balance some of these tensions. Even the placement of the new US Capitol between Maryland and Virginia can be seen as a symbolic compromise between the regions.

Skill 1.4   Political and economic relations between the colonies and Europe

The New England colonies were primarily settled by English colonists, but other nations had a presence in the New World as well. Although one colony was founded as strictly a philanthropic enterprise, and three others were founded primarily for religious reasons, the other nine were started for economic reasons. Settlers came to these colonies came for different reasons, but primarily they sought religious or political freedom, economic prosperity, or the opportunity to own land. Despite sentiments about freedom or economic independence, the colonies remained connected to the political and economic developments in Europe.

The Dutch West India Company founded a colony in what is now New York, establishing it as New Holland. It was eventually captured by English settlers and named New York, but many of the Dutch families that had been granted large segments of land by the Dutch government were allowed to keep their estates. As hostility built between England and the colonies over the taxation of tea, colonists turned to the Dutch to supply them with this important import.

To the north of the Anglo-American colonies, the French were establishing a significant presence in what is now eastern Canada. Spain was advancing in its colonization of parts of the Caribbean, where much of the early slave trade originated. Consequently, the American colonies found themselves swept into international political affairs whenever the homeland, Britain, found itself in conflict with Europe.

The case of Britain's rivalry with France is an example. England and France were historic rivals who found themselves with a new common border in the New World. Disputes over control of the Ohio River between French and British colonies were one of the primary causes leading into the Seven Years' War among many of the European powers. Anglo-American colonists, still considering themselves British subjects, fought against the French and their Indian allies. George Washington emerged as an effective military leader during this conflict.

Later, the animosity between the English and French would work to the advantage of the revolutionary colonists, who received aid from France in their struggle against England. Holland, with its long connection to the American colonies, was the second nation after France to recognize their independence. Spain, while not officially recognizing the independence of the colonies, joined the Revolutionary War on the side of the colonists owing to a disagreement with Britain over possession of Gibraltar. Thus, from the earliest times the fortunes of the colonists were caught up in international affairs, and even relied on their political and economic connections with Europe to advance and gain eventual independence.

The war for independence occurred due to a number of changes, the two most important ones being economic and political. By the end of the French and Indian War in 1763, Britain's American colonies were thirteen out of a total of thirty-three scattered around the earth. Like all other countries, Britain strove for having a strong economy and a favorable balance of trade. This delicate balance required wealth, self-sufficiency and a powerful army and navy. This is why the overseas colonies developed.

The English colonies, with only a few exceptions, were considered commercial ventures founded to make a profit for the crown, or the company, or whoever financed its beginnings. The colonies would provide raw materials for the industries in the Mother Country, be a market for finished products by buying them and assist the Mother Country in becoming powerful and strong. In the case of Great Britain, a strong merchant fleet would provide training for the Royal Navy as well as provide places as bases of operation.

Trade explains the major reason for British encouragement and support of colonization, especially in North America. So between 1607 and 1763, at various times for various reasons, the British Parliament enacted different laws to assist the government in getting and keeping this trade balance. One series of laws required that most of the manufacturing be done only in England, such as the prohibition on exporting any wool or woolen cloth from the colonies, and no manufacture of beaver hats or iron products. This didn't concern the colonists as they had no money and no highly skilled labor to set up any industries, anyway. Other acts had greater impact.

The **Navigation Acts of 1651** put restrictions on shipping and trade within the British Empire by requiring that it was allowed only on British ships. This increased the strength of the British merchant fleet and greatly benefited the American colonists. Since they were British citizens, they could have their own vessels, and build and operate them as well. By the end of the war in 1763, the shipyards in the colonies were building one third of the merchant ships under the British flag. There were quite a number of wealthy, American, colonial merchants.

The **Navigation Act of 1660** restricted the shipment and sale of colonial products to England only. In 1663 another Navigation Act stipulated that the colonies had to buy manufactured products only from England and that any European goods going to the colonies had to go to England first. These acts were a protection from enemy ships and pirates and from competition from European rivals.

The New England and Middle Atlantic colonies at first felt threatened by these laws as they had started producing many of the same products being produced in Britain. But they soon found new markets for their goods and began their own **"triangular trade."** Colonial vessels started the first part of the triangle by sailing for Africa loaded with kegs of rum from colonial distilleries. On Africa's West Coast, the rum was traded for either gold or slaves. The second part of the triangle was from Africa to the West Indies where slaves were traded for molasses, sugar, or money. The third part of the triangle was home, bringing sugar or molasses (to make more rum), gold, and silver.

The major concern of the British government was that the trade violated the 1733 **Molasses Act**. Planters had wanted the colonists to buy all of their molasses in the British West Indies but these islands could give the traders only about one eighth of the amount of molasses needed for distilling the rum. The colonists were forced to buy the rest of what they needed from the French, Dutch, and Spanish islands, thus evading the law by not paying the high duty on the molasses bought from these islands. If Britain had enforced the Molasses Act, economic chaos and ruin would have occurred. So the government followed the policy of "salutary neglect," deliberately failing to enforce the mercantile laws.

In 1763, after the war, money was needed to pay the British war debt, for the defense of the empire, and to pay for the governing of thirty-three colonies scattered around the earth. It was decided to adopt a new colonial policy and pass laws to raise revenue. It was reasoned that the colonists were subjects of the king, and since the king and his ministers had spent a great deal of money defending and protecting them, it was only right and fair that the colonists should help pay the costs of defense. The earlier laws were for the purposes of regulating production and trade which generally put money into colonial pockets. These new laws would take some of that rather hard-earned money out of their pockets and it would be done, in colonial eyes, unjustly and illegally.

Skill 1.5 Comparisons of the ethnic and religious diversity of American colonists and intellectual heritage of Anglo American colonials

The thirteen English colonies were successful and by the time they had gained their independence from Britain, were more than able to govern themselves. They had a rich historical heritage of law, tradition, and documents leading the way to constitutional government conducted according to laws and customs. The settlers in the British colonies highly valued individual freedom, democratic government, and getting ahead through hard work.

While some eighty percent of the American colonists were of European descent, the proportion of these who were of English descent decreased during the 1700s as more and more settlers from other countries settled in the colonies. Settlers from Germany, Scotland and Ireland made up nearly a third of colonials from Europe, often settling in separate communities. By 1775, approximately one fifth of the colonial population was of African ancestry, primarily living in slavery in the southern colonies. Some free black people did live and work in the northern colonies.

The colonists were a diverse group in terms of religion, as well. Of those who were members of a church – and many colonists did not belong to a church – the vast majority were Protestant Christians. In Maryland and Delaware there were significant groups of Roman Catholics, and a small number of Jews living in the northern colonies.

Within Protestantism, there were several divisions. In the northern Puritan regions, the Congregational Church was organized, and received support from the colonies. In the South, the Church of England was widespread. In the more ethnically diverse middle colonies, a more diverse religious group existed. The Quakers, who had been driven out of the Puritan regions, settled in Rhode Island and Pennsylvania. Immigrants from Scotland founded Presbyterian churches. Baptist churches began to emerge after the Great Awakening of the 1740s ignited religious sentiments among many Protestants. Other denominations also took hold in the colonies, including Lutherans, Mennonites and Dutch Reformed churches.

In the Puritan regions, personal responsibility toward one's community was a basic value that was based on the religious commitment one made to the church. The earliest settlements were centered on the church and the meetings among church members to decide public matters eventually transformed into the New England town meeting, a community-based system of government that is still used today. In educational matters, Puritans felt it important that everyone be able to study the Bible and so ensured that their children received an elementary education.

Publicly funded grammar schools were established in New England to provide secondary education. The country's first college, Harvard, was established in Cambridge, Massachusetts, as were several others, including Yale, Dartmouth and Brown in other parts of New England.

In the middle colonies, the more diverse population led to a less homogenous region in terms of community relationships. The large number of Germans in the area meant that the German language remained in common use in many small communities. Marriage within these communities was encouraged. The Quaker Church was more inclusive than the Congregationalists in the north, holding that all people were equal before God, and that women had an equal position in the church. Presbyterian Church members were arranged into synods who were able to make decisions on church matters without an authoritarian hierarchy. These "democratic" systems of church organizations supported democratic values that made their way into civic matters. A public responsibility toward the less fortunate was another Quaker tenet that culminated in the establishment of institutions such as public hospitals.

Education in the middle colonies was influenced largely by the Enlightenment movement, which emphasized scholarly research and public service. Benjamin Franklin embodied these principles in Philadelphia, which became a center of learning and culture, owing largely to its economic success and ease of access to European books and tracts.

In the South, the wealthy elite landowners looked to England for culture. The Church of England was legally established throughout the colonies, and received public money in support. Wealthy planters were able to exercise their influence over their local regions through their authority over the local church organization. A hierarchical social system developed, with the wealthy planters at the top, followed by merchants, smaller farmers, and slaves. In the back country, Scots-Irish settlers lived in small farm communities outside of this system. During the Great Awakening, the hierarchy was threatened as Baptist congregations formed. Many planters sought to disrupt these congregations, sometimes with violence.

In education, as in many things, wealthy southerners looked to England. Some would send their sons to London for schooling, and to learn the manners of British gentlemen. British tutors were hired for wealthy southern children. Among the Roman Catholic communities in Maryland, some families sent their sons to Jesuit schools in France. Education for less wealthy southerners was not as widely available as it was in the North. As other groups moved into the area, such as the German Lutherans, elementary education became more common.

Skill 1.6   Events leading up to and occurring during the American Revolution

International events that helped set the stage for the American Revolution

By the 1750s in Europe, Spain was no longer the most powerful nation and the remaining rivalry was between Britain and France. For nearly twenty-five years, between 1689 and 1748, a series of armed conflicts involving these two powers had been taking place. These conflicts had spilled over into North America. The War of the League of Augsburg in Europe, 1689 to 1697, had been King William's War. The War of the Spanish Succession, 1702 to 1713, had been Queen Anne's War. The War of the Austrian Succession, 1740 to 1748, was called King George's War in the colonies. The two nations fought for possession of colonies, especially in Asia and North America, and for control of the seas, but none of these conflicts was decisive.

The final conflict, which decided once and for all who was the most powerful, began in North America in 1754, in the Ohio River Valley. It was known in America as the **French and Indian War** and in Europe as the **Seven Years' War**, since it began there in 1756. In America, both sides had advantages and disadvantages.

The British colonies were well established and consolidated in a smaller area. British colonists outnumbered French colonists 23 to 1. Except for a small area in Canada, French settlements were scattered over a much larger area, roughly half of the continent, and were smaller. However, the French settlements were united under one government and were quick to act and cooperate when necessary. In addition, the French had many more Indian allies than the British. The British colonies had separate, individual governments and very seldom cooperated, even when needed. In Europe, at that time, France was the more powerful of the two nations.

Both sides had stunning victories and humiliating defeats. If there was one person who could be given the credit for British victory, it would have to be **William Pitt**. He was a strong leader, enormously energetic, supremely self-confident, and determined on a complete British victory. Despite the advantages and military victories of the French, Pitt succeeded. In the army he got rid of the incompetents and replaced them with men who could do the job. He sent more troops to America, strengthened the British navy, gave to the officers of the colonial militias equal rank to the British officers - in short, he saw to it that Britain took the offensive and kept it to victory. Of all the British victories, perhaps the most crucial and important was winning Canada.

The French depended on the St. Lawrence River for transporting supplies, soldiers, and messages. It was the link between New France and the Mother Country. Tied into this waterway system were the connecting links of the Great Lakes, Mississippi River and its tributaries along which were scattered French forts, trading posts, and small settlements. When, in 1758, the British captured Louisburg on Cape Breton Island, New France was doomed. Louisburg gave the British navy a base of operations preventing French reinforcements and supplies getting to their troops. Other forts fell to the British: Frontenac, Duquesne, Crown Point, Ticonderoga, and Niagara, those in the upper Ohio Valley, and, most importantly, Quebec and finally Montreal. Spain entered the war in 1762 to aid France but it was too late. British victories occurred all around the world: in India, in the Mediterranean, and in Europe.

In 1763, France, Spain, and Britain met in Paris to draw up the **Treaty of Paris.** Great Britain got most of India and all of North America east of the Mississippi River, except for New Orleans. Britain received control of Florida from Spain and returned Cuba and the islands of the Philippines, taken during the war, to Spain. France lost nearly all of its possessions in America and India though it was allowed to keep four islands: Guadeloupe, Martinique, Haiti on Hispaniola, and St. Pierre and Miquelon. France gave Spain New Orleans and the vast territory of Louisiana, west of the Mississippi River. Britain was now the most powerful nation, bar none.

Where did all of this leave the British colonies? Their colonial militias had fought with the British and so they too benefited. The militias and their officers gained much fighting experience which was very valuable later. The thirteen colonies also began to realize that cooperating with each other was the only way to defend themselves. That last lesson wouldn't be fully implemented until the time came for the war for independence and establishing a national government, but a start had been made. Shortly after the start of the war in 1754, the French and their Indian allies had defeated Major George Washington and his militia at Fort Necessity. This left the entire northern frontier of the British colonies vulnerable and open to attack. In the wake of this, Benjamin Franklin proposed to the thirteen colonies that they unite permanently to be able to defend themselves.

Delegates from seven of the thirteen colonies met at Albany, New York, along with the representatives from the Iroquois Confederation and British officials. Franklin's proposal, known as the Albany Plan of Union, was rejected by the colonists, along with a similar proposal from the British. Delegates simply did not want each of the colonies to lose its right to act independently. However, the seed was planted.

Social and political divergence of the colonies from England

As the proportion of English-born colonists decreased and the diversity of settlers increased, fewer and fewer colonists felt a cultural tie to the country that held so much influence over the colonies' trade and government. Divisions between the colonies became more pronounced as settlers of differing religious and national groups established themselves.

Government of the colonies differed depending on the type of colony. Each colony had a lower legislative assembly that was elected and a higher council and governor that were elected or appointed in different ways depending on the how the colony was organized initially. In most colonies, the councils and governors were appointed by the King of England or by British property owners or agencies. In corporate colonies, the council and governors were elected by colonial property owners who maintained a close connection to England.

Thus, while the colonies were allowed to tax themselves and regulate much of their daily lives through representation in the colonial assemblies, Britain maintained control of international affairs and international trade by controlling the upper levels of colonial government. In practice, Britain allowed the colonies to go about their business without interference, largely because the colonies were providing important raw materials to the home country.

The first glimmers of dissent from the colonies came during the French and Indian War, in which colonial militias were raised to fight the French in America. Conflict arose with Britain over who should control these militias, with the colonies wanting the assemblies to have authority. Following the British victory over the French, Britain found itself in debt from the war and looked to the colonies to provide revenue. Britain began enforcing taxes on colonial trade that it had ignored prior to the war and began passing new regulations.

The developing sense of unity among the colonies and the emergence of revolution

The war's effect on the colonies was to provide them with a sense of unity that they had lacked before. This newfound unity was to prove important in the growth of dissent against Britain's increased involvement in colonial affairs. It began in 1763 when Parliament decided to have a standing army in North America to reinforce British control. In 1765, the **Quartering Act** was passed requiring the colonists to provide supplies and living quarters for the British troops.

The **Sugar Act of 1764** required efficient collection of taxes on any molasses that were brought into the colonies and gave British officials free license to conduct searches of the premises of anyone suspected of violating the law. The colonists were taxed on newspapers, legal documents, and other printed matter under the **Stamp Act of 1765**. Feelings reached a peak with the passage of the Stamp Act, which was a direct tax on colonists. Nine colonies assembled in New York to call for the repeal of the Act. At the same time, a group of New York merchants organized a protest to stop the importation of British goods. Similar protests arose in Philadelphia and Boston and other merchant cities, often erupting in violence. As Britain's representatives in the colonies, the governors and members of the cabinet and council were sometimes the targets of these protests.

Britain repealed the Stamp Act, but continued to tax external trade items such as tea through the **Townshend Act**, provoking the growth of the movement to halt importation of British goods. This boycott eventually led Britain to repeal much of the Townshend Act.

Before 1763, except for trade and supplying raw materials, the colonies had mostly been left to themselves. England looked on them merely as part of an economic or commercial empire. Little consideration was given as to how they were to conduct their daily affairs, so the colonists became very independent, self-reliant, and extremely skillful at handling those daily affairs. This, in turn, gave rise to leadership, initiative, achievement, and vast experience.

In fact, there was a far greater degree of independence and self-government in America than could be found in Britain or the major countries on the Continent or any other colonies anywhere. There were a number of reasons for this:

1. The religious and scriptural teachings of previous centuries put forth the worth of the individual and equality in God's sight. Freedom of worship and freedom from religious persecution were major reasons to live in the New World.
2. European Protestants, especially Calvinists, believed and taught the idea that government originates from those governed, that rulers are required to protect individual rights and that the governed have the right and privilege to choose their rulers.
3. Trading companies put into practice the principle that their members had the right to make the decisions and shape the policies affecting their lives.
4. The colonists believed and supported the idea that a person's property should not be taken without his consent, based on the English document, the Magna Carta, and English common law.

5. From about 1700 to 1750, population increases in America came about through immigration and generations and generations of descendants of the original settlers. The immigrants were mainly Scots-Irish who hated the English, Germans who cared nothing about England, and black slaves who knew nothing about England. The descendants of the original settlers had never been out of America at any time.

6. In America, as new towns and counties were formed, there began the practice' of representation in government. Representatives to the colonial legislative assemblies were elected from the district in which they lived, chosen by qualified property-owning male voters, and representing the interests of the political district from which they were elected. Each of the 13 colonies had a royal governor appointed by the king, representing his interests in the colonies. Nevertheless, the colonial legislative assemblies controlled the purse strings by having the power to vote on all issues involving money to be spent by the colonial governments.

Contrary to this was the established government in England. Members of Parliament were not elected to represent their own districts. They were considered representative of classes, not individuals. If some members of a professional or commercial class or some landed interests were able to elect representatives, then those classes or special interests were represented. It had nothing at all to do with numbers or territories. Some large population centers had no direct representation at all, yet the people there considered themselves represented by men elected from their particular class or interest somewhere else. Consequently, it was extremely difficult for the English to understand why the American merchants and landowners claimed they were not represented because they themselves did not vote for members of Parliament.

The colonists' protest of, "**No taxation without representation**" was meaningless to the English. Parliament represented the entire nation, was completely unlimited in legislation, and had become supreme. The colonists were incensed at this English attitude and considered their colonial legislative assemblies equal to Parliament, a position which was totally unacceptable in England. There were now two different environments: the older, traditional British system in the Mother Country, and the American system with its new ideas and different ways of doing things. In a new country, a new environment has little or no tradition, institutions or vested interests. New ideas and traditions grew extremely fast, pushing aside what was left of the old ideas and old traditions. By 1763, Britain had changed its perception of its American colonies to their being a "territorial" empire. The stage was set and the conditions were right for a showdown.

When Britain proposed that the East India Company be allowed to import tea to the colonies without customs duty, the colonists were faced with a dilemma. They could purchase the tea at a much lower price than the smuggled Dutch tea they had been drinking, however tea was still subject to the Townshend Act, and to purchase it would be an acceptance of this act. The **Boston Tea Party** was the result, where a group of colonists seized a shipment of British tea in Boston Harbor and dumped it into the sea.

Britain responded with a series of even more restrictive acts, driving the colonies to come together in the **First Continental Congress** to make a unified demand that Britain remove these **Intolerable Acts**, as they were called by the colonists.

Britain stood firm and sought to dissolve the colonial assemblies that were coming forth in opposition to British policies, and were stockpiling weapons and preparing militias. When the British military in America were ordered to break up the illegal meeting of the Massachusetts' assembly outside Boston, they were met with armed resistance at **Lexington and Concord**, and the Revolutionary War was underway.

By 1776, the colonists and their representatives in the Second Continental Congress realized that things were past the point of no return. The **Declaration of Independence** was drafted and declared July 4, 1776. George Washington labored against tremendous odds to wage a victorious war. The turning point in the Americans' favor occurred in 1777 with the American victory at Saratoga. This victory led to the French to aligning themselves with the Americans against the British. With the aid of Admiral deGrasse and French warships blocking the entrance to Chesapeake Bay, British General Cornwallis trapped at Yorktown, Virginia, surrendered in 1781 and the war was over. The Treaty of Paris officially ending the war was signed in 1783.

During the war, and after independence was declared, the former colonies now found themselves independent states. The Second Continental Congress conducted the war with representation by delegates from thirteen separate states. Yet the Congress had no power to act for the states or to require them to accept and follow its wishes. A permanent united government was desperately needed. On November 15, 1777, the **Articles of Confederation** were adopted, creating a league of free and independent states.

Skill 1.7 **The strengths and weaknesses of the Articles of Confederation**

Articles of Confederation - This was the first political system under which the newly independent colonies tried to organize themselves. It was drafted after the Declaration of Independence in 1776, was passed by the Continental Congress on November 15, 1777, ratified by the thirteen states, and took effect on March 1, 1781.

The newly independent states were unwilling to give too much power to a national government. They were already fighting Great Britain. They did not want to replace one harsh ruler with another. After many debates, the form of the Articles was accepted. Each state agreed to send delegates to the Congress. Each state had one vote in the Congress. The Articles gave Congress the power to declare war, appoint military officers, and coin money. The Congress was also responsible for foreign affairs. The Articles of Confederation limited the powers of Congress by giving the states final authority. Although Congress could pass laws, at least nine of the thirteen states had to approve a law before it went into effect. Congress could not pass any laws regarding taxes. To get money, Congress had to ask each state for it, no state could be forced to pay.

Thus, the Articles created a loose alliance among the thirteen states. The national government was weak, in part, because it didn't have a strong chief executive to carry out laws passed by the legislature. This weak national government might have worked if the states were able to get along with each other. However, many different disputes arose and there was no way of settling them. Thus, the delegates went to meet again to try to fix the Articles; instead they ended up scrapping them and created a new Constitution that learned from these earlier mistakes.

The central government of the new United States of America consisted of a Congress of two to seven delegates from each state with each state having just one vote. The government under the Articles solved some of the postwar problems but had serious weaknesses. Some of its powers included: borrowing and coining money, directing foreign affairs, declaring war and making peace, building and equipping a navy, regulating weights and measures, asking the states to supply men and money for an army. The delegates to Congress had no real authority as each state carefully and jealously guarded its own interests and limited powers under the Articles. Also, the delegates to Congress were paid by their states and had to vote as directed by their state legislatures. The serious weaknesses were the lack of power: to regulate finances, over interstate trade, over foreign trade, to enforce treaties, and military power. Something better and more efficient was needed.

In May of 1787, delegates from all states except Rhode Island began meeting in Philadelphia. At first, they met to revise the Articles of Confederation as instructed by Congress; but they soon realized that much more was needed. Abandoning the instructions, they set out to write a new Constitution, a new document, the foundation of all government in the United States and a model for representative government throughout the world.

The first order of business was the agreement among all the delegates that the convention would be kept secret. No discussion of the convention outside of the meeting room would be allowed. They wanted to be able to discuss, argue, and agree among themselves before presenting the completed document to the American people.

The delegates were afraid that if the people were aware of what was taking place before it was completed the entire country would be plunged into argument and dissension. It would be extremely difficult, if not impossible, to settle differences and come to an agreement. Between the official notes kept and the complete notes of future President James Madison, an accurate picture of the events of the Convention is part of the historical record.

The delegates went to Philadelphia representing different areas and different interests. They all agreed on a strong central government but not one with unlimited powers. They also agreed that no one part of government could control the rest. It would be a republican form of government (sometimes referred to as representative democracy) in which the supreme power was in the hands of the voters who would elect the men who would govern for them.

One of the first serious controversies involved the small states versus the large states over representation in Congress. Virginia's Governor Edmund Randolph proposed that state population determine the number of representatives sent to Congress, also known as the **Virginia Plan**. New Jersey delegate William Paterson countered with what is known as the **New Jersey Plan**, each state having equal representation.

After much argument and debate, the **Great Compromise** was devised, known also as the Connecticut Compromise, as proposed by Roger Sherman. It was agreed that Congress would have two houses. The Senate would have two Senators, giving equal powers in the Senate. The House of Representatives would have its members elected based on each state's population. Both houses could draft bills to debate and vote on with the exception of bills pertaining to money, which must originate in the House of Representatives.

Another controversy involved economic differences between North and South. One concerned the counting of the African slaves for determining representation in the House of Representatives. The southern delegates wanted this but didn't want it to determine taxes to be paid. The northern delegates argued the opposite: count the slaves for taxes but not for representation. The resulting agreement was known as the **"three-fifths"** compromise. Three-fifths of the slaves would be counted for both taxes and determining representation in the House.

The last major compromise, also between North and South, was the **Commerce Compromise**. The economic interests of the northern part of the country were ones of industry and business whereas the south's economic interests were primarily in farming. The Northern merchants wanted the government to regulate and control commerce with foreign nations and with the states. Southern planters opposed this idea as they felt that any tariff laws passed would be unfavorable to them.

The acceptable compromise to this dispute was that Congress was given the power to regulate commerce with other nations and the states, including levying tariffs on imports. However, Congress did not have the power to levy tariffs on any exports. This increased Southern concern about the effect it would have on the slave trade. The delegates finally agreed that the importation of slaves would continue for 20 more years with no interference from Congress. Any import tax could not exceed 10 dollars per person. After 1808, Congress would be able to decide whether to prohibit or regulate any further importation of slaves.

Once work was completed and the document was presented, nine states needed to approve for it to go into effect. There was no little amount of discussion, arguing, debating, and haranguing. The opposition had three major objections:

1. The states felt they were being asked to surrender too much power to the national government.
2. The voters did not have enough control and influence over the men who would be elected by them to run the government.
3. A lack of a "bill of rights" guaranteeing hard-won individual freedoms and liberties.

Eleven states finally ratified the document and the new national government went into effect. It was no small feat that the delegates were able to produce a workable document that satisfied all opinions, feelings, and viewpoints. The separation of powers of the three branches of government and the built-in system of checks and balances to keep power balanced were a stroke of genius. It provided for the individuals and the states as well as an organized central authority to keep a new inexperienced young nation on track.

They created a system of government so flexible that it has continued in its basic form to this day. As Benjamin Franklin said, *"though it may not be the best there is";* he said that he, *"wasn't sure that it could be possible to create one better".* A fact that might be true considering that the Constitution has lasted, through civil war, foreign wars, depression, and social revolution for over 200 years. It is truly a living document because of its ability to remain strong while allowing itself to be changed with changing times.

Skill 1.8   The debate over the ratification of the U.S. Constitution

Ratification of the **U.S. Constitution** was by no means a foregone conclusion. The representative government had powerful enemies, especially those who had seen firsthand the failure of the Articles of Confederation. The strong central government had powerful enemies, including some of the guiding lights of the American Revolution.

Those who wanted to see a strong central government were called **Federalists**, because they wanted to see a federal government reign supreme. Among the leaders of the Federalists were Alexander Hamilton and John Jay. These two, along with James Madison, wrote a series of letters to New York newspapers, urging that that state ratify the Constitution. These became known as the **Federalist Papers**.

In the Anti-Federalist camp were Thomas Jefferson and Patrick Henry. These men and many others like them were worried that a strong national government would descend into the kind of tyranny that they had just worked so hard to abolish. In the same way that they took their name from their foes, they wrote a series of arguments against the Constitution called the **Anti-Federalist Papers.**

In the end, both sides got most of what they wanted. The Federalists got their strong national government, which was held in place by the famous "checks and balances." The Anti-Federalists got the **Bill of Rights**, the first ten Amendments to the Constitution and a series of laws that protect some of the most basic of human rights. The states that were in doubt for ratification of the Constitution signed on when the Bill of Rights was promised.

COMPETENCY 0002   Understand major political, economic, and social developments in U.S. history from 1791 to 1877

Skill 2.1   Origin and development of American political parties

The vast majority of the settlers in New England shared similar origins, coming from England and Scotland. Towns were carefully planned and laid out the same way. The form of government was the town meeting where all adult males met to make the laws. The legislative body, the General Court, consisted of upper and lower houses.

The early presidential administrations established much of the form and many of the procedures still present today, including the development of the party system. **George Washington**, the first President, established a cabinet form of government, with individual advisors overseeing the various functions of the executive branch and advising the President, who makes a final decision. Divisions within his cabinet and within Congress during his administration eventually led to the development of political parties, which Washington opposed. Washington was also instrumental in establishing the power of the federal government when he rode at the head of militia forces to put down a rebellion in Pennsylvania. Washington was elected to two terms and served from 1789 to 1797.

Washington's Vice President, **John Adams**, was elected to succeed him. Adams' administration was marked by the new nation's first entanglement in international affairs. Britain and France were at war. President Adams' **Federalist Party** supported the British, and Vice President **Thomas Jefferson**'s **Republican Party** supported the French. The nation was brought nearly to the brink of war with France, but Adams managed to negotiate a treaty that avoided full conflict. In the process, however, he lost the support of his party and was defeated after one term by Thomas Jefferson.

Through the early 1790s, Jefferson as Secretary of State and **Alexander Hamilton** as Secretary of the Treasury led the two political parties that developed. Jefferson and Hamilton were different in many ways. Not least were their views on what should be the proper form of government of the United States. This difference helped to shape the parties that formed around them.

Hamilton wanted the federal government to be stronger than the state governments. Jefferson believed that the state governments should be stronger. Hamilton supported the creation of the first Bank of the United States. Jefferson opposed it because he felt that it gave too much power to wealthy investors who would help run it.

HISTORY   27

Jefferson interpreted the Constitution strictly. He argued that nowhere did the Constitution give the federal government the power to create a national bank. Hamilton interpreted the Constitution loosely. He pointed out that the Constitution gave Congress the power to make all laws "necessary and proper" to carry out its duties. He reasoned that since Congress had the right to collect taxes, then Congress had the right to create the bank.

Hamilton wanted the government to encourage economic growth. He favored the growth of trade, manufacturing, and the rise of cities as the necessary parts of economic growth. He favored the business leaders and mistrusted the common people. Jefferson believed that the common people, especially the farmers, were the backbone of the nation. He thought that the rise of big cities and manufacturing would corrupt American life.

When Congress began to pass many of Hamilton's ideas and programs, Jefferson and James Madison, decided to organize support for their own views.
They met with several important New York politicians, including its governor, **George Clinton,** and **Aaron Burr**, a strong critic of Hamilton. Jefferson asked Clinton and Burr to help defeat Hamilton's program by getting New Yorkers to vote for Jefferson's supporters in the next election. Before long, leaders in other states began to organize support for either Jefferson or Hamilton.

Jefferson's supporters called themselves **Democratic-Republicans**. Hamilton and his supporters were known as Federalists, because they favored a strong federal government. The Federalists had the support of the merchants and ship owners in the Northeast and some planters in the South. During the course of the American Revolution a large number of Tories had left the country either to return to England or move into Canada.

Skill 2.2   Challenges confronted by the government and its leaders in the early years of the Republic

Within a few months from the adoption of the Articles of Confederation, it became apparent that there were serious defects in the system of government established for the new republic. There was a need for change that would create a national government with adequate powers to replace the Confederation, which was actually only a league of sovereign states.

In 1786, an effort to regulate interstate commerce ended in what is known as the **Annapolis Convention**. Because only five states were represented, this Convention was not able to accomplish definitive results. The debates, however, made it clear that a government with as little authority could not regulate foreign and interstate commerce as the government established by the Confederation.

Congress was, therefore, asked to call a convention to provide a constitution that would address the emerging needs of the new nation. The convention met under the presidency of George Washington, with fifty-five of the sixty-five appointed members present. A constitution was written in four months.

The Constitution of the United States is the fundamental law of the republic. It is a precise, formal, written document of the *extraordinary*, or *supreme* type of constitution. The founders of the Union established it as the highest governmental authority. There is no national power superior to it. The foundations were so broadly laid as to provide for the expansion of national life and to make it an instrument which would last for all time. To maintain its stability, the framers created a difficult process for making any changes to it. No amendment can become valid until it is ratified by three-fourths of all of the states.

The British system of government was part of the basis of the final document. But significant changes were necessary to meet the needs of a partnership of states that were tied together as a single federation, yet sovereign in their own local affairs. This constitution established a system of government that was unique and advanced far beyond other systems of its day.

There were, to be sure, differences of opinion. The compromises that resolved these conflicts are reflected in the final document. The first point of disagreement and compromise was related to the Presidency. Some wanted a strong, centralized, individual authority. Others feared autocracy or the growth of monarchy. The compromise was to give the President broad powers but to limit the amount of time, through term of office, that any individual could exercise that power. The power to make appointments and to conclude treaties was controlled by the requirement of the consent of the Senate.

The second conflict was between large and small states. The large states wanted power proportionate to their voting strength; the small states opposed this plan. The compromise was that all states should have equal voting power in the Senate but to make the membership of the House of Representatives determined in proportion to population.

The third conflict was about slavery. The compromise was:

- fugitive slaves should be returned by states to which they might flee for refuge
- no law would be passed for 20 years prohibiting the importation of slaves

The fourth major area of conflict was how the President would be chosen. One side of the disagreement argued for election by direct vote of the people. The other side thought Congress should choose the President. One group feared the ignorance of the people; the other feared the power of a small group of people. The compromise was the **Electoral College**.

The Constitution binds the states in a governmental unity in everything that affects the welfare of all. At the same time, it recognizes the right of the people of each state to independence of action in matters that relate only to them. Since the federal Constitution is the law of the land, all other laws must conform to it.

The debates conducted during the Constitutional Congress represent the issues and the arguments that led to the compromises in the final document. The debates also reflect the concerns of the Founding Fathers that the rights of the people be protected from abrogation by the government itself and the determination that no branch of government should have enough power to continually dominate the others. There is, therefore, a system of checks and balances.

From the beginning of the Confederation, there were differences of opinion about the new government. One faction favored a loose confederacy in which the individual states would retain all powers of sovereignty except the absolute minimum required for the limited cooperation of all the states. (This approach was tried under the Articles of Confederation.)

The other faction that steadily gained influence demanded that the central government be granted all the essential powers of sovereignty, and only the powers of local self-government should be left to the states.

The **Judiciary Act** set up the U.S. **Supreme Court** provided for a Chief Justice and five associate justices. It also established federal district and circuit courts. One of the most important acts of Congress was to pass the first ten amendments to the Constitution called the Bill of Rights, which emphasizes the rights of individuals.

Article III of the Constitution established the Judicial Branch of government headed by the **Supreme Court**. The Supreme Court has the power to rule that a law passed by the legislature, or an act of the executive branch is illegal and unconstitutional. Citizens, businesses, and government officials can appeal the Supreme Court to review a decision made in a lower court if someone believes that the ruling by a judge is unconstitutional.

The Judicial branch also includes lower federal courts known as federal district courts. These courts try lawbreakers and review cases referred from other courts.

The first Supreme Court **Chief Justice John Marshall** made extremely significant contributions to the American judiciary. He established three basic principles of law, which became the foundation of the judicial system and the federal government:

- He began the power of judicial review, the right of the Supreme Court to determine the constitutionality of laws passed by Congress.
- He stated that only the Supreme Court has the power to set aside laws passed by state legislatures when they contradict the U.S. Constitution.
- He established the right of the Supreme Court to reverse decisions of state courts.

Another challenge was The United States' unintentional and accidental involvement in what was known as the **War of 1812.** This resulted from political and economic struggles between France and Great Britain. Napoleon's goal was complete conquest and control of Europe, including Great Britain. Although British troops were temporarily driven off the mainland of Europe, the British Navy still controlled the seas, the seas across which France had to travel to carry the products it traded. America traded with both nations, especially with France and its colonies.

The British decided to destroy the American trade with France, for two main reasons:

- Products and goods from the U.S. gave Napoleon what he needed to keep up his struggle with Britain. The British argued that the Americans were aiding Britain's enemy.
- Britain felt threatened by the increasing strength and success of the U.S. merchant fleet who were becoming major competitors with the ship-owners and merchants in Britain.

The British issued the **Orders in Council,** which was a series of measures prohibiting American ships from entering any French ports, not only in Europe but also in India and the West Indies. At the same time, Napoleon began efforts for a coastal blockade of the British Isles. He issued a series of Orders prohibiting all nations, including the United States, from trading with the British. He threatened seizure of every ship entering French ports after they stopped at any British port or colony, even threatening to seize every ship inspected by British cruisers or that paid any duties to their government. British were stopping American ships and impressing American seamen to service on British ships. Americans were outraged.

In 1807, Congress passed the **Embargo Act** forbidding American ships from sailing to foreign ports. It could not be completely enforced and it hurt business and trade in America so in 1809 it was repealed. Two additional acts passed by Congress after James Madison became president attempted to regulate trade with other nations and to get Britain and France to remove the restrictions they had put on American shipping. The catch was that whichever nation removed restrictions, the U.S. agreed not to trade with the other one. Napoleon was the first to do this, prompting Madison to issue orders prohibiting trade with Britain. This did not work either, and although Britain eventually rescinded the Orders in Council, war came in June of 1812.

During this war, Americans were divided over whether or not it was necessary to even fight and also over what territories should be fought for and taken. The nation was still young and not prepared for war. The primary American objective was to conquer Canada, but it failed.

Two naval victories and one military victory stand out for the United States. Oliver Perry gained control of Lake Erie, and Thomas MacDonough fought on Lake Champlain. Both of these naval battles successfully prevented the British invasion of the United States from Canada.

Nevertheless, the troops did land below Washington, DC, on the Potomac and marched into the city and burned the public buildings, including the White House. **Andrew Jackson**'s victory at New Orleans was a great morale booster to Americans, giving them the impression the U.S. had won the war. The battle actually took place after Britain and the United States had reached an agreement, and it had no impact on the war's outcome. This war ended Christmas Eve, 1814, with the signing of the **Treaty of Ghent**.

The Treaty of Ghent brought peace, released prisoners of war, restored all occupied territory, and set up a commission to settle boundary disputes with Canada.

The war proved to be a turning point in American history. European events had profoundly shaped U.S. policies, especially foreign policies. Thus, in President Monroe's message to Congress on December 2, 1823, he delivered what is known as the **Monroe Doctrine.** The United States was informing the powers of the Old World that the American continents were no longer open to European colonization and that any effort to extend European political influence into the New World would be considered by the United States "as dangerous to our peace and safety." The United States would not interfere in European wars or internal affairs and expected Europe to stay out of American affairs.

Skill 2.3 Westward expansion and its effects on the political, economic, cultural, and social development of the nation

Between the growing economy, expansion westward of the population, and improvements in travel and mass communication, the federal government did face periodic financial depressions. Contributing to these downward spirals were land speculations, availability and soundness of money and currency, failed banks, failing businesses, and unemployment. Sometimes conditions outside the nation would help trigger it; at other times, domestic politics and presidential elections affected it.

Westward expansion occurred for a number of reasons, the most important being economic. Cotton was highly important to the southern states. The effects of the Industrial Revolution, which began in England, were now being felt in the United States. With the invention of power-driven machines, the demand for cotton fiber greatly increased for the yarn needed in spinning and weaving. Eli Whitney's cotton gin made the separation of the seeds from the cotton much more efficient and faster. This, in turn, increased the demand and more farmers became involved in the raising and selling of cotton.

The innovations and developments of better methods of long-distance transportation moved the cotton in greater quantities to textile mills in England as well as to mills in New England and the Middle Atlantic states. As prices increased along with increased demand, southern farmers began expanding by clearing more land to grow more cotton. Movement, settlement, and farming headed west to utilize the fertile soils. This, in turn, increased need for a large supply of cheap labor. The system of slavery expanded, both in numbers and in the movement to lands "west" of the South.

Many people in other fields of economic endeavor began to migrate: trappers, miners, merchants, ranchers, and others were all seeking their fortunes. The Lewis and Clark expedition stimulated the westward push. Fur companies hired men, known as "Mountain Men," to go westward, searching for the animal pelts to supply the market and meet the demands of the East and Europe. These men explored and discovered the many passes and trails that would eventually be used by settlers in their trek to the west. The **California Gold Rush** drew gold-seekers west. Missionaries who traveled west with the fur traders encouraged increased settlement. They sent word back east for more settlers and the results were tremendous. By the 1840s, the population increases in the Oregon country alone were at a rate of about a thousand people a year.

It was the belief of many that the United States was destined to control all of the land between the two oceans or as one newspaper editor termed it, "**Manifest Destiny**." This mass migration westward put the U.S. government on a collision course with the Indians, and with Great Britain, Spain, and Mexico. The fur traders and missionaries ran up against the Indians in the Northwest as well as the claims of Great Britain for the Oregon country. The U.S. and Britain had shared the Oregon country but by the 1840s, with the increases in the free and slave populations and the demand of the settlers for control and government by the U.S., the conflict had to be resolved. In a treaty signed in 1846 by both nations, a peaceful resolution occurred with Britain giving up its claims south of the 49th parallel.

In the American Southwest, the results were exactly the opposite. Spain had claimed this area since the 1540s, had spread northward from Mexico City, and, in the 1700s, had established missions, forts, villages, towns, and very large ranches. After the purchase of the Louisiana Territory in 1803, Americans began moving into Spanish territory. A few hundred American families in what is now Texas were allowed to live there but had to agree to become loyal subjects to Spain.

In 1821, Mexico successfully revolted against Spanish rule, won independence, and chose to be more tolerant towards the American settlers and traders. The Mexican government encouraged and allowed extensive trade and settlement, especially in Texas. Many of the new settlers were southerners who had brought with them their slaves. Slavery was outlawed in Mexico and technically illegal in Texas although the Mexican government looked the other way.

With the influx of so many Americans and the liberal policies of the Mexican government, concern grew over the possible growth and development of an American state within Mexico. Settlement restrictions, cancellation of land grants, outlawing slavery, and increased military activity brought everything to a head. The order of events included the fight for Texas independence, the brief **Republic of Texas**, eventual annexation of Texas, statehood, and finally war with Mexico.

The Texas controversy was not the sole reason for war. Since American settlers had begun pouring into the Southwest, cultural differences played a prominent part. Language, religion, law, customs, and government were different between the two groups. A clash was bound to occur.

The impact of the entire westward movement resulted in the final borders of the present-day contiguous United States; a war with Mexico; the ever-growing controversy over slave versus free states, and finally the Civil War itself.

Skill 2.4 Territorial acquisitions that form the United States and the factors that influenced these acquisitions

Because the nation extended its borders into the lands west of the Mississippi, thousands of settlers streamed in. Equality for everyone, as stated in the Declaration of Independence, did not yet apply to minority groups, black Americans or American Indians. Voting rights and the right to hold public office were restricted in varying degrees in each state. All of these factors decidedly affected the political, economic, and social life of the country and all three were focused in the attitudes of the three sections of the country on slavery.

European events had profoundly shaped U.S. policies, especially foreign policies. After 1815, the U.S. became much more independent from European influence and began to be treated with growing respect by European nations who were impressed that the young United States showed no hesitancy in going to war with the world's greatest naval power.

After the U.S. purchased the **Louisiana Territory from France**, Jefferson appointed Captains Meriwether Lewis and William Clark to explore it, to find out exactly what had been bought. Their expedition went all the way to the Pacific Ocean, and they returned two years later with maps, journals, and artifacts. This led the way for future explorers to make available more knowledge about the territory and resulted in the westward movement and the belief in the doctrine of Manifest Destiny.

The **Red River Cession** was the next acquisition of land and came about as part of a treaty with Great Britain in 1818. It included parts of what later became North and South Dakota and Minnesota. In 1819, Florida, both east and West, was ceded to the U.S. by Spain along with parts of Alabama, Mississippi, and Louisiana. The Republic of Texas was annexed in 1845, and after the war with Mexico in 1848, the U.S. government paid $15 million for what would become the states of California, Utah, and Nevada, and parts of four other states.

In 1846, the **Oregon Country** was ceded to the U.S., which extended the western border to the Pacific Ocean. The northern U.S. boundary was established at the 49th parallel. The states of Idaho, Oregon, and Washington were formed from this territory. In 1853, the **Gadsden Purchase** rounded out the present boundary of the 48 contiguous states with payment to Mexico of $10 million for land that makes up the present states of New Mexico and Arizona.

Skill 2.5   Major issues and events of the Mexican War and their impact on the United States

The slavery issue in Texas grew into a crisis. By 1836, Texas was an independent republic with its own constitution. During its fight for independence, Americans were sympathetic to and supportive of the Texans, and some recruited volunteers who crossed into Texas to help the struggle.

Problems arose when the Texas petitioned Congress for statehood. Texas wanted to allow slavery, but Northerners in Congress then opposed admission to the Union because it would disrupt the balance between free and slave states and give Southerners in Congress increased influence. There were others who believed that granting statehood to Texas would lead to a war with Mexico, which had refused to recognize Texas independence. For the time being, statehood was put on hold.

Friction increased between land-hungry Americans swarming into western lands and the Mexican government, which controlled these lands. The clash was not only political but also cultural and economic. The Spanish influence permeated all parts of southwestern life: law, language, architecture, and customs. By this time, the doctrine of Manifest Destiny was in the hearts and on the lips of those seeking new areas of settlement and a new life. Americans were demanding U.S. control of not only the Mexican Territory but also Oregon. Peaceful negotiations with Great Britain secured Oregon, but it took two years of war to gain control of the southwestern U.S.

In addition, the Mexican government owed debts to U.S. citizens whose property was damaged or destroyed during its struggle for independence from Spain. By the time war broke out in 1845, Mexico had not paid its war debts. The government was weak, corrupt, tom by revolutions, and insolvent. Mexico was also bitter over American expansion into Texas and the 1836 Revolution, which had resulted in Texas independence. In the 1844 Presidential election, the Democrats pushed for annexation of Texas and Oregon, and after **James Polk** won the election, they started the procedure to admit Texas to the Union.

When Texas statehood occurred, diplomatic relations between the U.S. and Mexico were ended. President Polk wanted the U.S. to control the entire southwest, from Texas to the Pacific Ocean. He sent a diplomatic mission with an offer to purchase New Mexico and Upper California, but the Mexican government refused to even receive the diplomat. Consequently, in 1846, each nation claimed aggression on the part of the other and war was declared. The treaty signed in 1848 and a subsequent one in 1853 completed the southwestern boundary of the United States, reaching to the Pacific Ocean, as President Polk wished.

Skill 2.6   Slavery and other political, economic, and social factors that led to the growth of sectionalism and the Civil War

The drafting of the Constitution, its ratification and implementation, united thirteen independent states into a Union under one central government. The two crucial compromises that had been made concerning slaves had pacified Southerners, especially the slave-owners, but the issue of slavery was not settled, and from then on, **sectionalism** became stronger and more apparent each year, putting the entire country on a collision course.

Slavery in the English colonies began in 1619 when 20 Africans arrived in the colony of Virginia at Jamestown. From then on, slavery had a foothold, especially in the agricultural South, where a large amount of labor was needed for the extensive plantations. Free men refused to work for wages on the plantations when land was available for settling on the frontier.

Therefore, slave labor was the only recourse plantation owners perceived. If it had been profitable to use slaves in New England and the Middle colonies, then perhaps slavery would have been more widespread. Slavery was profitable in the South, but not in the other two colonial regions.

The West quickly became involved in the controversy as well as the North and South. By 1860, the country was made up of three major regions, and the people in all three regions had a number of beliefs and institutions in common. Each, however, region had its own unique characteristics.

The North had a great deal of agriculture, but it was also industrial with towns and factories growing at a very fast rate. The South was largely agricultural, and it was becoming increasingly dependent on one crop, cotton. In the West, restless pioneers moved into new frontiers seeking land, wealth, and opportunity. Many were from the South and were slave owners, bringing their slaves with them. In different parts of the country, the views on tariffs, public lands, internal improvements at federal expense, banking and currency, and the issue of slavery were decidedly different.

This period of U.S. history was a period of compromises, breakdowns of the compromises, desperate attempts to restore and retain harmony among the three sections, short-lived intervals of the uneasy balance of interests, and ever-increasing conflict.

The issue of tariffs was a divisive issue during this period, especially between 1829 and 1833. The Embargo Act of 1807 and the War of 1812 had completely cut off the source of manufactured goods for Americans; thus, it was necessary to build factories to produce what was needed. After 1815 when the war had ended, Great Britain's strategy was to be ahead of its industrial rivals by supplying its goods in America. To protect and encourage the U.S.'s own industries and their products, Congress passed the Tariff of 1816, which required high duties to be levied on manufactured goods coming into the United States. Southern leaders, such as John C. Calhoun of South Carolina, supported the tariff with the assumption that the South would develop its own industries.

For a brief period after 1815, the nation enjoyed the "Era of Good Feelings." People were moving into the West; industry and agriculture were growing; a feeling of national pride united Americans in their efforts and determination to strengthen the country. However, over-speculation in stocks and lands for quick profits backfired. Cotton prices were rising, and many Southerners bought land for cultivation at inflated prices. Manufacturers in the industrial North purchased land to build more factories in an attempt to have a part of this prosperity.

Settlers in the West rushed to buy land to reap the benefits of the increasing prices of meat and grain. To have the money for all of these economic activities, all of these groups were borrowing heavily from the banks, and the banks themselves encouraged this by giving loans on insubstantial security.

In late 1818, the Bank of the United States and its branches stopped renewal of personal mortgages and required state banks to immediately pay their bank notes in gold, silver, or in national bank notes. The state banks were unable to do this so they closed their doors and were unable to do any business at all. Since mortgages could not be renewed, people lost properties, and foreclosures were rampant throughout the country.

At the same time, cotton prices collapsed in the English market. Its high price had caused the British manufacturers to seek cheaper cotton from India for their textile mills. With the fall of cotton prices, the demand for American manufactured goods declined, revealing how fragile the economic prosperity had been.

In 1824, Congress, favoring the financial interests of the manufacturers in New England and the Middle Atlantic States, passed a higher tariff. This was proposed by Henry Clay and called the American System, and the purpose was for road-building and other infrastructure as well as creating the national bank. In addition, the 1824 tariff was closely tied to the presidential election of that year. Before becoming law, **Calhoun** had proposed the very high tariffs in an effort to get Eastern business interests to vote with the agricultural interests in the South (who were against it). Supporters of candidate Andrew Jackson sided with whichever side served their best interests.

The bill became law, to Calhoun's surprise, due mainly to the political maneuvering of **Martin van Buren** and **Daniel Webster**. By the time the higher 1828 tariff was passed, feelings were extremely bitter in the South, where many believed that the New England manufacturers greatly benefited from it. Vice President Calhoun, speaking for his home state of South Carolina, promptly declared that if any state felt that a federal law was unconstitutional, that state could **nullify** it.

In 1832, Congress took the action of lowering the tariffs to a degree but not enough to please South Carolina, which promptly declared the tariff null and void, threatening to secede from the Union.

In 1833, Congress lowered the tariffs again, this time at a level acceptable to South Carolina. Although President Jackson believed in states' rights, he also firmly believed in and determined to keep the preservation of the Union. A constitutional crisis had been averted, but sectional divisions were getting deeper and more pronounced. Meanwhile, the **abolition movement** was growing rapidly, becoming an important issue in the North.

Skill 2.7 Individuals, events, and issues of the Civil War

South Carolina was the first state to **secede** from the Union, and the first shots of the war were fired on Fort Sumter in Charleston Harbor. Both sides quickly prepared for war.

The North had more in its favor: a larger population; superiority in finances and transportation facilities; manufacturing, agricultural, and natural resources. The North possessed most of the nation's gold, had about 92% of all industries, and almost all known supplies of copper, coal, iron, and various other minerals. Since most of the nation's railroads were in the North and Midwest, men and supplies could be moved wherever needed; food could be transported from the farms of the Midwest to workers in the East and to soldiers on the battlefields. Trade with nations overseas could go on as usual due to control of the navy and the merchant fleet. The Northern states numbered 24 and included western states (California and Oregon) as well as the border states of Maryland, Delaware, Kentucky, Missouri, and West Virginia.

The slavery issue flared again and would not to be done away with until the end of the Civil War. It was obvious that the newly acquired territory would be divided up into territories and later become states. In addition to the two factions of Northerners who advocated prohibition of slavery and of Southerners who favored slavery existing there, a third faction arose supporting the doctrine of "popular sovereignty" which stated that people living in territories and states should be allowed to decide for themselves whether or not slavery should be permitted. In 1849, California applied for admittance to the Union and the furor began.

The result was the **Compromise of 1850**, a series of laws designed as a final solution to the issue. Concessions made to the North included the admission of California as a free state and the abolition of slave trading in Washington, D.C. The laws also provided for the creation of the New Mexico and Utah territories. As a concession to Southerners, the residents there would decide whether to permit slavery when these two territories became states. In addition, Congress authorized implementation of stricter measures to capture runaway slaves in the controversial **Fugitive Slave Act**.

A few years later, Congress took up consideration of new territories between Missouri and present-day Idaho. Again, heated debate over permitting slavery in these areas flared up. Those opposed to slavery used the Missouri Compromise to prove their point showing that the land being considered for territories was part of the area the Compromise had designated as banned to slavery.

But on May 25, 1854, Congress passed the **Kansas-Nebraska Act**, which nullified this provision, created the territories of Kansas and Nebraska, and provided for the people of these two territories to decide for themselves whether or not to permit slavery to exist there. Feelings were so deep and divided that any further attempts to compromise would meet with little, if any, success. Political and social turmoil swirled everywhere. Kansas was called **Bleeding Kansas** because of the extreme violence and bloodshed throughout the territory between pro-slavery and anti-slavery factions.

The Supreme Court in 1857 handed down an explosive decision. **Dred Scott** was a slave whose owner had taken him from slave state Missouri to free state Illinois, and into Minnesota Territory, where Dred Scott was free under the provisions of the Missouri Compromise, and then finally back to slave state Missouri. Abolitionists presented a court case stating that since Scott had lived in a free state and free territory, he was in actuality a free man.

Two lower courts had ruled before the Supreme Court became involved, one ruling in favor and one against. The Supreme Court decided that residing in a free state and free territory did not make Scott a free man because Scott (and all other slaves) was not a U.S. citizen or state citizen of Missouri. Therefore, he did not have the right to sue in state or federal courts. The Court went a step further and ruled that the old **Missouri Compromise** was now unconstitutional because Congress did not have the power to prohibit slavery in the Territories.

Anti-slavery supporters were stunned. They had just formed the new **Republican Party**, and one of its platforms was keeping slavery out of the Territories. Now, according to the decision in the Dred Scott case, this basic party principle was unconstitutional. The only way to ban slavery in new areas was by a Constitutional amendment, requiring ratification by three-fourths of all states. At this time, this was out of the question because the supporters would be unable to get a majority due to Southern opposition.

In 1858, **Abraham Lincoln** and Stephen A. Douglas were running for the office of U.S. Senator from Illinois and participated in a series of debates, which directly affected the outcome of the 1860 presidential election. Douglas, a Democrat, was up for re-election and believed that if he won the race, he had a good chance of becoming President in 1860. Lincoln, a Republican, was not an abolitionist but believed that slavery was wrong morally. He firmly supported the Republican Party principle that slavery must not be allowed to extend any further.

Douglas, on the other hand, had originated the doctrine of "**popular sovereignty**" and was responsible for supporting and getting through Congress the inflammatory Kansas-Nebraska Act. In the course of the debates, Lincoln challenged Douglas to show that popular sovereignty reconciled with the Dred Scott decision.

Either way he answered Lincoln, Douglas would lose crucial support from one group or the other. If he supported the Dred Scott decision, Southerners would support him, but he would lose Northern support. If he stayed with popular sovereignty, Northern support would be his, but Southern support would be lost. His reply to Lincoln stated that Territorial legislatures could exclude slavery by refusing to pass laws supporting it, and that gave him enough support and approval to be re-elected to the Senate. But it cost him the Democratic nomination for President in 1860.

Southerners came to the realization that Douglas supported popular sovereignty but not necessarily for the expansion of slavery. Two years later, Lincoln received the nomination of the Republican Party for President.

In 1859, abolitionist **John Brown** and his followers seized the federal arsenal at Harper's Ferry in what is now West Virginia. His purpose was to take the guns stored in the arsenal, give them to slaves nearby, and lead them in a widespread rebellion. Colonel Robert E. Lee of the United States Army captured him and his men and, after being found guilty at trial, he was hanged. Southerners supposed that the majority of Northerners approved of Brown's actions, but in actuality, most of them were stunned and shocked. Southern newspapers took great pains to quote a small but well-known minority of abolitionists who applauded and supported Brown's actions. This merely served to widen the gap between the two sections.

The final straw came with the election of Lincoln to the Presidency the next year. Due to a split in the Democratic Party, there were four candidates from four political parties. With Lincoln receiving a minority of the popular vote and a majority of electoral votes, the Southern states, one by one, voted to secede from the Union as they had promised they would do if Lincoln and the Republicans were victorious.

As 1860 began, the nation had extended its borders north, south, and west. Industry and agriculture were flourishing. Although the U.S. did not involve itself actively in European affairs, the relationship with Great Britain was much improved and it and other nations that dealt with the young nation accorded it more respect and admiration. Nevertheless, war was on the horizon. The country was deeply divided along political lines concerning slavery and the election of Abraham Lincoln.

Although the colonies had won independence, had written a Constitution forming a union of those states under a central government, had fought wars and signed treaties, had purchased and explored vast areas of land, had developed industry and agriculture, had improved transportation, had seen population expansion westward, and had increased the number of states admitted to the Union annually, the issue of human slavery had to be settled once and for all.

One historian stated that before 1865, the nation referred to itself as "the United States *are* . . ." but after 1865, "the United States *is* ...." It took the Civil War to finally, completely unify all states into one Union.

The Southern states numbered eleven and included South Carolina, Georgia, Florida, Alabama, Mississippi, Louisiana, Texas, Virginia, North Carolina, Tennessee, and Arkansas. These states made up the Confederacy. Although outnumbered in population, the South was completely confident of victory. They knew that all they had to do was fight a defensive war, protecting their own territory until the North, who had to invade and defeat an area almost the size of Western Europe, tired of the struggle and gave up.

Another advantage of the South was that a number of its best officers had graduated from the U.S. Military Academy at West Point and had had long years of army experience, some even exercising varying degrees of command in the Indian wars and the war with Mexico. Men from the South were conditioned to living outdoors and were more familiar with horses and firearms than many men from northeastern cities. Since cotton was such an important crop, Southerners felt that British and French textile mills were so dependent on raw cotton that they would be forced to help the Confederacy in the war.

The South had specific reasons and goals for fighting the war, more so than the North. The major aim of the Confederacy never wavered: to win independence, the right to govern themselves as they wished, and to preserve slavery.

The Northerners were not as clear in their reasons for conducting war. At the beginning, most believed, along with Lincoln, that preservation of the Union was paramount. Only a few abolitionists looked on the war as a way to end slavery. However, by war's end, more and more northerners had come to believe that freeing the slaves was just as important as restoring the Union.

The war strategies for both sides were relatively clear and simple. The South planned a defensive war, wearing down the North until it agreed to peace on Southern terms. The exception was to gain control of Washington, D.C., go North through the Shenandoah Valley into Maryland and Pennsylvania in order to drive a wedge between the Northeast and mid-West, interrupt the lines of communication, and end the war quickly. The North had three basic strategies:

- blockade the Confederate coastline in order to cripple the South

- seize control of the Mississippi River and interior railroad lines to split the Confederacy in two
- seize the Confederate capital of Richmond, Virginia, driving southward and

  joining up with Union forces coming east from the Mississippi Valley

- blockade the Confederate coastline in order to cripple the South

- seize control of the Mississippi River and interior railroad lines to split the Confederacy in two
- seize the Confederate capital of Richmond, Virginia, driving southward and joining up with Union forces coming east from the Mississippi Valley

The South was winning until the Battle of Gettysburg, which took place July 1 - 3, 1863. Until Gettysburg, Lincoln's commanders, **McDowell, McClellan, Burnside, and Hooker** had only limited success. **Lee**, on the other hand, had many able officers including **Jackson and Stuart** on whom he depended heavily.

Jackson died at Chancellorsville and was replaced by Longstreet. Lee decided to invade the North and depended on **J.E.B. Stuart** and his cavalry to keep him informed of the location of Union troops and their strengths.

Four things worked against Lee at Gettysburg:

- The Union troops gained the best positions and the best ground first, making it easier to make a stand there.
- Lee's move into Northern territory put him and his army a long way from food and supply lines.
- Lee thought that his Army of Northern Virginia was invincible and could fight and win under any conditions or circumstances.
- Stuart and his men did not arrive at Gettysburg until the end of the second day of fighting, and by then, it was too little too late. He and the men had had to detour around Union soldiers, and he was delayed in getting the information Lee needed.

Consequently, Lee made the mistake of failing to listen to Longstreet and following the strategy of regrouping back into Southern territory to the supply lines. Lee thought that regrouping was retreating and almost an admission of defeat.

He was convinced the army would be victorious. **Longstreet** was concerned about the Union troops occupying the best positions and felt that regrouping to a better position would be an advantage. He was also very concerned about the distance from supply lines.

It was not the intention of either side to fight there but the fighting began when a Confederate brigade stumbled into a unit of Union cavalry while looking for shoes. The third and last day Lee launched the final attempt to break Union lines. **General George Pickett** sent his division of three brigades under Generals Garnet, Kemper, and Armistead against Union troops on Cemetery Ridge under command of General Winfield Scott Hancock. Union lines held, and Lee and the defeated Army of Northern Virginia made their way back to Virginia. Although Lincoln's commander George Meade successfully turned back a Confederate charge, he and the Union troops failed to pursue Lee and the Confederates. Nonetheless, this battle was the turning point for the North. After this, Lee never again had the troop strength to launch a major offensive.
The day after Gettysburg, on July 4, Vicksburg, Mississippi, surrendered to Union **General Ulysses Grant**, thus severing the western Confederacy from the eastern part.

In September 1863, the Confederacy won its last important victory at Chickamauga. In November, the Union victory at Chattanooga made it possible for Union troops to go into Alabama and Georgia, splitting the eastern Confederacy in two. Lincoln gave Grant command of all Northern armies in March of 1864.

Grant led his armies into battles in Virginia while Phil Sheridan and his cavalry did as much damage as possible. In a skirmish at a place called Yellow Tavern, Virginia, Sheridan's and Stuart's forces met, with Stuart being fatally wounded. The Union won the Battle of Mobile Bay and in May 1864, William Tecumseh Sherman began his march to successfully demolish Atlanta, then on to Savannah. He and his troops turned northward through the Carolinas to Grant in Virginia. On April 9, 1865, Lee formally surrendered to Grant at Appomattox Courthouse, Virginia.

The effects of the Civil War

The Civil War took more American lives than any other war in history. The South lost one-third of its soldiers in battle compared to about one-sixth for the North. More than half of the total deaths were caused by disease and the horrendous conditions of field hospitals. Both sections paid a tremendous economic price but the South suffered more severely from direct damages.

Destruction was pervasive, with towns, farms, trade, industry, lives, and homes of men, women, and children all destroyed. The entire Southern way of life was lost. The deep resentment, bitterness, and hatred that remained for generations gradually lessened as the years went by, but legacies of it surface and remain to this day.

After the war, the South had no voice in the political, social, and cultural affairs of the nation, almost eliminating the influence of the traditional Southern ideals. The Northern Yankee Protestant ideals of hard work, education, and economic freedom became the standard of the United States and helped influence the development of the nation into a modern, industrial power.

The effects of the Civil War were tremendous. The Civil War changed the methods of waging war; it has been called the first modern war. It introduced weapons and tactics that, when improved later, were used extensively in wars of the late 1800s and 1900s. Civil War soldiers were the first to fight in trenches, first to fight under a unified command, first to wage a defense called "major cordon defense," a strategy of advance on all fronts. They were also the first to use repeating and breech-loading weapons. Observation balloons were first used during the war along with submarines, ironclad ships, and mines. Telegraphy and railroads were put to use first in the Civil War. It was considered a modern war because of the vast destruction and was "total war" involving the use of all resources of the opposing sides. There was probably no way it could have ended other than total defeat and unconditional surrender of one side or the other.

By executive proclamation and constitutional amendment, slavery was officially and finally ended although there remained deep prejudice and racism, still raising its ugly head today. The Union was preserved and the states were finally truly united. **Sectionalism**, especially in the area of politics, remained strong for another 100 years but not to the degree nor with the violence that existed before 1861. The Civil War may have been American democracy's greatest failure because from 1861 to 1865, calm reason that is basic to democracy fell to human passion. Yet, democracy did survive.

The victory of the North established that no state has the right to end or leave the Union. Because of unity, the U.S. became a major global power. Lincoln had never proposed to punish the South. He was most concerned with restoring the South to the Union in a program that was flexible and practical rather than rigid and unbending. In fact, he never really felt that the states had succeeded in leaving the Union but that they had left the 'family circle" for a short time. His plans consisted of two major steps: All Southerners taking an oath of allegiance to the Union promising to accept all federal laws and proclamations dealing with slavery would receive a full pardon.

The only ones excluded from this were men who had resigned from civil and military positions in the federal government to serve in the Confederacy, those who were part of the Confederate government, those in the Confederate army above the rank of lieutenant, and Confederates who were guilty of mistreating prisoners of war and blacks.

A state would be able to write a new constitution, elect new officials, and return to the Union fully equal to all other states on certain conditions: a minimum number of persons (at least 10% of those who were qualified voters in their states before secession from the Union who had voted in the 1860 election) must take an oath of allegiance.

Skill 2.8   The effects of Reconstruction on the political, economic, and social life of the nation

As the war dragged on to its bloody, destructive conclusion, Lincoln was concerned and anxious to get the states restored to the Union. Lincoln showed flexibility in his thinking as he made changes to his **Reconstruction** program to make it as easy and painless as possible. Unfortunately, Lincoln was assassinated before Congress could approve many of his proposed changes. After Andrew Johnson became President and the Radical Republicans gained control of Congress, harsh measures of Reconstruction were implemented.

The economic and social chaos in the South after the war was severe, with starvation and disease rampant, especially in the cities. The U.S. Army provided some relief of food and clothing for both whites and blacks, but the major responsibility fell to the Freedmen's Bureau. Though the bureau agents helped southern whites to a certain extent, their main responsibility was to the freed slaves. They were to assist freedmen in becoming self-supporting and protect them from being taken advantage of by others. Northerners looked on it as an honest effort to help the South out of the chaos. Most white Southerners charged the bureau with causing racial friction by encouraging the freedmen to consider former owners as enemies.

Federal troops were stationed throughout the South and protected Republicans who took control of Southern governments. However, before being allowed to rejoin the Union, the Confederate states had been required to agree to all federal laws. Between 1866 and 1870, all of them had returned to the Union, but Northern interest in Reconstruction was fading. Reconstruction officially ended when the last federal troops left the South in 1877.

Reconstruction had a limited success since it set up public school systems and expanded legal rights of black Americans. Nevertheless, white "redeemer governments" rapidly worked to undo much of the changes resulting from Reconstruction. Further, many bitterly resentful white Southerners fought the new political system by joining a secret society called the **Ku Klux Klan**, using violence to keep black Americans from enjoying basic rights.

The Emancipation Proclamation in 1863, together with the 13th Amendment in 1865, ended slavery in the United States, but these measures did not erase the centuries of racial prejudices among whites that held blacks to be inferior in intelligence and morality. These prejudices, along with fear of economic competition from newly freed slaves, led to a series of state laws that permitted or required businesses, landlords, school boards and others to physically segregate blacks and whites in their everyday lives.

Segregation laws were foreshadowed in the **Black Codes**, strict laws proposed by some southern states during the Reconstruction period which sought to essentially recreate the conditions of pre-war servitude. Under these codes, blacks were to remain subservient to their white employers, and were subject to fines and beatings if they failed to work.

Freedmen, as newly freed slaves were called, were afforded some civil rights protection during the Reconstruction period, however beginning around 1876, so called Redeemer governments began to take office in southern states after the removal of Federal troops that had supported Reconstruction goals. The Redeemer state legislatures began passing segregation laws which came to be known as **Jim Crow** laws.

The Jim Crow laws varied from state to state, but the most significant of them required separate school systems and libraries for blacks and whites. Ticket windows, waiting rooms and seating areas on trains and, later, other public transportation were also segregated. Restaurant owners were permitted or sometimes required to provide separate entrances and tables and counters for blacks and whites, so that the two races would not see one another while dining. Public parks and playgrounds were constructed for each race. Landlords were not allowed to mix black and white tenants in apartment houses in some states.

The Jim Crow laws were given credibility in 1896 when the Supreme Court handed down its decision in the case **Plessy v. Ferguson**. In 1890, Louisiana had passed a law requiring separate train cars for blacks and whites. To challenge this law, in 1892, Homer Plessy, a man who had a black great grandparent and so was considered legally "black" in that state, purchased a ticket in the white section and took his seat. Upon informing the conductor that he was black, he was told to move to the black car. He refused and was arrested. His case was eventually elevated to the Supreme Court.

The Court ruled against Plessy, thereby ensuring that the Jim Crow laws would continue to proliferate and be enforced. The Court held that segregating races was not unconstitutional as long as the facilities for each were identical. This became known as the **"separate but equal"** principle. In practice, facilities were seldom equal. Black schools were not funded at the same level, for instance. Streets and parks in black neighborhoods were not maintained. This trend continued throughout the following decades. Even the federal government adopted segregation as official policy when President Woodrow Wilson segregated the civil service in the 1910s.

The 13th Amendment abolished slavery and involuntary servitude, except as punishment for crime. The amendment was proposed on January 31, 1865. It was declared ratified by the necessary number of states on December 18, 1865. The Emancipation Proclamation had freed slaves held in states that were considered to be in rebellion. This amendment freed slaves in states and territories controlled by the Union. The Supreme Court has ruled that this amendment does not bar mandatory military service.

The 14th Amendment provides for **Due Process and Equal Protection** under the Law. It was proposed on June 13, 1866 and ratified on July 28, 1868. The drafters of the Amendment took a broad view of national citizenship. The law requires that states provide equal protection under the law to all persons - not just all citizens. This amendment also came to be interpreted as overturning the Dred Scott case, which said that blacks were not and could not become citizens of the United States.

The full potential of interpretation of this amendment was not realized until the 1950s and 1960s, when it became the basis of ending segregation in the Supreme Court case *Brown v. Board of Education*. This amendment includes the stipulation that all children born on American soil, with very few exceptions, are U.S. citizens. There have been recommendations that this guarantee of citizenship be limited to exclude the children of illegal immigrants and tourists, but this has not yet occurred. There is no provision in this amendment for loss of citizenship.

After the Civil War, many Southern states passed laws that attempted to restrict the movements of blacks and prevent them from bringing lawsuits or testifying in court. In **the Slaughterhouse Cases** (1871) the Supreme Court ruled that the Amendment applies only to rights granted by the federal government. In the **Civil Rights Cases**, the Court held that the guarantee of rights did not outlaw racial discrimination by individuals and organizations. In the next few decades the Court overturned several laws barring blacks from serving on juries or discriminating against the Chinese immigrants in regulating the laundry businesses.

The Fifteenth Amendment grants voting rights regardless of race, color or previous condition of servitude. It was ratified on February 3, 1870.

Lincoln and President Johnson had considered the conflict of Civil War as a "rebellion of individuals," but Congressional Radical Republicans, such as Charles Sumner in the Senate, considered the Southern states as complete political organizations that were now in the same position as any unorganized territory and should be treated as such. Radical House leader Thaddeus Stevens considered the Confederate states not as territories, but as conquered provinces and felt they should be treated that way. President Johnson refused to work with Congressional moderates, insisting on having his own way. As a result the Radicals gained control of both houses of Congress, and when Johnson opposed their harsh measures, they came within one vote of impeaching him

General Grant was elected President in 1868, and then served two scandal-ridden terms. He was an honest, upright person but he greatly lacked political experience. His greatest weakness was a blind loyalty to his friends. He absolutely refused to believe that his friends were dishonest and stubbornly would not admit to their using him to further their own interests. One of the sad results of the war was the rapid growth of business and industry with large corporations controlled by unscrupulous men. However, after 1877, some degree of normalcy returned and there was time for rebuilding, expansion, and growth.

COMPETENCY 0003 **Understand major political, economic, and social developments in U.S. history from 1877 to 1945**

Skill 3.1 **Continued westward expansion and the factors and events that contributed to the emergence of the United States as a world power between 1898 and 1920**

The post-Reconstruction era represents a period of great transformation and expansion for the United States, both economically and geographically, particularly for the South, which was recovering from the devastation of the Civil War and migration west of the Mississippi River. Great numbers of former slaves moved west, away from their former masters and lured by the promise of land. White migration was also spurred by similar desires for land and resources, leading to boom economies of cotton, cattle and grain starting in Kansas and spreading westward. Although industrial production grew fastest in the South during this period, it was still predominantly agricultural, which featured land tenancy and sharecropping, which did not really advance the remaining freed slaves economically since most of the land was still owned by the large plantation landowners who retained their holdings from before the Civil War. The economic chasm dividing white landowners and black freedmen only widened as the tenants sank further into debt to their landlords.

Westward movement of significant populations from the eastern United States originated with the discovery of gold in the West in the 1840s and picked up greater momentum after the Civil War. Settlers were lured by what they perceived as unpopulated places with land for the taking. However, when they arrived, they found that the lands were populated by earlier settlers of Spanish descent and Native Americans, who did not particularly welcome the newcomers. These original inhabitants frequently clashed with those who were moving west.

Despite having signed treaties with the United States government years earlier, virtually all were ignored and broken as westward settlement accelerated and the government was called upon to protect settlers who were en route and when they had reached their destinations. This led to a series of wars between the United States and the various Native American nations. Although the bloodshed during these encounters was great, it paled compared to the number of Native Americans who died from epidemics of deadly diseases for which they had no resistance. Eventually, the government sought to relocate inconveniently located peoples to Indian reservations, and to Oklahoma, which was lacked the resources they need and was geographically remote from their home range. The justification for this westward expansion at the expense of the previous inhabitants was that it was America's "Manifest Destiny" to "tame" and settle the continent from coast-to-coast.

Another major factor affecting the opening of the West to migration of Americans and displacement of native peoples was the expansion of the railroad. The **transcontinental railroad** was completed in 1869, joining the West Coast with the existing rail infrastructure terminating at Omaha, Nebraska, its westernmost point. This not only enabled unprecedented movement of people and goods, it also hastened the near extinction of bison, which the Indians of the Great Plains, in particular, depended on for their survival.

Once the American West was subdued and firmly under United States control, the United States started looking beyond its shores. Overseas markets were becoming important as American industry produced goods more efficiently and manufacturing capacity grew. Out of concern for the protection of shipping, the United States modernized and built up the Navy, which by 1900 ranked third in the world, giving it the means to become an imperial power. The first overseas possessions were **Midway Island** and **Alaska**, which had been purchased in 1867.

By the1880s, Secretary of State James G. Blaine pushed for expanding U.S. trade and influence to Central and South America, and in the 1890s, President Grover Cleveland invoked the **Monroe Doctrine** to intercede in Latin American affairs when it looked as though Great Britain was going to exert its influence and power in the Western Hemisphere. In the Pacific, the United States lent its support to American sugar planters who overthrew the Kingdom of **Hawaii** and eventually annexed it as U.S. territory.

During the 1890s, Spain controlled such overseas possessions as Puerto Rico, the Philippines, and Cuba. Cubans rebelled against Spanish rule, and the U.S. government found itself besieged by demands from Americans to assist the Cubans in their revolt. The event that proved a turning point for the **Spanish-American War** in 1898 was the explosion of the *USS Maine.* Two months later, Congress declared war on Spain, and the U.S. quickly defeated Spain. The war with Spain also triggered the dispatch of the fleet under Admiral **George Dewey** to the Philippines, followed by Army troops. Victory over the Spanish proved fruitful for American territorial ambitions.

Although Congress passed legislation renouncing claims to annex Cuba, in a rare moment of idealism, the United States gained control of the island of **Puerto Rico**; a permanent deep-water naval harbor at Guantanamo Bay, Cuba; the Philippines; and various other Pacific islands formerly possessed by Spain. The decision to occupy the **Philippines** rather than grant it immediate independence, led to a guerrilla war, the "Philippines Insurrection" that lasted until 1902. U.S. rule over the Philippines lasted until 1942, but unlike the guerrilla war years, American rule was relatively benign. The peace treaty gave the U.S. possession of **Puerto Rico, the Philippines, Guam and Hawaii.**

This success enlarged and expanded the U.S. role in foreign affairs. Under the administration of **Theodore Roosevelt**, the U.S. armed forces were built up, greatly increasing military strength. Roosevelt's foreign policy was summed up in the slogan of "Speak softly and carry a big stick," backing up the efforts in diplomacy with a strong military. During the years before the outbreak of World War I, evidence of U.S. emergence as a world power could be seen in a number of actions.

Using the Monroe Doctrine of non-involvement of Europe in the affairs of the Western Hemisphere, President Roosevelt forced Italy, Germany, and Great Britain to remove their blockade of Venezuela. He gained the rights to construct the **Panama Canal** by threatening force. He assumed the finances of the Dominican Republic to stabilize it and prevent any intervention by Europeans. In 1916 under President **Woodrow Wilson**, U.S. troops were sent to the Dominican Republic to keep order.

The **Panic of 1893** was a sharp decline in the United States economy that resulted in several bank failures, widespread unemployment, and a drop in farm crop prices. The panic owed partly to a run on the gold supply when people began exchanging U.S. silver notes for gold. The federal reserve of gold soon reached its minimum level, and no more notes could be redeemed. The price of silver fell and thousands of companies went bankrupt, including several major railroads. High unemployment continued for over five years following the panic. The economy and the practice of using silver and gold to back U.S. Treasury notes became central issues in the 1896 presidential elections. **William McKinley** won the election, which restored confidence, and the economy began to recover before McKinley was assassinated.

Skill 3.2   Industrialization and business-labor developments

There was a marked degree of industrialization before and during the Civil War, but at war's end, industry in America was small. Of course, industry before, during, and after the Civil War was centered mainly in the North. Yet post- war, dramatic changes took place: machines replaced hand labor, extensive nationwide railroad service made possible the wider distribution of goods, new products were invented and made available in large quantities, and large amounts of money from bankers and investors was made available for the expansion of business operations.

Cities became the centers of this new business activity resulting in mass population movements and tremendous growth. This new boom in business resulted in huge fortunes for some Americans and extreme poverty for many others. The resulting discontent led to a number of reform movements, prompting measures to control the power and size of big business and help the poor. The use of machines in industry enabled workers to produce a large quantity of goods much faster than by hand. With the increase in business, hundreds of workers were hired, assigned to perform a certain job in the production process. This was a method of organization called "**division of labor**" and by increasing the rate of production, businesses lowered prices for their products making the products affordable for more people. As a result, sales and businesses were increasingly successful and profitable.

A great variety of new products or inventions became available such as the typewriter, the telephone, barbed wire, the electric light, the phonograph, and the automobile. From this list, the one that had the greatest effect on America's economy was the automobile.

The increase in business and industry was greatly affected by the many rich natural resources that were found throughout the nation. The industrial machines were powered by the abundant water supply. The construction industry as well as products made from wood depended heavily on lumber from the forests. Coal and iron ore in abundance were needed for the steel industry, which profited and increased from the use of steel in such things as skyscrapers, automobiles, bridges, railroad tracks, and machines. Other minerals such as silver, copper, and petroleum played a large role in industrial growth, especially petroleum, from which gasoline was refined as fuel for the increasingly popular automobile.

As business grew, new methods of sales and promotion were developed. Salesmen (as they were all male back then) went to all parts of the country, promoting the varied products, opening large department stores in the growing cities, offering the varied products at reasonable affordable prices. People who lived too far from the cities, making it impossible to shop there, had the advantage of using a mail order service, buying what they needed from catalogs furnished by the companies. Developments in communication, such as the telephone and telegraph, increased the efficiency and prosperity of big business.

Investments in corporate stocks and bonds resulted from business prosperity. In their eager desire to share in the profits, individuals began investing heavily. Their investments made available the needed capital for companies to expand their operations. From this, banks increased in number throughout the country, making loans to businesses and significant contributions to economic growth. At the same time, during the 1880s, government made little effort to regulate businesses. This gave rise to **monopolies** where larger businesses were rid of their smaller competitors and assumed complete control of their industries.

Some owners in the same business would join or merge to form one company. Others formed what were called "**trusts**," a type of monopoly in which rival businesses were controlled but not formally owned. Monopolies had some good effects on the economy. Out of them grew the large, efficient corporations, which made important contributions to the growth of the nation's economy. Also, the monopolies enabled businesses to keep their sales steady and avoid sharp fluctuations in price and production.

At the same time, the downside of monopolies was the unfair business practices of the business leaders. Some acquired so much power that they took unfair advantage of others. Those who had little or no competition would require their suppliers to supply goods at a low cost, sell the finished products at high prices, and reduce the quality of the product to save money.

Skilled laborers were organized into a labor union called the **American Federation of Labor**, in an effort to gain better working conditions and wages for its members. Farmers joined organizations such as the National Grange and Farmers Alliances. Farmers were producing more food than people could afford to buy. This was the result of both new farmlands rapidly sprouting on the plains and prairies, and the development and availability of new farm machinery and newer and better methods of farming. They tried selling their surplus abroad but faced stiff competition from other nations selling the same farm products.

Other problems contributed significantly to their situation. Items they needed for daily life were priced exorbitantly high. Having to borrow money to carry on farming activities kept them constantly in debt. Higher interest rates, shortage of money, falling farm prices, dealing with the so-called middlemen, and the increasingly high charges by the railroads to haul farm products to large markets all contributed to the desperate need for reform to relieve the plight of American farmers.

The **Wagner Act** (The National Labor Relations Act) established a legal basis for unions, set collective bargaining as a matter of national policy required by the law, provided for secret ballot elections for choosing unions, and protected union members from employer intimidation and coercion. This law was later amended by the Taft-Hartley Act (1947) and by the Landrum Griffin Act (1959). The Wagner Act itself was upheld by the Supreme Court in 1937.

One of the most common tactics of the union was the **strike**. Half a million Southern mill workers walked off the job in the Great Uprising of 1934, establishing the precedent that without workers, industry could not move forward. Then, in 1936, the United Rubber Workers staged the first **sit-down strike** where instead of walking off the job, they stayed at their posts but refused to work. The United Auto Workers used the sit-down strike against General Motors in 1936.
Strikes were met with varying degrees of resistance by the companies. Sometimes, "**scabs**" were brought in to replace the striking workers. In 1936, the Anti-Strikebreaker Act (the Byrnes Act) made it illegal to transport or aid strikebreakers in interstate or foreign trade. In part this was an attempt to stem the violence often associated with management's attempts to bully the workers back into their jobs.

As the leaders of industry were often powerful community figures, they sometimes employed law enforcement to disrupt the strikes. During a strike in 1937 of the Steel Workers Organizing Committee against Republic Steel, police attacked a crowd gathered in support of the strike, killing ten and injuring eighty. This came to be called **The Memorial Day Massacre**.

A number of acts were designed to provide fair compensation and other benefits to workers. The Davis-Bacon Act was passed in 1931 and provided that employers of contractors and subcontractors on public construction should be paid the prevailing wages. The states sometimes took matters into their own hands. Wisconsin created the first unemployment insurance act in the country in 1932. The Public Contracts Act (the **Walsh-Healey Act**) of 1936 established labor standards, including minimum wages, overtime pay, child and convict labor provisions and safety standards on federal contracts. The **Fair Labor Standards** Act created a $0.25 minimum wage, stipulated time-and-a-half pay for hours over 40 per week. The Social Security Act was approved in 1935.

There were also efforts to clean up or unionize particular industries. The Supreme Court upheld the Railway Labor Act in 1930, including its prohibition of employer interference or coercion in the choice of bargaining representatives which was later applied to other organize labor unions. The Guffey Act stabilized the coal industry and improved labor conditions in 1935, though a year later it was declared unconstitutional. General Motors recognized the **United Auto Workers** and US Steel recognized the **Steel Workers Organizing Committee**, both in 1937. Then in 1938 Merchant Marine Act created a Federal Maritime Labor Board.

One of labor's biggest unions was formed in 1935. The Committee for Industrial Organization (**CIO**) was formed within the AFL to carry unionism to the industrial sector. By 1937, however, the CIO had been expelled from the AFL over charges of dual unionism or competition. It then became known as the Congress of Industrial Organizations.

Federal labor efforts included:

- The Anti-Injunction Act of 1932 which prohibited Federal injunctions in most labor disputes.
- The Wagner-Peyser Act which created the United States Employment Service within the Department of Labor in 1933.
- The Secretary of Labor calling for the first National Labor Legislation Conference to get better cooperation between the Federal Government and the States in defining a national labor legislation program in 1934.
- The U.S. joining the International Labor Organization, also in 1934.
- And the National Apprenticeship Act establishing the Bureau of Apprenticeship within the Department of Labor in 1937.

Skill 3.3   The effects of immigration, internal migration, urbanization and the industrial experience

Between 1870 and 1916, more than 25 million immigrants came into the United States adding to the phenomenal population growth taking place. This tremendous growth aided business and industry in two ways. First, the number of consumers increased creating a greater demand for products thus enlarging the markets for the products. And second, with increased production and expanding business, more workers were available for newly created jobs. The completion of the nation's transcontinental railroad in 1869 contributed greatly to the nation's economic and industrial growth. Some examples of the benefits of using the railroads include: raw materials were shipped quickly by the mining companies and finished products were sent to all parts of the country. Many wealthy industrialists and railroad owners saw tremendous profits steadily increasing due to this improved method of transportation.

Innovations in new industrial processes and technology grew at a pace unmatched at any other time in American history. **Thomas Edison** was the most prolific inventor of that time, using a systematic and efficient method to invent and improve on current technology in a profitable manner. The abundance of resources, together with growth of industry and the pace of capital investments led to the growth of cities. Populations were shifting from rural agricultural areas to urban industrial areas and by the early 1900s a third of the nation's population lived in cities. Industry needed workers in its factories, mills and plants and rural workers were being displaced by advances in farm machinery and their increasing use and other forms of automation.

The dramatic growth of population in cities was fueled by growing industries, more efficient transportation of goods and resources, and the people who migrated to those new industrial jobs, either from rural areas of the United States or immigrants from foreign lands. Increased urban populations, frequently packed into dense tenements, often without adequate sanitation or clean water, led to public health challenges that required cities to establish sanitation, water and public health departments to cope with and prevent epidemics. Political organizations also saw the advantage of mobilizing the new industrial working class and created vast patronage programs that sometimes became notorious for corruption in big-city machine politics, like **Tammany Hall** in New York. **Populism** is the philosophy concerned with the common sense needs of average people. Populism often finds expression as a reaction against perceived oppression of the average people by the wealthy elite in society. The prevalent claim of populist movements is that they will put the people first. Populism is often, though not always, connected with religious fundamentalism, racism, or nationalism. Populist movements claim to represent the majority of the people and call them to stand up to institutions or practices that seem detrimental to their well being.

Populism flourished in the late 19th and early 20th centuries. Several political parties were formed out of this philosophy, including the Greenback Party, the Populist Party, the Farmer-Labor Party, the Single Tax movement of Henry George, the Share Our Wealth movement of Huey Long, the Progressive Party, and the Union Party. In the 1890s, the People's Party won the support of millions of farmers and other working people. This party challenged the social ills of the monopolists of the "Gilded Age."

The tremendous change that resulted from the industrial revolution led to a demand for reform that would control the power wielded by big corporations. The gap between the industrial moguls and the working people was growing. This disparity between rich and poor resulted in a public outcry for reform at the same time that there was an outcry for governmental reform that would end the political corruption and elitism of the day.

The late 1800s and early 1900s were a period of the efforts of many to make significant reforms and changes in the areas of politics, society, and the economy. There was a need to reduce the levels of poverty and to improve the living conditions of those affected by it. Regulations of big business, ridding governmental corruption and making it more responsive to the needs of the people were also on the list of reforms to be accomplished. Until 1890, there was very little success, but from 1890 on, the reformers gained increased public support and were able to achieve some influence in government. Since some of these individuals referred to themselves as "**progressives**," the period of 1890 to 1917 is referred to by historians as the **Progressive Era**.

This fire was fueled by the writings of investigative journalists known as "**muckrakers**" who published scathing exposés of political and business wrongdoing and corruption. The result was the rise of a group of politicians and reformers who supported a wide array of populist causes. Although these leaders came from many different backgrounds and were driven by different ideologies, they shared a common fundamental belief that government should be eradicating social ills and promoting the common good and the equality guaranteed by the Constitution.

The reforms initiated by these leaders and the spirit of **Progressivism** were far-reaching. Politically, many states enacted the initiative and the referendum. The adoption of the recall occurred in many states. Several states enacted legislation that would undermine the power of political machines. On a national level the two most significant political changes were firstly the ratification of the 17th amendment, which required that all U.S. Senators be chosen by popular election, and, secondly, the ratification of the **19th Amendment**, which granted women the right to vote.

Major economic reforms of the period included aggressive enforcement of the **Sherman Antitrust Act**, passage of the Elkins Act, and the Hepburn Act, which gave the Interstate Commerce Commission greater power to regulate the railroads. The Pure Food and Drug Act prohibited the use of harmful chemicals in food. The Meat Inspection Act regulated the meat industry to protect the public against tainted meat. Over 2/3 of the states passed laws prohibiting child labor, workmen's compensation was mandated, and the **Department of Commerce and Labor** was created.

Responding to concern over the environmental effects of the timber, ranching, and mining industries, President Theodore Roosevelt set aside 238 million acres of federal lands to protect them from development. Wildlife preserves were established, the national park system was expanded, and the National Conservation Commission was created. The Newlands Reclamation Act also provided federal funding for the construction of irrigation projects and dams in semi-arid areas of the country.

The Wilson Administration carried out additional reforms. The Federal Reserve Act created a national banking system, providing a stable money supply. The Sherman Act and the Clayton Antitrust Act defined unfair competition, made corporate officers liable for the illegal actions of employees, and exempted labor unions from antitrust lawsuits. The Federal Trade Commission was established to enforce these measures. Finally, the 16th amendment was ratified, establishing an income tax. This measure was designed to relieve the poor of a disproportionate burden in funding the federal government and make the wealthy pay a greater share of the nation's tax burden.

Skill 3.4 Causes and consequences of U.S. intervention in World War I

U.S. involvement in World War I did not occur until 1916. When the war began in 1914, triggered by the assassination of Austrian Archduke Francis Ferdinand and his wife in Sarajevo, President Woodrow Wilson declared that the U.S. was neutral. Most Americans were opposed to any involvement anyway and were content to stay out of the matter as Europe marched off to war.

In 1916, Wilson was reelected to a second term based on a slogan proclaiming his efforts at keeping America out of the war. For a few months after, he put forth most of his efforts to stopping the war but German submarines began unlimited warfare against American merchant shipping. The development of the German *unterseeboat* or **U-boat** allowed them to efficiently attack merchant ships that were supplying their European enemies from Canada and the US. In 1915, a German U-boat sunk the passenger liner RMS **Lusitania**, killing over 1,000 civilians including over 100 Americans. This attack outraged the American public and turned public opinion against Germany. The attack on the Lusitania became a rallying point for those advocating US involvement in the European conflict.

Great Britain intercepted and decoded a secret message from Germany to Mexico urging Mexico to go to war against the U.S. The publishing of this information, known as the **Zimmerman Note,** along with continued German destruction of American ships resulted in the eventual entry of the U.S. into the conflict, the first time the country prepared to fight in a conflict not on American soil. Though unprepared for war, governmental efforts and activities resulted in massive defense mobilization with America's economy directed to the war effort. Though America made important contributions of war materials, its greatest contribution to the war was manpower, soldiers desperately needed by the Allies.

Some ten months before the war ended, President Wilson had proposed a program called the **Fourteen Points** as a method of bringing the war to an end with an equitable peace settlement. In these Points he had five points setting out general ideals; there were eight pertaining to immediately working to resolve territorial and political problems; and the fourteenth point counseled establishing an organization of nations to help keep world peace.

When Germany agreed in 1918 to an armistice, it assumed that the peace settlement would be drawn up on the basis of these Fourteen Points. However, the peace conference in Paris ignored these points and Wilson had to be content with efforts at establishing the **League of Nations**. Italy, France, and Great Britain, having suffered and sacrificed far more in the war than America, wanted retribution. The treaties punished severely the Central Powers, taking away arms and territories and requiring payment of reparations. Germany was punished more than the others and, according to one clause in the treaty, was forced to assume the responsibility for causing the war.

President Wilson lost in his efforts to get the U.S. Senate to approve the peace treaty. The Senate at the time was a reflection of American public opinion and its rejection of the treaty was a rejection of Wilson. The approval of the treaty would have made the U.S. a member of the League of Nations but Americans had just come off a bloody war to ensure that democracy would exist throughout the world. Americans just did not want to accept any responsibility that resulted from its new position of power and were afraid that membership in the League of Nations would embroil the U.S. in future disputes in Europe.

The harsh treatment of Germany would not be forgotten, especially by the Germans themselves as they sought to rebuild their nation. World War I left European leaders skittish of another major conflict, and the United States once again adopted a policy of isolationism. It seemed as though few real lessons had been learned, and the seeds were sown for another conflict.

Skill 3.5   How national and international decisions and conflicts between World War I and World War II affected the United States

Some ten months before World War I ended, President Wilson proposed a program called the **Fourteen Points** as a method of bringing the war to an end with an equitable peace settlement. Five points set out general ideals; eight pertained to immediately working to resolve territorial and political problems; and the fourteenth point counseled establishing an organization of nations to help keep world peace.

When Germany agreed in1918 to an armistice, it assumed that the peace settlement would be drawn up on the basis of these Fourteen Points. However, the peace conference in Paris ignored the points, and Wilson had to be content with efforts at establishing the **League of Nations**. Italy, France, and Great Britain, who had sacrificed more in the war than America did, wanted retribution. Their treaties severely punished the Central Powers--taking away arms and territories and requiring payment of reparations. Germany was punished the most, and had to assume the responsibility for causing the war.

The decade of the 1920s saw tremendous changes in the United States, signifying the beginning of its development into its modern society. The shift from farm to city life was occurring in tremendous numbers. Social changes and problems were occurring at such a fast pace that it was extremely difficult and perplexing for many Americans to adjust to them.

Politically the **Eighteenth Amendment** to the Constitution, the Prohibition Amendment, prohibited selling alcoholic beverages throughout the U.S. and resulted in problems affecting society. The passage of the **Nineteenth Amendment** gave women their right to vote in all elections. The decade of the 1920s also showed a marked change in roles and opportunities for women with more and more women seeking and finding careers outside the home.

The **U.S. economy** experienced a tremendous period of boom. Restrictions on business because of war no longer existed, and the conservatives in control adopted policies that helped and encouraged big business. To keep foreign goods from competing with American goods, tariffs were raised to the highest level. American manufacturers developed new products, and many different items became readily available. These included refrigerators, radios, washing machines, and, most importantly, the automobile. Much of the stock speculation involved paying a small part of the cost and borrowing the rest. This led eventually to the stock market crash.

Pre-war empires lost tremendous amounts of territories as well as the wealth of natural resources in them. New, independent nations were formed and some predominately ethnic areas came under control of 1929, financial ruin for many investors and a weakening of nations of different cultural backgrounds. Some national boundary changes overlapped and created tensions and hard feelings as well as political and economic confusion. The wishes and desires of every national or cultural group could not possibly be realized and satisfied, resulting in disappointments for both those who were victorious and those who were defeated.

The Depression hit the United States tremendously hard resulting in bank failures, loss of jobs due to cut-backs in production and a lack of money leading to a sharp decline in spending which in turn affected businesses, factories and stores, and higher unemployment. Farm products were not affordable so the farmers suffered even more. Foreign trade sharply decreased, and in the early 1930s, the U.S. economy was effectively paralyzed. Europe was affected even more so.

The influence of the automobile, the entertainment industry, and the rejection of the morals and values of pre-World War I life, resulted in the fast-paced **Roaring Twenties**, and had significant effects on events leading to the Depression-era 1930s and another world war. Many Americans greatly desired the pre-war life and supported political policies and candidates in favor of the return to what was considered normal. It was desired to end government's strong role and adopt a policy of isolating the country from world affairs, a result of the war.

Americans in the 1920s heavily invested in corporation stocks, providing companies a large amount of capital1930s, set the stage for expanding their businesses. The more money investors put into the stock market, the more the value of the stocks increased. This, in turn, led to widespread speculation that increased stock value to a point beyond the level that was justified by earnings and dividends.

Prohibition of the sale of alcohol had caused the increased activities of **bootlegging** and the rise of underworld **gangs** and illegal **speakeasies**, as well as the **jazz** music and dances that accompanied them. The customers of these clubs were considered "modern," reflected by extremes in clothing, hairstyles, and attitudes towards authority and life. Movies and, to a certain degree, other types of entertainment, along with increased interest in sports figures and the accomplishments of national heroes, such as **Lindbergh**, influenced Americans to admire, emulate, and support individual accomplishments.

As wild and uninhibited modern behavior became, this decade witnessed an increase in a religious tradition known as "**revivalism**," or emotional preaching.

Although many Americans demanded law and order, the administration of President **Warren G. Harding** was marked by widespread corruption and scandal, not unlike the administration of **Ulysses S. Grant**. Neither of them apparently knew about the corruption. The decade of the 1920s also saw the resurgence of such racist organizations as the **Ku Klux Klan,** Adolf Hitler and his **Nationalist Socialist Party,** and World War II.

World War I had seriously damaged the **economies of the European countries,** both the victors and the defeated, leaving them deeply in debt. There was difficulty on both sides paying off war debts and loans. It was difficult to find jobs, and some countries such as Japan and Italy found themselves without enough resources but more than enough people. Solving these problems by expanding the territory merely set up conditions for war later.

Germany suffered with runaway inflation ruining the value of its money and wiping out the savings of German citizens. Even though the U.S. lent money to Germany and this helped the government to restore some order, and helped to provide a short existence of some economic stability in Europe, the Great Depression served to undo any good that had been done. Mass unemployment, poverty, and despair greatly weakened the democratic governments that had been formed and greatly strengthened the increasing power and influence of extreme political movements, such as communism, fascism, and national-socialism. These ideologies promised to put an end to the economic problems.

The extreme form of patriotism called *nationalism* that had been the chief cause of World War I grew even stronger after the war ended in 1918. The political, social, and economic unrest fueled nationalism, and it became an effective tool enabling dictators to gain and maintain power from the 1930s to the end of World War II in 1945. In the Soviet Union, **Josef Stalin** succeeded in gaining political control and establishing a strong harsh dictatorship.

Benito Mussolini and the Fascist party, promising prosperity and order in Italy, gained national support and set up a strong government. In Japan, although **Emperor Hirohito** was considered ruler, actual control and administration of government was held by military officers. In Germany, the results of war, harsh treaty terms, loss of territory, great economic chaos and collapse all enabled **Adolf Hitler** and his Nazi party to gain complete power and control.

Germany, Italy, and Japan initiated a policy of aggressive territorial expansion In 1931, Japanese forces seized control of Manchuria, a part of China containing rich natural resources, In 1937, Japan began an attack on China, occupying most of its eastern part by 1938. Italy invaded Ethiopia in Africa in 1935, having it totally under its control by 1936.

In Germany, almost immediately after taking power, in direct violation of the World War I peace treaty, Hitler began the buildup of the armed forces. He sent troops into the Rhineland in 1936, invaded Austria in 1938 and united it with Germany, seized control of the Sudetenland in 1938 (part of western Czechoslovakia and containing mostly Germans), the rest of Czechoslovakia in March 1939, and, on September 1, 1939, began World War II in Europe by invading Poland. In 1940, Germany invaded and controlled Norway, Denmark, Belgium, Luxembourg, the Netherlands, and France.

Skill 3.6   The causes of the Great Depression, its effects on U.S. society, and the impact of the New Deal on American life

The 1929 Stock Market Crash was the powerful event that is generally interpreted as the beginning of the Great Depression in America. Although the crash of the Stock Market was unexpected, it was not without identifiable causes. The 1920s had been a decade of social and economic growth and hope. But the attitudes and actions of the 1920s regarding wealth, production, and investment created several trends that quietly set the stage for the 1929 disaster.

Uneven distribution of wealth: In the 1920s, the distribution of wealth between the rich and the middle class was grossly disproportionate. In 1929, the combined income of the top 0.1% of the population was equal to the combined income of the bottom 42%. The top 0.1% of the population controlled 34% of all savings, while 80% of Americans had no savings. Capitalism was making the wealthy richer at the expense of the workers. Between 1920 and 1929, the amount of disposable income per person rose 9%. The top 0.1% of the population, however, enjoyed an increase in disposable income of 75%. One reason for this disparity was increased manufacturing productivity during the 1920s. Average worker productivity in manufacturing increased 32% during this period. Yet, wages in manufacturing increased only 8%. The wages of the workers rose very slowly, failing to keep pace with increasing productivity. As production costs fell and prices remained constant, profits soared. But profits were retained by the companies and owners.

The Legislative and Executive branches of the Coolidge administration tended to favor business and the wealthy. The Revenue Act of 1926 reduced income taxes for the wealthy significantly. This bill lowered taxes so that a person with a million-dollar income saw his/her taxes reduced from $600,000 to $200,000. Despite the rise of labor unions, even the Supreme Court ruled in ways that further widened the gap between the rich and the middle class. In the case of Adkins v. Children's Hospital (1923), the Court ruled that minimum wage legislation was unconstitutional.

This kind of disparity in the distribution of wealth weakened the economy. Demand was unable to equal supply. The surplus of manufactured goods was beyond the reach of the poor and the middle class. The wealthy, however, could purchase all they wanted with a smaller and smaller portion of their income. This meant that in order for the economy to remain stable, the wealthy had to invest their money and spend money on luxury items while others bought on credit.

The majority of the population did not have enough money to buy what was necessary to meet their needs. The concept of buying on credit caught on very quickly. Buying on credit, however, creates artificial demand for products people cannot ordinarily afford. This has two effects: First, at some point, there is less need to purchase products (because they have already been bought). Second, at some point, paying for previous purchases makes it impossible to purchase new products. This exacerbated the problem of a surplus of goods.

The economy also relied on investment and luxury spending by the rich in the 1920s. Luxury spending, however, only occurs when people are confident with regard to the economy and the future. Should these people lose confidence, that luxury spending would come to an abrupt halt. This is precisely what happened when the stock market crashed in 1929. Investing in business produces returns for the investor. During the 1920s, investing was very healthy. Investors, however, began to expect greater returns on their investments. This led many to make speculative investments in risky opportunities.

The disproportionate distribution of wealth between the rich and the middle class mirrors the uneven distribution of wealth between industries. In 1929, half of all corporate wealth was controlled by just 200 companies. The automotive industry was growing exceptionally quickly, but agriculture was steadily declining. In fact, in 1921 food prices dropped about 70% due to surplus. The average income in agriculture was only about one-third of the national average across all industries.

Two industries, automotive and radio, drove the economy in the 1920s. During this decade, the government tended to support new industries rather than agriculture. During WWI, the government had subsidized farms and paid ridiculously high prices for grains. Farmers had been encouraged to buy and farm more land and to use new technology to increase production. The nation was feeding much of Europe during and in the aftermath of the war. But when the war ended, these farm policies were cut off. Prices plummeted, farmers fell into debt, and farm prices declined. The agriculture industry was on the brink of ruin before the stock market crash.

The concentration of production and economic stability in the automotive industry and the production and sale of radios was expected to last forever. But there comes a point when the growth of an industry slows due to market saturation. When these two industries declined, due to decreased demand, they caused the collapse of other industries upon which they were dependent (e.g., rubber tires, glass, fuel, construction, etc.).

Another factor contributing to the Great Depression was the **economic condition of Europe.** The U.S. was lending money to European nations to rebuild. Many of these countries used this money to purchase U.S. food and manufactured goods. But they were not able to pay off their debts. While the U.S. was providing money, food, and goods to Europe, however, it was not willing to buy European goods. Trade barriers were enacted to maintain a favorable trade balance.

Risky speculative investments in the stock market were another major factor contributing to the stock market crash of 1929 and the ensuing depression. Stock market speculation was spectacular throughout the 1920s. In 1929, shares traded on the New York Stock Exchange reached 1,124,800,410. In 1928 and 1929 stock prices doubled and tripled (RCA stock prices rose from 85 to 420 within one year). The opportunity to achieve such profits was irresistible. In much the same way that buying goods on credit became popular, buying stock on margin allowed people to invest a very small amount of money in the hope of receiving exceptional profit. This created an investing craze that drove the market higher and higher. But brokers were also charging higher interest rates on their margin loans (nearly 20%). If, however, the price of the stock dropped, the investor owed the broker the amount borrowed plus interest.

Several other factors are cited by some scholars as contributing to the Great Depression. First, in 1929, the Federal Reserve increased interest rates. Second, some believe that as interest rates rose and the stock market began to decline, people began to hoard money. This was certainly the case after the crash. There is a question that it was a cause of the crash.

In September 1929, stock prices began to slip somewhat, yet people remained optimistic. On Monday, October 21, prices began to fall quickly. The volume traded was so high that the tickers were unable to keep up. Investors were frightened, and they started selling very quickly. This caused further collapse. For the next two days prices stabilized somewhat. On **Black Thursday**, October 24, prices plummeted again. By this time investors had lost confidence. On Friday and Saturday an attempt to stop the crash was made by some leading bankers. But on Monday the 28th, prices began to fall again, declining by 13% in one day. The next day, **Black Tuesday, October 29**, saw 16.4 million shares traded. Stock prices fell so far, that at many times no one was willing to buy at any price.

Unemployment quickly reached 25% nationwide. People thrown out of their homes created makeshift domiciles of cardboard, scraps of wood and tents. With unmasked reference to President Hoover, who was quite obviously overwhelmed by the situation and incompetent to deal with it, these communities were called "**Hoovervilles**." Families stood in bread lines, rural workers left the dust bowl of the plains to search for work in California, and banks failed. More than 100,000 businesses failed between 1929 and 1932. The despair that swept the nation left an indelible scar on all who endured the Depression.

When the stock market crashed, businesses collapsed. Without demand for products other businesses and industries collapsed. This set in motion a domino effect, bringing down the businesses and industries that provided raw materials or components to these industries. Hundreds of thousands became jobless. Then the jobless often became homeless. Desperation prevailed. Little had been done to assess the toll hunger, inadequate nutrition, or starvation took on the health of those who were children during this time. Indeed, food was cheap, relatively speaking, but there was little money to buy it.

Everyone who lived through the Great Depression was permanently affected in some way. Many never trusted banks again. Many people of this generation later hoarded cash so they would not risk losing everything again. Some permanently rejected the use of credit.

In the immediate aftermath of the stock market crash, many urged President Herbert Hoover to provide government relief. Hoover responded by urging the nation to be patient. By the time he signed relief bills in 1932, it was too late.

Hoover's bid for re-election in 1932 failed. The new president, Franklin D. Roosevelt, won the White House on his promise to the American people of a "new deal." Upon assuming the office, Roosevelt and his advisers immediately launched a massive program of innovation and experimentation to try to bring the Depression to an end and get the nation back on track. Congress gave the president unprecedented power to act to save the nation. During the next eight years, the most extensive and broadly-based legislation in the nation's history was enacted. The legislation was intended to accomplish three goals: relief, recovery, and reform.

The first step in the "**New Deal**" was to relieve suffering. This was accomplished through a number of job-creation projects. The second step, the recovery aspect, was to stimulate the economy. The third step was to create social and economic change through innovative legislation.

The National Recovery Administration attempted to accomplish several goals:

- Restore employment
- Increase general purchasing power
- Provide character-building activity for unemployed youth
- Encourage decentralization of industry and thus divert population from crowded cities to rural or semi-rural communities
- Develop river resources in the interest of navigation and cheap power and light
- Complete flood control on a permanent basis
- Enlarge the national program of forest protection and develop forest resources
- Control farm production and improve farm prices
- Assist home builders and home owners
- Restore public faith in banking and trust operations
- Recapture the value of physical assets, whether in real property, securities, or other investments

These objectives and their accomplishment implied a restoration of public confidence and courage.

Among the "alphabet organizations" set up to work out the details of the recovery plan, the most prominent were:

- **Agricultural Adjustment Administration** (AAA), designed to readjust agricultural production and prices thereby boosting farm income
- **Civilian Conservation Corps** (CCC), designed to give wholesome, useful activity in the forestry service to unemployed young men
- **Civil Works Administration** (CWA) and the **Public Works Administration** (PWA), designed to give employment in the construction and repair of public buildings, parks, and highways
- **Works Progress Administration** (WPA), whose task was to move individuals from relief rolls to work projects or private employment

The **Tennessee Valley Authority** (TVA) was of a more permanent nature, designed to improve the navigability of the Tennessee River and increase productivity of the timber and farm lands in its valley. This program built 16 dams that provided water control and hydroelectric generation.

The **Public Works Administration** employed Americans on over 34,000 public works projects at a cost of more than $4 billion. Among these projects was the construction of a highway that linked the Florida Keys and Miami, the Boulder Dam (now the Hoover Dam), and numerous highway projects.

To provide economic stability and prevent another crash, Congress passed the **Glass-Steagall Act**, which separated banking and investing. The Securities and Exchange Commission was created to regulate dangerous speculative practices on Wall Street. The Wagner Act guaranteed a number of rights to workers and unions in an effort to improve worker-employer relations.

The **Social Security Act of 1935** established pensions for the aged and infirm as well as a system of unemployment insurance.

Much of the recovery program was to respond to an emergency, but certain permanent national policies emerged. The intention of the public was to employ their government in supervising and, to an extent, regulating business operations—from corporate activities to labor problems. This included protecting bank depositors and the credit system of the country, employing gold resources and currency adjustments to aid permanent restoration of normal living, and, if possible, establishing a line of subsistence below which no useful citizen would be permitted to sink.

Many of the steps taken by the Roosevelt administration have had far-reaching effects. They alleviated the economic disaster of the Great Depression, enacted controls that would mitigate the risk of another stock market crash, and provided greater security for workers. The nation's economy, however, did not fully recover until America entered World War II.

Skill 3.7   Causes, key events, and consequences of U.S. participation in World War II

After war began in Europe in 1939, U.S. **President Franklin D. Roosevelt** announced that the United States was neutral. Most Americans, although hoping for an Allied victory, wanted the U.S. to stay out of the war. President Roosevelt and his supporters, called "interventionists," favored all aid except war to the Allied nations fighting Axis aggression. They were fearful that an Axis victory would seriously threaten and endanger all democracies. On the other hand, the "isolationists" were against any U.S. aid being given to the warring nations, accusing President Roosevelt of leading the U.S. into a war very much unprepared to fight. Roosevelt's plan was to defeat the Axis nations by sending the Allied nations the equipment needed to fight; ships, aircraft, tanks, and other war materials.

In Asia, the U.S. had opposed Japan's invasion of Southeast Asia, an effort to gain Japanese control of that region's rich resources. Consequently, the U.S. stopped all important exports to Japan, whose industries depended heavily on petroleum, scrap metal, and other raw materials. Later Roosevelt refused the Japanese withdrawal of its funds from American banks. General Tojo became the Japanese premier in October 1941 and quickly realized that the U.S. Navy was powerful enough to block Japanese expansion into Asia. Deciding to cripple the Pacific Fleet, the Japanese aircraft, without warning, bombed the Fleet December 7, 1941, while at anchor in **Pearl Harbor** in Hawaii. Temporarily it was a success. It destroyed many aircraft and disabled much of the U.S. Pacific Fleet. In the end, it was a costly mistake as it quickly motivated the Americans to prepare for war.

Military strategy in the European theater of war as developed by **Roosevelt, Churchill, and Stalin** was to concentrate on Germany's defeat first, then Japan's. The start was made in North Africa, pushing Germans and Italians off the continent, beginning in the summer of 1942 and ending successfully in May, 1943. Before the war, Hitler and Stalin had signed a non-aggression pact in 1939, which Hitler violated in 1941 by invading the Soviet Union. The German defeat at Stalingrad, which marked a turning point in the war, was brought about by a combination of entrapment of German troops by Soviet troops and the death of many more Germans by starvation and freezing due to the horrendous winter conditions. All of this occurred at the same time the Allies were driving them out of North Africa.

The liberation of Italy began in July 1943 and ended May 2, 1945. The third part of the strategy was **D-Day, June 6, 1944,** with the Allied invasion of France at Normandy. At the same time, starting in January, 1943, the Soviets began pushing the German troops back into Europe greatly assisted by supplies from Britain and the United States. By April, 1945, Allies occupied positions beyond the Rhine and the Soviets moved on to Berlin, surrounding it by April 25. Germany surrendered May 7 and the war in Europe was finally over.

The years between WWI and WWII had produced significant advancement in aircraft technology. But the pace of aircraft development and production was dramatically increased during WWII. Major developments included flight-based weapon delivery systems such as the long-range bomber, the first jet fighter, the first cruise missile, and the first ballistic missile, although the cruise and ballistic missiles were not widely used during the war. Glider planes were heavily used in WWII because they were silent upon approach. Another significant development was the broad use of paratrooper units. Finally, hospital planes came into use to extract the seriously wounded from the front and transport them to hospitals for treatment.

Weapons and technology in other areas also improved rapidly during the war. These advances were critical in determining the outcome of the war. Used for the first time were devices such as radar and electronic computers. More new inventions were registered for patents than ever before. Most of these new ideas were aimed to either kill or prevent soldiers from being killed.

The war began with essentially the same weaponry that had been used in WWI. The aircraft carrier joined the battleship on the seas. Light tanks were developed to meet the needs of a changing battlefield, and other armored vehicles were developed. Submarines were also perfected during this period. Numerous other weapons of modern warfare were also developed or invented to meet the needs of battle during WWII: the bazooka, the rocket propelled grenade, anti-tank weapons, assault rifles, cruise missiles, rocket artillery, guided weapons, torpedoes, self-guiding weapons and napalm.

The **Yalta Conference** took place in Yalta in February 1945, between the Allied leaders Winston Churchill, Franklin Roosevelt and Joseph Stalin. With the defeat of Nazi Germany within sight, the three allies met to determine the shape of post-war Europe. Germany was to be divided into four zones of occupation, as was the capital city of Berlin. Germany was also to undergo demilitarization and to make reparations for the war. Poland was to remain under control of Soviet Russia. Roosevelt also received a promise from Stalin that the Soviet Union would join the new United Nations.

Following the surrender of Germany in May, 1945, the Allies called the Potsdam Conference in July, between Clement Attlee, Harry Truman and Stalin. **The Potsdam Conference** addressed the administration of post-war Germany and provided for the forced migration of millions of Germans from previously occupied regions.

Meanwhile, in the Pacific, in the six months after the attack on Pearl Harbor, Japanese forces moved across Southeast Asia and the western Pacific Ocean. By August, 1942, the Japanese Empire was at its largest size and stretched northeast to Alaska's Aleutian Islands, west to Burma, south to what is now Indonesia. Invaded and controlled areas included Hong Kong, Guam, Wake Island, Thailand, part of Malaysia, Singapore, the Philippines, and bombed Darwin on the north coast of Australia.

The raid of **General Doolittle's** bombers on Japanese cities and the American naval victory at **Midway** along with the fighting in the **Battle of the Coral Sea** helped turn the tide against Japan. **Island-hopping** by U.S. Seabees and Marines and the grueling bloody battles fought resulted in gradually pushing the Japanese back towards Japan. After victory was attained in Europe, concentrated efforts were made to secure Japan's surrender, but it took dropping two atomic bombs on the cities of **Hiroshima** and **Nagasaki** to finally end the war in the Pacific.

The development and use of the atomic bomb during WWII was probably the most profound military development of the war years. This invention made it possible for a single plane to carry a single bomb that was sufficiently powerful to destroy an entire city. It was believed that possession of the bomb would serve as a deterrent to any nation because it would make aggression against a nation with a bomb a decision for mass suicide.

Two nuclear bombs were dropped in 1945 on the cities of Nagasaki and Hiroshima. They caused the immediate deaths of 100,000 to 200,000 people, and far more deaths over time. This was (and still is) a controversial decision. Those who opposed the use of the atom bomb argued that was an unnecessary act of mass killing, particularly of non-combatants. Proponents argued that it ended the war sooner, thus resulting in fewer casualties on both sides. The development and use of nuclear weapons marked the beginning of a new age in warfare that created greater distance from the act of killing and eliminated the ability to minimize the effect of war on non-combatants.

Japan formally surrendered on September 2, 1945, aboard the U.S. battleship Missouri, anchored in Tokyo Bay. The war was finally ended.

After Japan's defeat, the Allies began a military occupation directed by American **General Douglas MacArthur**, who introduced a number of reforms eventually ridding Japan of its military institutions transforming it into a democracy. A constitution was drawn up in 1947 transferring all political rights from the emperor to the people, granting women the right to vote, and denying Japan the right to declare war. War crimes trials of twenty-five war leaders and government officials were also conducted. The U.S. did not sign a peace treaty until 1951. The treaty permitted Japan to rearm but took away its overseas empire.

Again, after a major world war came efforts to prevent war from occurring again throughout the world. Preliminary work began in 1943 when the U.S., Great Britain, the Soviet Union, and China sent representatives to Moscow where they agreed to set up an international organization that would work to promote peace around the earth. In 1944, the four Allied powers met again and made the decision to name the organization the **United Nations**. In 1945, a charter for the U. N. was drawn up and signed, taking effect in October of that year.

COMPETENCY 0004   Understand major political, economic, and social developments in U.S. history from 1945 to the present

Skill 4.1   U.S. foreign policy during the Cold War and the impact of the Cold War on U.S. politics

After the end of the Second World War, the United States perceived its greatest threat to be the expansion of Communism in the world. To that end, it devoted a larger and larger share of its foreign policy, diplomacy, and both economic and military might to combating it.

In the aftermath of the Second World War, with the Soviet Union having emerged as the *second* strongest power on Earth, the United States embarked on a policy known as "**Containment**" of the Communist menace. This involved what came to be known as the "**Marshall Plan**" and the "**Truman Doctrine**." The Marshall Plan involved the economic aid that was sent to Europe in the aftermath of the Second World War aimed at preventing the spread of communism.

The Truman Doctrine offered military aid to those countries that were in danger of communist upheaval. This led to the era known as the **Cold War** in which the United States took the lead along with the Western European nations against the Soviet Union and the Eastern Bloc countries. It was also at this time that the United States finally gave up on George Washington's' advice against "European entanglements" and joined the **North Atlantic Treaty Organization** or **NATO**. This was formed in 1949 and was comprised of the United States and several Western European nations for the purposes of opposing communist aggression.

In the 1950s, the United States embarked on what was called the **Eisenhower Doctrine** after the then President Eisenhower. This aimed at trying to maintain peace in a troubled area of the world, the Middle East. However, unlike the Truman Doctrine in Europe, it would have little success.

See Skills 4.2 and 10.5 for more information on the Cold War.

Skill 4.2   U.S. foreign policy in the second half of the 20th century

The first "hot war" in the post-World War II era was the **Korean War**, which began June 25, 1950 and ended with a truce on July 27, 1953. Troops from Communist North Korea invaded democratic South Korea in an effort to unite both sections under Communist control. The United Nations organization asked its member nations to furnish troops to help restore peace. Many nations responded and President Truman sent American troops to help the South Koreans.

The war dragged on for three years and ended with a truce, not a peace treaty. Like Germany then, Korea remained divided and does so to this day, with the two Koreas facing each other across the longest militarized border in the world, the Demilitarized Zone, or **DMZ**.

In 1954, the French were forced to give up their colonial claims in Indochina, the present-day countries of **Vietnam**, **Laos**, and **Cambodia**. Afterwards, the Communist northern part of Vietnam began battling with the democratic southern part over control of the entire country. In the late 1950s and early 1960s, U.S. Presidents Eisenhower and Kennedy sent to Vietnam a number of military advisers and military aid to assist and support South Vietnam's non-Communist government. During Lyndon Johnson's presidency, the war escalated with thousands of American troops being sent to participate in combat with the South Vietnamese. The war was extremely unpopular in America and caused such serious divisiveness among its citizens that Johnson decided not to seek reelection in 1968. It was in President Richard Nixon's second term in office that the U.S. signed an agreement ending war in Vietnam and restoring peace. This was done January 27, 1973, and by March 29, the last American combat troops and American prisoners of war left Vietnam for home. It was the longest war in U.S. history and to this day carries the perception that it was a "lost war."

In 1962, during the administration of President **John F. Kennedy**, Premier Khrushchev and the Soviets decided, as a protective measure for Cuba against an American invasion, to install nuclear missiles on the island. In October, American U-2 spy planes photographed over Cuba what were identified as missile bases under construction. The decision the White House faced was how to handle the situation without starting a war. The only recourse was removal of the missile sites and prevention of more sites. Kennedy announced that the U.S. had set up a "quarantine" of Soviet ships heading to Cuba. It was in reality a blockade but the "blockade" could not be used as a blockade was actually considered an act of war.

A week of incredible tension and anxiety gripped the entire world until Khrushchev capitulated. Soviet ships carrying missiles for the Cuban bases turned back and the crisis eased. What precipitated the crisis was Khrushchev's underestimation of Kennedy. The President made no effort to prevent the erection of the Berlin Wall and was reluctant to commit American troops to invade Cuba and overthrow Fidel Castro. The Soviets assumed this was a weakness and decided they could install the missiles without any interference.

As tensions eased in the aftermath of the crisis, several agreements were made. The missiles in Turkey were removed, as they were obsolete. A telephone "hot line" was set up between Moscow and Washington to make it possible for the two heads of government to have instant contact with each other. The U.S. agreed to sell its surplus wheat to the Soviets.

Probably the highlight of the foreign policy of **President Richard Nixon**, after the end of the Vietnam War and withdrawal of troops, was his 1972 trip to China. Since 1949, when the Communists gained control of China, the policy of the U.S. government had been to refuse to recognize the Communist government. Instead the U.S. regarded the legitimate government of **China** to be that of Chiang Kai-shek, exiled on the island of Taiwan.

In 1971, Nixon sent Henry Kissinger on a secret trip to Peking to investigate whether or not it would be possible for America to give recognition to China. In February 1972, President and Mrs. Nixon spent a number of days in the country visiting well-known Chinese landmarks, dining with the two leaders, Mao Zedong and Chou En-lai. Agreements were made for cultural and scientific exchanges, eventual resumption of trade, and future unification of the mainland with Taiwan. In 1979, formal diplomatic recognition was achieved. With this one visit, the pattern of the Cold War was essentially shifted.

In the administration of **President Jimmy Carter**, Egyptian President Anwar el-Sadat and Israeli Prime Minister Menachem Begin met at presidential retreat **Camp David** and agreed, after a series of meetings, to sign a formal treaty of peace between the two countries. In 1979, the Soviet invasion of Afghanistan was perceived by Carter and his advisers as a threat to the rich oil fields in the Persian Gulf but at the time, U.S. military capability to prevent further Soviet aggression in the Middle East was weak. The last year of Carter's presidential term was taken up with the fifty-three American hostages held in Iran. The shah had been deposed and control of the government and the country was in the hands of Muslim leader, Ayatollah Ruhollah Khomeini.

Khomeini's extreme hatred for the U.S. was the result of the 1953 overthrow of Iran's Mossadegh government, sponsored by the CIA. To make matters worse, the CIA proceeded to train the shah's ruthless secret police force. So when the terminally ill exiled shah was allowed into the U.S. for medical treatment, a fanatical mob stormed into the American embassy taking the fifty-three Americans as prisoners, supported and encouraged by Khomeini.

President Carter froze all Iranian assets in the U.S., set up trade restrictions, and approved a risky rescue attempt, which failed. He had appealed to the UN for aid in gaining release for the hostages and to European allies to join the trade embargo on Iran. Khomeini ignored UN requests for releasing the Americans and Europeans refused to support the embargo so as not to risk losing access to Iran's oil. American prestige was damaged and Carter's chances for reelection were doomed. The hostages were released on the day of Ronald Reagan's inauguration as President when Carter released Iranian assets as ransom.

The foreign policy of **President Ronald Reagan** was, in his first term, focused primarily on the Western Hemisphere, particularly in Central America and the West Indies. U.S. involvement in the domestic revolutions of El Salvador and Nicaragua continued into Reagan's second term when Congress held televised hearings on what came to be known as the **Iran-Contra Affair**. A cover-up was exposed showing that profits from secretly selling military hardware to Iran had been used to give support to rebels, called Contras, who were fighting in Nicaragua.

In 1983 in Lebanon, 241 American Marines were killed when an Islamic suicide bomber drove an explosive-laden truck into U.S. Marines headquarters located at the airport in Beirut. This tragic event came as part of the unrest and violence between the Israelis and the Palestinian Liberation Organization (PLO) forces in southern Lebanon.

In the same month, 1,900 U.S. Marines landed on the island of **Grenada** to rescue a small group of American medical students at the medical school and depose the leftist government.

Perhaps the most intriguing and far-reaching event towards the end of Reagan's second term was the arms-reduction agreement Reagan reached with Soviet General Secretary **Mikhail Gorbachev**. Gorbachev began easing East-West tensions by stressing the importance of cooperation with the West and easing the harsh and restrictive life of the people in the Soviet Union. Though regarded as a fierce Cold Warrior, having compared the Soviet Union to an "evil empire," Reagan proved willing to talk repeatedly with the Soviets, and a new level of accord was reached. In retrospect, it was clearly a prelude to the events occurring during the administration of **President George Bush.**

After Bush took office, it appeared for a brief period that democracy would gain a hold and influence in China with democracy protests in **Tianamen Square**, but the brief movement was quickly and decisively crushed. The biggest surprise was the fall of the **Berlin Wall**, resulting in the unification of all of Germany, the loss of power of the Communists in other Eastern European countries, and the fall of Communism in the Soviet Union and the breakup of its republics into independent nations. The countries of Poland, Hungary, Romania, Czechoslovakia, Albania, and Bulgaria replaced Communist rule for a democratic one.

The former **Yugoslavia** broke apart into individual ethnic enclaves with the republics of Serbia, Croatia, and Bosnia-Herzegovina embarking on wars of ethnic cleansing between Catholics, Orthodox, and Muslims. In Russia, as in the other former republics and satellites, democratic governments were put into operation and the difficult task of changing communist economies into ones of capitalistic free enterprise began. It appeared that the tensions and dangers of the post-World War II "Cold War" between the U.S. and Soviet-led Communism were over.

President Bush, in December of 1989, sent U.S. troops to invade **Panama** and arrest the Panamanian dictator Manuel Noriega. Although he had periodically assisted CIA operations with intelligence information, at the same time, Noriega laundered money from drug smuggling and gunrunning through Panama's banks. When a political associate tried unsuccessfully to depose him and an off-duty U.S. Marine was shot and killed at a roadblock, Bush acted. Noriega was brought to the U.S. where he stood trial on charges of drug distribution and racketeering.

During the time of the American hostage crisis, Iraq and Iran fought a war in which the U.S. and most of Iraq's neighbors supported Iraq. In a five-year period, **Saddam Hussein** received from the U.S. $500 million worth of American technology, including lasers, advanced computers, and special machine tools used in missile development. The Iraq-Iran war was a bloody one resulting in a stalemate with a UN truce ending it. Deeply in debt from the war and totally dependent on oil revenues, Saddam invaded and occupied Kuwait. The U.S. made extensive plans to put into operation strategy to successfully carry out **Operation Desert Storm**, the liberation of Kuwait. In four days, February 24-28, 1991, the war was over and Iraq had been defeated, its troops driven back into their country. Saddam remained in power although Iraq's economy was seriously damaged.

President Bill Clinton sent U.S. troops to Haiti to protect the efforts of Jean-Bertrand Aristide to gain democratic power and to Bosnia to assist UN peacekeeping forces. He also inherited from the Bush administration the problem of Somalia in East Africa, where U.S. troops had been sent in December 1992 to support UN efforts to end the starvation of the Somalis and restore peace. The efforts were successful at first, but eventually failed due to the severity of the intricate political problems within the country. After U.S. soldiers were killed in an ambush along with 300 Somalis, American troops were withdrawn and returned home.

Less than nine months into the presidency of **George W. Bush** (son of the previous President Bush), the United States experienced terrorist attacks on U.S. soil by Islamist militants thought to be directed by Osama bin Laden. The subsequent U.S.-led attacks on Afghanistan and Iraq were part of what President Bush defined as "the war on terror." Though Britain, Canada, Spain and some other countries supported initial war efforts, this approach alienated many foreign governments and peoples. Bush's policies were viewed by many as alarmingly isolationist and self-interested; only time will give us a clear analysis on the legacy of U.S. foreign policy during the first decade of the 21st century.

Skill 4.3   Civil rights and other social reform movements in the United States

The economic boom following the war led to prosperity for many Americans in the 1950s. This prosperity did not extend to the poor blacks of the south, however, and the economic disparities between the races became more pronounced. After World War II and the Korean War, efforts began to relieve the problems of millions of African-Americans, including efforts to end discrimination in education, housing, and jobs and the grinding widespread poverty.

Taking inspiration from similar struggles in India at the time led by Mahatma Ghandi, a burgeoning civil rights movement began to gain momentum under such leaders as **Dr. Martin Luther King, Jr**. The phrase "the civil rights movement" generally refers to the nation-wide effort made by black people and those who supported them to gain rights equal to whites and to eliminate segregation. Discussion of this movement is generally understood in terms of the period of the 1950s and 1960s, although efforts continue into the 21st century. Further, other groups, such as Native Americans, women, Hispanic and Asian peoples, and those with disabilities and of different sexual orientations have also struggled for equal rights under the law throughout the 20th and 21st centuries.

Since 1941, a number of anti-discrimination laws have been passed by Congress. These acts have protected the civil rights of several groups of Americans. These laws include:

- Fair Employment Act of 1941
- Civil Rights Act of 1964
- Immigration and Nationality Services Act of 1965
- Voting Rights Act of 1965
- Civil Rights Act of 1968
- Age Discrimination in Employment Act of 1967
- Age Discrimination Act of 1975
- Pregnancy Discrimination Act of 1978
- Americans with Disabilities Act of 1990
- Civil Rights Act of 1991
- Employment Non-Discrimination Act

The concept of **minority rights** encompasses two ideas: the first consists of the individual rights of members of ethnic, racial, class, religious or sexual minorities; the second concerns the collective rights of minority groups. Various civil rights movements have sought to guarantee that the individual rights of persons are not denied on the basis of being part of a minority group. These movements worked for guarantees of minority representation and affirmative action quotas, as well as other measures to ensure present equality and redress past wrongs.

The "Civil Rights Movement" of the 1950's and 1960's

Some **key people** in the African-American movement for civil rights include:

Rosa Parks -- A black seamstress from Montgomery Alabama who, in 1955, refused to give up her seat on the bus to a white man. This event is generally understood as the spark that lit the fire of the Civil Rights Movement. She has been generally regarded as the "mother of the Civil Rights Movement."

Martin Luther King, Jr.-- the most prominent member of the Civil Rights movement. King promoted nonviolent methods of opposition to segregation. The "Letter from Birmingham Jail" explained the purpose of nonviolent action as a way to make people notice injustice. He led the march on Washington in 1963, at which he delivered the "I Have a Dream" speech. He received the 1968 Nobel Prize for Peace.

James Meredith – the first African American to enroll at the University of Mississippi.

Emmett Till – a teenage boy who was murdered in Mississippi while visiting from Chicago. The crime of which he was accused was "whistling at a white woman in a store." He was beaten and murdered, and his body was dumped in a river. His two white abductors were apprehended and tried. They were acquitted by an all-white jury. After the acquittal, they admitted their guilt, but remained free because of double jeopardy laws.

Ralph Abernathy – A major figure in the Civil Rights Movement who succeeded Martin Luther King, Jr., as head of the Southern Christian Leadership Conference

W.E.B. DuBois, another outstanding African-American leader and spokesman, believed that only continuous and vigorous protests against injustices and inequalities coupled with appeals to black pride would effect changes. The results of his efforts was the formation of the Urban League and the NAACP which today continue to seek to eliminate discriminations and secure equality and equal rights.

Malcolm X – a political leader and part of the Civil Rights Movement. He was a prominent Black Muslim.

Stokeley Carmichael – one of the leaders of the Black Power movement who called for independent development of political and social institutions for blacks. Carmichael called for black pride and maintenance of black culture. He was head of the Student Nonviolent Coordinating Committee.

Key events of the Civil Rights Movement include:

***Brown vs. Board of Education*, 1954** in which the Supreme Court declared that *Plessy vs. Ferguson* was unconstitutional. This was the ruling that had established "Separate but Equal" as the basis for segregation. With this decision, the Court ordered immediate desegregation.

The murder of Emmett Till, 1955 (as noted above)

Rosa Parks and the Montgomery Bus Boycott, 1955-56 – After refusing to give up her seat on a bus in Montgomery, Alabama, Parks was arrested, tried, and convicted of disorderly conduct and violating a local ordinance. When word reached the black community a bus boycott was organized to protest the segregation of blacks and whites on public buses. The boycott lasted 381 days, until the ordinance was lifted.

Strategy shift to "direct action" – nonviolent resistance and civil disobedience, 1955-1965, which consisted mostly of bus boycotts, sit-ins, and freedom rides.

Formation of the Southern Christian Leadership Conference, 1957. This group, formed by Martin Luther King, Jr., John Duffy, Rev. C. D. Steele, Rev. T. J. Jemison, Rev. Fred Shuttlesworth, Ella Baker, A. Philip Randolph, Bayard Rustin, and Stanley Levison, who provided training and assistance to local efforts to fight segregation. Non-violence was its central doctrine and its major method of fighting segregation and racism.

The Desegregation of Little Rock, 1957. Following up on the decision of the Supreme Court in *Brown vs. Board of Education*, the Arkansas school board voted to integrate the school system. The National Association for the Advancement of Colored People (NAACP) chose Arkansas as the place to push integration because it was considered a relatively progressive Southern state. However, the governor called up the National Guard to prevent nine black students from attending Little Rock's Central High School.

Sit-ins – In 1960, students began to stage "sit-ins" at local lunch counters and stores as a means of protesting the refusal of those businesses to desegregate. The first was in Greensboro, NC. Similar campaigns took place throughout the South. Demonstrators began to protest segregated parks, beaches, theaters, museums, and libraries. When arrested, the protesters made "jail-no-bail" pledges. This called attention to their cause and put the financial burden of providing jail space and food on the cities.

Freedom Rides – Activists traveled by bus throughout the Deep South to desegregate bus terminals (required by federal law). These protesters undertook extremely dangerous protests. Many buses were firebombed, attacked by the KKK, and protesters were beaten. They were crammed into small, airless jail cells and mistreated in many ways. Key figures in this effort included John Lewis, James Lawson, Diane Nash, Bob Moses, James Bevel, Charles McDew, Bernard Lafayette, Charles Jones, Lonnie King, Julian Bond, Hosea Williams, and Stokely Carmichael.

The Birmingham Campaign, 1963-64. A campaign was planned to use sit-ins, kneel-ins in churches, and a march to the county building to launch a voter registration campaign. The City obtained an injunction forbidding all such protests. The protesters, including Martin Luther King, Jr., believed the injunction was unconstitutional, and defied it. They were arrested. While in jail, King wrote his famous "Letter from Birmingham Jail." When the campaign began to falter, the "Children's Crusade" called students to leave school and join the protests. The events became news when more than 600 students were jailed.

The next day more students joined the protest. The media was present and broadcast to the nation, vivid pictures of fire hoses being used to knock down children and dogs attacking some of them. The resulting public outrage led the Kennedy administration to intervene. About a month later, a committee was formed to end hiring discrimination, arrange for the release of jailed protesters, and establish normative communication between blacks and whites. Four months later, the KKK bombed the Sixteenth Street Baptist Church, killing four girls.

The March on Washington, 1963. This was a march on Washington for jobs and freedom. It was a combined effort of all major civil rights organizations. The goals of the march were: meaningful civil rights laws, a massive federal works program, full and fair employment, decent housing, the right to vote, and adequate integrated education. It was at this march that Martin Luther King, Jr., made the famous "I Have a Dream" speech.

Mississippi Freedom Summer, 1964. Students were brought from other states to Mississippi to assist local activists in registering voters, teaching in "Freedom Schools" and in forming the Mississippi Freedom Democratic Party. Three of the workers disappeared – murdered by the KKK. It took six weeks to find their bodies. The national uproar forced President Johnson to send in the FBI. Johnson was able to use public sentiment to effect passage in Congress of the **Civil Rights Act of 1964.**

Selma to Montgomery marches, 1965. Attempts to obtain voter registration in Selma, Alabama had been largely unsuccessful due to opposition from the city's sheriff. Martin Luther King, Jr., came to the city to lead a series of marches. He and over 200 demonstrators were arrested and jailed. Police met each successive march with violent resistance. In March, a group of over 600 intended to walk from Selma to Montgomery (54 miles). News media were on hand when, six blocks into the march, state and local law enforcement officials attacked the marchers with billy clubs, tear gas, rubber tubes wrapped in barbed wire, and bullwhips. They were driven back to Selma. National broadcast of the footage provoked a nation-wide response.

President Johnson again used public sentiment to achieve passage of the **Voting Rights Act of 1965**. This law changed the political landscape of the South irrevocably by suspending poll taxes, literacy tests and other voter tests for voter registration.

In 1968, Reverend Martin Luther King, Jr. was assassinated in Memphis, Tennessee, sparking racial riots in many American cities.

Other social justice movements: Numerous groups have used various forms of protest, attempts to sway public opinion, legal action, and congressional lobbying to obtain full protection of their civil rights under the Constitution.

Indians rights activists have been working to change destructive U.S. policies toward indigenous peoples for many generations. This has included changes to treaties signed in the 19th century, reclaiming hunting, fishing and grazing rights, and establishing greater equality in U.S. citizenship.

The **disability rights** movement was a successful effort to guarantee access to public buildings and transportation, equal access to education and employment, and equal protection under the law in terms of access to insurance, and other basic rights of American citizens. As a result of these efforts, public buildings and public transportation must be accessible to persons with disabilities. Discrimination in hiring or housing on the basis of disability is also illegal.

A **prisoners' rights** movement has been working for many years to ensure the basic human rights of persons incarcerated for crimes. **Immigrant rights** movements have worked for employment and housing rights, as well as preventing abuse of immigrants through hate crimes. In some states, immigrant rights movements have led to bi-lingual education and public information access. Another group movement to obtain equal rights is the **lesbian, gay, bisexual and transgender** social reform movement. This movement seeks equal housing, freedom from social and employment discrimination and from hate crimes, and equal recognition of relationships under the law.

The women's rights movement

Over the course of more than150 years, we have seen three movements in the women's rights movement. The first wave occurred in the 19th and early 20th century, the second in the mid-20th century, close on the heels of the black civil right movement. The third and current wave continues to work toward equality for women in all arenas. The movement has fought throughout history for:

- The right to vote
- The right to work
- The right to fair wages
- The right to bodily integrity and autonomy
- The right to own property
- The right to an education
- The right to hold public office
- Marital and parental rights
- The right to serve in the military
- The right to enter into legal contracts

The movement for women's rights has resulted in many social and political changes. Many of the ideas that seemed radical 100 (or even 50) years ago are now commonly accepted practices or social mores.

Many of the strategies and actions that early feminist activists such as Susan B. Anthony and Elizabeth Cady Stanton utilized in the 19th and early 20th centuries were the very methods employed by civil rights activists fighting racism in the mid to late 20th century. Similarly, many people active today within the women's movement are fundamentally committed to justice and the rights of all people. This has led many members of the women's movement to be involved in the black civil rights movement, the gay rights movement, and the other social movements.

Some of the advocates for women and leaders in the women's movement have been:
- Abigail Adams
- Susan B. Anthony
- Betty Friedan
- Audre Lourde
- Lucretia Mott
- Alice Paul
- Elizabeth Cady Stanton
- Gloria Steinem
- Ida B. Wells

Skill 4.4   Major political and social developments since World War II

The impact of the Cold War on migration patterns was very significant. Until the middle of the twentieth century, voluntary migrations to America were primarily Europeans. After WWII, a large number of Europeans were admitted to the U.S. and Canada. These were considered the most desirable immigrants. Indeed, immigration policies based upon ethnicity or country of origin were not eliminated until the 1960s.

A significant change in immigration policy occurred after WWII. Both the U.S. and Canada began to distinguish between economically motivated voluntary immigrants and **political refugees**. The conditions that existed after the war made it clear that some immigrants must be treated differently on the basis of humanitarian concerns. Fear of persecution caused massive migrations. The United Nations created the International Refugee Organization in 1946. In the next three years this organization relocated over a million European refugees.

Immigration policy in the U.S. was carefully aligned with foreign policy. President Truman introduced the **Displaced Persons Act in 1948** which facilitated the admission of more than 400,000 persons from Europe. During the 1950s, however, the immigration policy became very restrictive. The McCarran-Walter Immigration Nationality Act of 1952 established a quota system and was clearly anti-Asian. The number of refugees from Eastern Europe far exceeded these quotas. Both President Truman and President Eisenhower urged extension of the quotas, and in time they were abandoned. Refugees from communist Europe were admitted under the President's Escapee Program of 1952 and the Refugee Relief Act of 1953.

Immigration by Asians had been restricted for some time and this policy did not change after WWII. The changes in immigration policies and the great influx of Europeans brought a wide variety of people into the U.S. To be sure, some were farmers and laborers, but many were highly trained and skilled scientists, teachers, inventors, and executives. This migration added to the American "melting pot" experience. The immigrants provided new sources of labor for a booming economy and the introduction of new cultural ideas and contributions to science and technology. The acceptance and assimilation of European immigrants was, for the most part, easier than the prejudiced assimilation of persons of Asian descent, particularly after the recent hostilities with Japan.

McCarthyism is a term that came to be used to describe the anti-communist movement within the federal government in the late 1940s and 1950s. The movement is named after Senator Joseph McCarthy of Wisconsin, who was one of its prime movers. Several congressional committees convened to investigate and interrogate citizens on their possible sympathies for or connections to the Communist Party. Failure to cooperate with these committees often resulted in the loss of ones job and placement on a "**blacklist**," which prevented one from being hired for many positions. After targeting the entertainment industry and educational institutions, McCarthy turned his sights on the Army. This proved unpopular with the American public, and his influence began to wane. McCarthy was eventually censured by the Senate for his overzealous attacks.

In 1960, **John F. Kennedy** was elected President. Kennedy espoused an ethic of national service, establishing the **Peace Corps** and similar programs in the mold of Roosevelt. He fostered the growing civil rights movement, and introduced a bill in Congress that proposed the end to legal discrimination against blacks, and the abolition of Jim Crow segregation laws.

Kennedy was assassinated before the bill was completely through Congress. His Vice President, Lyndon Johnson, carried on support for the bill. The bill was enacted as the **Civil Rights Act of 1964**, which President Johnson signed. The **Civil Rights Acts of 1964 and 1968** prohibited discrimination in housing sales and rentals, employment, public accommodations, and voter registration

Johnson was elected to his own full term as President in 1964, defeating the very conservative Barry Goldwater. Johnson had been a Roosevelt democrat during the 1930s, and proposed legislation and programs that were based on the principles of the New Deal. This included his **War on** Poverty. Once again, war interrupted domestic business as the United States became more fully involved in Vietnam. Controversy over the war led to a splintering of the Democratic Party during the run up to the presidential election of 1968, and several viable candidates emerged, including Robert Kennedy who was assassinated while campaigning. Johnson decided not to run for re-election.

Republican **Richard Nixon** won the election against Democratic nominee Hubert Humphrey. Nixon was more moderate than Goldwater, and indeed many of the liberal policies implemented by Kennedy and Johnson found their way into the Nixon administration.

The Vietnam War Era and American society

U.S. involvement in the **Vietnam War** from 1957 to 1973 was the second phase of three in Vietnam's history. The first phase began in 1946 when the Vietnamese fought French troops for control of the country. Vietnam prior to 1946 had been part of the French colony of Indochina since 1861 along with Laos and Kampuchea or Cambodia. In 1954, the defeated French left and the country became divided into Communist North and Democratic South. The United States' aid and influence continued as part of the U.S. "Cold War" foreign policy to help any nation threatened by Communism.

The second phase involved a much more direct U.S. commitment. The Communist Vietnamese considered the war one of national liberation, a struggle to avoid continual dominance and influence of a foreign power. Participants were the United States of America, Australia, New Zealand, South and North Vietnam, South Korea, Thailand, and the Philippines. With active U.S. involvement from 1957 to 1973, it was the longest war participated in by the U.S. to date. It was tremendously destructive and completely divided the American public in their opinions and feelings about the war. Many were frustrated and angered by the fact that it was the first war fought on foreign soil in which U.S. combat forces were totally unable to achieve their goals and objectives.

The Vietnam War also divided the Democratic Party, and the **1968 Democratic National Convention** in Chicago turned out to be a highly contentious and bitterly fought, both on the floor of the convention and outside, where thousands had gathered to protest the Vietnam War. Vice President Hubert H. Humphrey became the party's nominee, but he led a divided party.

In Vietnam, the forces of the **Viet Cong** and the **North Vietnamese Army (NVA)** launched a coordinated and devastating offensive on January 30, on the eve of Tet, the Lunar New Year, disproving the Johnson Administration officials who claimed that the Vietnamese Communists were no longer a viable military force. Although the **Tet Offensive** was a tactical defeat for the Viet Cong, it no longer could field a large enough military force to match American firepower in a set-piece engagement, it was a strategic defeat for the Americans, in public relations and the political will to continue in a seemingly endless conflict.

A cease-fire was arranged in January 1973 and a few months later, U.S. troops left for good. The third and final phase consisted of fighting between the Vietnamese but ended April 30, 1975, with the surrender of South Vietnam, the entire country being united under Communist ruler.

Meanwhile, on the home front, **poverty** remained a serious problem in the central sections of large cities. This economic disparity resulted in riots and soaring crime rates, which ultimately found its way to the suburbs. The escalation of the war in Vietnam and the social conflict and upheaval of support vs. opposition to U.S. involvement led to antiwar demonstrations, escalation of drug abuse, and a range of social difficulties. The continued issues of poverty and drug use had negative impacts on families and children as well.

One of the most significant issues of this period was the direct legacy of the war: the social, mental, and physical problems experienced by the Vietnam veterans who came home to unprepared spouses and families, and a country that was sometimes violently divided. Returning veterans faced not only readjustment to normal civilian life but also bitterness, anger, rejection, and no heroes' welcomes. Many suffered severe physical and deep psychological problems. The war set a precedent where both Congress and the American people actively challenged U.S. military and foreign policy. The conflict, though tempered markedly by time, still exists and still has a definite effect on people.

The conservative movement and the Reagan Revolution

In the decade preceding the election of Ronald Reagan in 1980, the United States had experienced increased inflation, an upswing in the crime rate, and a fuel shortage crisis. These factors contributed to a general dissatisfaction with the federal government, and a lack of confidence in the ability of the government to prevent or solve the nation's problems. It was a time of social division, as well. The 1973 Supreme Court decision in *Roe vs. Wade* upheld the legality of abortion, which angered many conservatives and became a rallying point for the right wing of the Republican Party, which had been out of favor for many years.

This conservative branch of the party had enjoyed prominence in 1964, when Barry Goldwater was selected to run for President on the Republican ticket. Goldwater was defeated, and the Republicans found more success four years later with the more moderate Richard Nixon. Then came the **Watergate** scandal, resulting in the first-ever resignation of a sitting American president, and was the most crucial domestic crisis of the 1970s. Nixon's presidency ended in disgrace with his resignation and in the meantime the Democrats retained their strong hold in both houses of Congress.

In 1976, Democrat Jimmy Carter was elected President, and it was on his watch that public dissatisfaction was to reach its peak. This dissatisfaction served to provide the conservative Republicans with an opportunity to offer a new direction, and the American public was receptive. Bolstering the more conservative Republicans were large numbers of religious activists who gathered behind television evangelists **Jerry Falwell** and **Pat Robertson**. This large bloc not only opposed abortion but pressed for a conservative agenda that invoked religious doctrine in interpreting and proposing social legislation.

In **Ronald Reagan**, the rising conservative movement found an eloquent and charismatic representative. Reagan was a former movie star who was comfortable in front of a camera. He had entered politics in California, eventually becoming governor. He had supported the conservative Goldwater in 1964, and had delivered a speech on his behalf at the nominating convention. Reagan was confident, and carried a positive message of American strength that resonated with many voters. He won the presidential election of 1980 against Jimmy Carter in a landslide. He was elected to a second term against Walter Mondale in 1984.

Reagan brought with him a cabinet of conservative advisors who believed in a conservative social agenda, limited government involvement in the economy, and American strength abroad. In 1988, Reagan's vice president, **George H.W. Bush**, was elected president and continued many of the conservative policies implemented by Reagan. The religious groups that had gained a foothold in the years surrounding Reagan's first election continued to grow and still maintain political influence, particularly in the Republican Party.

In 2000, conservative **George W. Bush**, the son of President George H.W. Bush, was elected President. George W. Bush populated his cabinet with many of the same people who had advised President Reagan twenty years earlier, thereby building on the conservative base that Ronald Reagan had laid.

On September 11, 2001, when members of right-wing Islamic terrorists attacked the World Trade Center in New York City, the Pentagon with hijacked jetliners, and downed another airplane in Pennsylvania, Bush was able to rally significant support from the larger populace. However, after Bush's eight years as president and the increasingly unpopular wars he waged in Afghanistan and Iraq, the conservative movement experienced the largest setback with the election of Barack Obama, the first African-American president. Only time can define what will emerge as the lasting effects of the conservative movement, effected by Ronald Reagan and the Christian right, on the Republican party as a political group and on the United States as a country.

Skill 4.5   Technological growth and development

During this period, extraordinary advances in science and technology opened new frontiers and pushed back an ever-growing number of boundaries. New technologies have made production faster, easier, and more efficient. To some degree, machines and humans have entered an age of competition. Yet these advances have facilitated greater control over nature, lightened the burden of labor, and extended human life span. These advances in science, knowledge and technology have also called into question for many the assumptions and beliefs that have provided meaning for human existence. Without the traditional belief structures that have given meaning to life, an emptiness and aimlessness has arisen for some that is a new by-product of technology and modern life. Advances in biology and medicine have **decreased infant mortality** and **increased life expectancy** dramatically. Antibiotics and new surgical techniques have saved countless lives. Inoculations have essentially erased many dreadful diseases. Yet others have resulted from the careless disposal of by-products and the effects of industrialization upon the environment and the individual.

Tremendous progress in communication and transportation has tied all parts of the earth and drawn them closer. There are still vast areas of unproductive land, extreme poverty, food shortages, rampant diseases, violent friction between cultures, the ever-present nuclear threat, environmental pollution, rapid reduction of natural resources, urban over-crowding, acceleration in global terrorism and violent crimes, and a diminishing middle class.

The **microchip** was developed in the 1950s as a way to reduce the size of transistor-based electronic equipment. By replacing individual transistors with a single chip of semiconductor material, more capability could be included in less space. This development led directly to the microprocessor, which is at the heart of every modern computer and most modern electronic products such as laptops, cell phones and PDAs (personal digital assistants), and other emerging technologies that invite instant communication.

New technologies have changed the way of life for many. In many places technology has resulted in a more mobile population. Popular culture has been shaped by mass production and the mass media. Mass production and technology has made electronic goods affordable to most. **Global satellite systems** and the **Internet** give us immediate contact around the world, funneling news and other data into our living rooms and offices at a rapid pace.

Outsourcing, the process of sending a segment of one's internal business to another vendor or location, is now possible and sometimes economically attractive because of technological advances. Call centers for European, American and large multinational companies are now located in India, Pakistan, and other countries. Similarly, multinational corporations locate plants in foreign countries to lower costs, and source raw materials from all over the world.

Nuclear energy was once hailed as a cheap and relatively clean alternative to fossil fuels, but fell largely out of favor in the US owing to some high-profile accidents at nuclear plants. Nuclear technology has continued to advance, and nuclear energy is gaining attention once again as a potential resource. Concerns about the damage to the environment by other sources of fuel such as coal, as well as the ongoing concern about U.S. dependence on foreign oil supplies, has contributed to the re-consideration of nuclear power.

One of the crucial considerations in the use of nuclear energy is safety. Nuclear fuels are highly radioactive and very dangerous should they enter the environment. The nuclear waste from creating nuclear energy is another important issue, as the dangerous by product must be carefully and safely stored. Internationally, there is concern that nuclear power plants may be outfitted to produce material for nuclear weapons, creating another level of controversy over the spread of nuclear technology.

Biotechnology is another area of rapid growth and development that also brings controversy. Advances in biotechnology have opened the possibility of cloning and genetically altering organisms. Serious ethical issues have been raised about this type of research, especially where it relates to human beings or human tissues. Nonetheless, the recent decoding of the human genome and stem cell research has already led to new treatments and prevention of disease, results that were unheard of even 15 years ago.

The U.S., like all industrialized countries, faces **complex ecological issues and problems.** Since the dawn of agriculture, humans have modified their environment to suit their needs and to provide food and shelter. These changes always impact the environment, sometimes adversely from a human perspective.

Agriculture, for instance, often involves loosening topsoil by plowing before planting. This in turn affects how water and wind act on the soil, and can lead to erosion. In extreme cases, erosion can leave a plot of agricultural land unsuitable for use. Technological advances have led to a modern method of farming that relies less on plowing the soil before planting, but more on chemical fertilizers, pesticides and herbicides. These chemicals find their way into groundwater, affecting the environment and ultimately human health.

Cities are large examples of how technological change has allowed humans to modify their environment to suit their needs. Further advances in transportation and building methods allow for larger and denser communities, which themselves impact the environment in many ways. Concentrated consumption of fuels by automobiles and home heating systems affect the quality of the air in and around cities. The lack of exposed ground means that rainwater runs off of roads and rooftops into sewer systems instead of seeping into the ground, and often makes its way into nearby streams or rivers, carrying urban debris with it.

In the area of **ecology**, scientific research is focused primarily on finding efficient fuel alternatives. Advances in solar and wind power technology have made these options feasible in some areas. Hybrid technology that uses electricity and fuel cells to supplement fossil fuels has found a market niche which is expanding every year. As economics and ecology continue to collide, perhaps advances can be made that are both environmentally and fiscally responsible.

Skill 4.6   The realities of globalization in the 21st century

Globalization refers to the complex of social, political, technological, and economic changes that result from increasing contact, communication, interaction, integration and interdependence of peoples of disparate parts of the world. The term is generally used to refer to the process of change or as the cause of turbulent change. Globalization may be understood in terms of positive social and economic change, as in the case of a broadening of trade resulting in an increase in the standard of living for developing countries.

Globalization may also be understood negatively in terms of the abusive treatment of developing countries in the interest of cultural or economic imperialism. These negative understandings generally point to cultural assimilation, plunder and profiteering, the destruction of the local culture and economy, and ecological indifference.

The period of European peace after the defeat of Napoleon and the reliance upon the gold standard in that time is often referred to as "The First Era of Globalization." The global economy expanded rapidly in the early twentieth century with the advent of the **airplane**, which made travel and trade easier and less time-consuming. Involved in this era of globalization was Europe, several European-influenced areas in the Americas, and Oceania. The exchange of goods based upon the common gold standard resulted in prosperity for all countries involved. Communication and the exchange of ideas between these countries also prospered. This period began to disintegrate with the crisis of the gold standard in the late 1920s and early 1930s. Since WWII, globalization of trade has been accomplished primarily through trade negotiations and treaties.

Globalization involves exchange of money, commodities, information, ideas, and people. Much of this has been facilitated by the great advances in technology in the last 150 years. The effects of globalization can be seen across all areas of social and cultural interaction. Economically, globalization brings about broader and faster trade and flow of capital, increased outsourcing of labor, the development of global financial systems (such as the introduction of the Euro), the creation of trade agreements, and the birth of international organizations to moderate the agreements.

From a social and cultural point of view, globalization results in greater exchange of all segments of the various cultures, including ideas, technology, food, clothing, fads, and culture. Travel and migration create multicultural societies. The media facilitates the exchange of cultural and social values. As values interact, a new shared set of values begins to emerge.

Trucks, trains, and ships carry cargo all over the world. Trains travel faster than ever as do ships. Roads are prevalent and enable distribution of cargo by trucks an efficient process. With all of this capability has come increasing demand. People traditionally obtained their goods using their own means or from traders who lived nearby. As technology improved, trade routes got longer, and demand for things from overseas grew. This demand fed the economic imperative of creating more supply, and vice versa. As more people discovered goods from overseas, the demand for those foreign goods increased. Because people could get goods from overseas with relative ease, they continued to get them and demand more.

Globalization has brought about welcome and unwelcome developments in the field of **epidemiology**. Vaccines and other cures for diseases can be shipped relatively quickly all around the world. For example, this has made it possible for HIV vaccines to reach the remotest areas of the world. Unfortunately, the preponderance of global travel has also meant a threat of spreading a disease by an infected person traveling on an international flight. It also has meant that diseases and viruses (as well as ecological threats) are "shipped" in to the U.S. from all across the world on boats and planes.

Technology has contributed to globalization with the development of the **Internet**. Instant communication between people thousands of miles apart is possible just by plugging in a computer and connecting to the Internet. The Internet is an extension of the telephone and cell phone revolutions; all three are developments in communications that have brought faraway places closer together. All three allow people to communicate no matter the distance. This communication can facilitate friendly chatter, remote business meetings, and distant trade opportunities. Cell phones and the Internet are often required to do business nowadays. Computer programs enable the tracking of goods and receipts quickly and efficiently.

Globalization has also brought financial and cultural exchange on a worldwide scale. Many businesses have investments in countries around the world. Financial transactions are conducted using a variety of currencies. A vivid example of the impact of economic globalization is reflected in the events of the recession of 2008-2009.

COMPETENCY 0500   **Understand major events, individuals, themes, and developments in Washington State history**

The Free Online Encyclopedia of Washington State History is an excellent online resource for teachers and students (www.historylinks.org). It claims to be "*the first and largest online encyclopedia of community history created expressly for the Internet. HistoryLink.org provides a free, authoritative, and easily accessible history reference for the benefit of students, teachers, journalists, scholars, researchers, and the general public.*" It contains over 5000 essays on many historical topics, including timelines, people-oriented stories, and detailed information about Washington's counties, cities and towns.

Skill 5.1   An historical perspective of native peoples (Indian tribes) in the state of Washington

For more than 10,000 years, native peoples have lived in the state of Washington. They came over the land bridge from East Asia and down through what is now Alaska and Canada. Their earliest known site is located at Sequim in western Washington. The influence of nature was profound, with the richness of the ocean, the lakes and rivers, the mountains and forests, providing abundant food and shelter. Like all indigenous peoples, the religion and culture of the Indian tribes of Washington were and are also grounded in their powerful connection with natural resources.

The many tribes of Washington developed in different ways, dependent largely upon geography. The Cascade Mountains divide the state into east and west. The western indigenous peoples over time built permanent structures and settled into a non-migratory lifestyle. The eastern peoples remained hunters and gatherers. Some eastern tribes, like the Chinooks, shared characteristics of both the river and ocean Indians as well as other inland groups.

Of the 35-40 tribes, some tribes are more well-known than others, or known for certain characteristics. For example, the Nez Perce of the Columbia Plateau were known for the many horses they owned and used. They were also one of the largest tribes in Washington (as well as parts of Oregon and Idaho). The Chinookans, a group of tribes in the same geographic region, often interacted with the Nez Perce although no official tribal network existed among them. They were all great fishers and traders; many had well-developed economic and social systems. Their technological skills were varied, involving bone, wood and stone.

One of the most well-known Indians in Washington was **Chief Seattle** (1786-1866), the namesake of the largest American city called after a Native American. Born on an island in Puget Sound, he was a warrior in his youth and grew into a revered elder and pacifist who negotiated effectively with the British and American settlers. As did many Indians of his era, he converted to Christianity. Seattle, viewed by many as a pragmatist, ultimately became the leader of the Suquamish, Duwamish and allied peoples. He lived through a very significant period of native history in Washington, beginning with the arrival of the first major onslaught of white explorers and traders through the devastating effects of white settlement on tribes and the movement of Indian people to the reservations.

Another well known native was **Chief Joseph** the Younger (1840-1904) of the Nez Perce. He became chief after his father and struggled to maintain the homeland of his Wallowa band of Nez Perce. He came of age during many of the struggles facing the Indian tribes as Washington was settled. Although not always successful, he relentlessly advocated peaceful resolution with both the government and with tribal councils, and strived to advance Indian rights both on the reservation and in Washington, DC.

See **Skill 5.2** for more information about the changes experienced by Washington Indians as settlers moved into the region.

Skill 5.2 Settlement and migration patterns and political interactions among diverse ethnic groups in Washington State in the 19th century

Although Spanish explorers sailed along the Washington coast as early as the 1600s, it was not until the late 1700s that Russian, British and Spanish ships began exploring the Pacific coastline in earnest. These forays were driven largely by the interest in fur trading with various tribes. The fur trading companies of Canada, England and the United States were instrumental in developing the area known as the Oregon Country (comprised of what are now the states of Oregon, Washington, Idaho and parts of Montana and Wyoming). Early explorers included British captain James Cook and his officer George Vancouver, and the trading companies of **Hudson's Bay** and **North West Company**.

Exploration of this territory by land began after the **Lewis and Clark Expedition** documented much about the area. This expedition reached the mouth of the Columbia River in 1805, and provided a clear path for Americans to journey to the Northwest. This eventually became known as the **Oregon Trail** and was the most commonly traveled route to Oregon and Washington.

The first American settlement in what later became Washington was **Fort Okanogan**, built in the early 1800s by the fur-trading company of John Astor. Various American fur companies set up a string of trading posts as well as forts for trade and protection. These developments, although impacted by the War of 1812 when the land traded hands several times, established the Northwest Territory as part of the growing United States.

Close behind the fur traders and early pioneers were Protestant and Catholic missionaries. Their goal was to convert native tribes to Christianity. Their interest in the Northwest was fueled by a visit from representatives of the Nez Perce tribe to St. Louis, asking for a mission to be established in their area. It is not clear what they were looking for, although it is believed that they saw the white man's religion as powerful.

This began a flood of missionaries, first the Methodists, then American Board missionaries (representing Congregational, Presbyterians and Dutch-Reformed Christians), and then Catholic priests. They were welcomed by the Nez Perce and Flathead tribes and settled throughout the Oregon Country. **Fr. Pierre John de Smet** was well-respected and often served as a peacemaker among tribes and between the native peoples and the Caucasian settlers.

In 1847, the **Whitman Massacre** (when medical missionary Marcus Whitman and his wife Narcissa were killed by Cayuse warriors) led to the Cayuses war. The Cayuses, like other tribes, felt invaded by the number of settlers moving into the region. These events highlighted the tensions between native and non-native people, and eventually contributed to the decline of the missionary period in the region. The wars between native peoples and settlers continued for the next 30 years, in spite of treaties signed in the mid 1850s. Smallpox and other European diseases also took their toll on the tribes.

By the 1880s, most of the Indians' land had been taken by white settlers, and most tribes were living on reservations. Treaties had been reached with tribal peoples, more readily with those in the western part of the state. The eastern tribes, as hunters and gatherers, needed more land to survive and some resisted treaties. Although the **Dawes Act** (1887) was referred to as the Act of Indian Emancipation, the results were less than stellar. Discrimination continued to exist and Indians were not granted citizenship as had been promised until a later date.

As the need for unskilled laborers grew for mining and building the railroad (see Skill 5.3 for more information), Washington saw increasing populations of Chinese and Scandinavian immigrants   The general population grew more than 350% between 1880 and 1890 alone. The railroad also brought African-Americans from the East. These were followed by the Japanese, and later the Italians and the Greeks. Russian Slavs grew in numbers, as did those from Eastern Europe.

Various degrees of segregation and assimilation existed, with Christian groups encouraging assimilation, especially among Indian peoples. Racism and bigotry were common against Asians and Blacks as well as Indians, although thriving communities within each ethnic group survived the various ethnic persecutions of the late 1800s. Immigrants of all nationalities suffered the usual indignities of prejudice and displacement, although those with white skin faired better.

Skill 5.3   Political, social and economic developments in Washington between 1880 and 1945

Rising tensions between the U.S. and Britain due to the influx of American settlers into what Britain saw as "their" land brought about the **Oregon Treaty** in the mid-19th century. Two years later, Congress officially named this land the Oregon Territory. Washington became and remained a territory until 1889 when it achieved statehood, 35 years after Oregon had become a state.

Washington's years as a territory saw many changes. Progress in transportation brought continued growth, both in terms of many new people as well as the development of new industries. Stagecoaches and steamboats moved people into and around the state, while growing railroad lines made the transportation of goods more feasible, along with more settlers from the East. The arrival of the railroad spurred rapid growth in Seattle and other cities.

Farming, mining, salmon canning and the building of infrastructure were major industries. The growth of the lumber industry took off once the railroad reached Seattle. Further, Seattle became a launching point for miners heading to Alaska at the turn of the century.

The shipbuilding industry grew rapidly during World War I, only to crash after the war. This reflects what some have referred to as Washington's "boom-bust" economy: as the need for raw materials rises, Washington booms, followed by a bust when the material is used up (as the early fur traders found at the end of the 18th century) or when the demand disappears. The war also moved the airplane industry forward; the **Boeing** Company was founded in 1916. Airplane-building in turn enhanced the timber industry because of the demand for light woods used in airplane construction.

The Great Depression was acute in Washington, as in many other states. The state saw many people from the Great Plains coming west away from the droughts. The rebuilding of the U.S. economy by New Deal projects was felt in Washington as well, particularly in the development of hydroelectric energy and irrigation for farming. The **Grand Coulee Dam** was built in the Columbia River, as was the **Booneville Dam** which was innovative in its use of "fish ladders" for salmon traveling upriver. Hydroelectric power also brought aluminum plants, drawn to area because of the relatively cheap source of electricity (needed for processing bauxite ore into aluminum).

The accompanying growth of political, social, and cultural institutions also followed the population and industrial developments during this period. The Progressive political movement emerged from the Populist reform movement and was quite strong in the Northwest. The movement was widespread, enjoying support from both rural and urban peoples, the Grange and the American Federation of Labor, as well as professional and business people. This led to, among other things, the passage of the right to vote for women in 1910, twelve years before universal suffrage for women in the U.S was enacted.

The arts, literature, music, education and journalism in Washington all began to develop in this period. Although the University of Washington was founded in 1861, it did not provide university-level courses until the latter part of the 1800s. Many ethnic groups thrived inside their somewhat segregated communities during this period, although greater acceptance of nonwhite minorities occurred as well. Cultural institutions were often grounded in their ethnic heritage, as reflected in newspapers, social societies, church and temple groups and schools. Ethnic groups were also active in labor unions and the politics of the day.

One of the most painful events in Washington history occurred at the end of this era: the **internment of Japanese-American citizens** during World War II. African-Americans continued to face racism on the job and at home, although there were gradual changes, especially within labor unions during the Second World War. The NAACP and the Urban League were active in Seattle particularly.

Another civil rights issue in this period involved the efforts of Indian tribes to reclaim some autonomy and develop their own governing bodies. The Yakima, Nez Perce, Colville, Spokanes, Umatillas and other tribes rejected federal initiatives such as the **Indian Reorganization Act** of 1938. Unfortunately, this meant that they lost even more of their land to white owners after 80 years of mistreatment, discrimination and poor management by the U.S. Bureau of Indian Affairs.

Skill 5.4   Modern social, political and economic issues in the state of Washington

After World War II, the Indian tribes of Washington fared better than others in Oregon and around the country. Effective tribal councils and governments brought some groups economic prosperity and development. The Yakimas held a significant share of stock in the American Indian National Bank, giving them an economic foothold. They, along with the Cowlitz tribes, also won successful suits against the U.S. for having taken land in previous actions without adequate payment to the tribes. Taking direct action such as **"fish-ins"** (named after the sit-ins held by black civil rights leaders in the American south) also provided tribes with the opportunity to renegotiate older treaties regarding access to fisheries during seasons other than those delineated by the state game commission.

The **Washington State Board against Discrimination** was established by the legislature in 1947 to address civil rights issues, including public accommodations, housing, employment and education. Their actions over the next 20 years did much to bring greater equality for ethnic minorities, especially African-Americans. Blacks moved into various positions of political power; an example is **Charles Stokes**, the first black legislator in Washington who later became the first black state Supreme Court justice. Similarly, women also entered the political arena in greater numbers. By 1980, Washington was second in the nation in the percentage of women in the state legislature.

Efforts were also made to right the wrongs experienced by Japanese-Americans during the war; many in Washington felt shame about what had occurred. The post-World War II era also saw an influx of Hispanic immigrants; similarly, after the Vietnam War, many immigrants came from Southeast Asia. Over time, statewide commissions have been established to protect the rights of various groups.

Economically, Washington has experienced the boom-bust cycle several times since World War II. However, unlike the depression the timber industry experienced after World War I, the growth of new home construction after 1945 caused it to flourish rather than decline. Due to improved irrigation followed the dam projects of the 1930s, the farming industry grew, especially **apple orchards** which provide approximately one-third of the nation's apple crop. The airplane-building industry continued to thrive, utilizing the aluminum plants in the region, until Boeing laid off many workers in the late 1960s, causing a slump in Washington's economy.

Since then, Seattle, as a major port, has engaged in significant foreign trade. Tourism and recreational activities have grown and also contribute to Washington's current economic picture. A significant addition to the Washington economic scene since World War II is the development of high technology industries in the state. The largest and most well-known of these companies is **Microsoft**, established in 1975 in New Mexico and relocated to Washington in 1979. Over the last thirty years, Microsoft has risen to dominate the market in operating systems for home computers, as well as other forms of software; it has factories and offices around the world.

Concern for the environment is an ongoing issue in Washington. For example, by the 1980s, only 10% of the old growth forests remained. Along with Oregon, Washington has been a leader in attending to environmental issues related to water, land, and forests. At times, there has been conflict between environmental and economic interests. This is often reflected by the two geographic sections of the state: the more liberal, urban, technologically-oriented western part of the state versus the rural, more conservative east where forestry and farming are still major industries.

A major environmental problem in recent years involved the **Hanford nuclear plant**, established during the war to make plutonium. In 1966, it was opened to generate electricity – the largest nuclear power plant in the nation when it went on-line. It remained in operation until 1988. Over time, leaks from hazardous waste were discovered as well as the knowledge that people living downwind from the plant had been exposed to radiation. The result has been a multi-billion dollar clean-up effort.

COMPETENCY 0600   **Understand the development of major world civilizations 8000BCE to 600CE.**

Skill 6.1   Human origins and prehistory

Anthropology, the scientific study of human culture, and archeology, the scientific study of past civilizations through the objects left behind, are the fields from which we often draw to understand human origins. Although written records only go back about 4,500 years, scientists have pieced together evidence that documents the existence of humans (or "man-apes) as far back as 600,000 years ago. Knowledge about early humans comes from many different sources, including fossils derived from **burial pits**, the occasional bones found in rock deposits, and archaeological excavations of tools, pottery, and well paintings. Even then, study of living primitives can yield clues about ancient men and women.

The first human-like creatures arose in many parts of the world about 1 million years ago. By slow stages, these creatures developed into types of people who discovered fire and tools. These creatures had human-sized brains and inbred to produce **Cro-Magnon** type creatures circa 25,000 years ago, from which **homo sapiens** descended. These primitive humans demonstrated wide behavior patterns and great adaptability. Little is known in the way of details, including when language began to develop. They are believed to have lived in small communities that developed on the basis of the need to hunt. **Cave paintings** reveal a belief that magic pictures of animals could conjure up real ones. Some figurines seem to indicate belief in fertility gods and goddesses. Belief in some form of afterlife is indicated by burial formalities.

Fire and weapons were in use quite early. Archaeological evidence points to the use of hatchets, awls, needles and cutting tools in the **Paleolithic**, or Old Stone Age, one million years ago. Artifacts of the **Neolithic** or New Stone Age, dating from 6,000-8,000 BCE, include indications of polished tools, domesticated animals, the wheel, and some agriculture. Pottery and textiles have been found dating to the end of the New Stone Age. The discovery of metals in the **Bronze Age**, 3,000 BCE, is concurrent with the establishment of what are believed to be the first civilizations. The Iron Age followed quickly on the heels of the Bronze Age.

By 4,000 BCE humans lived in villages, engaged in animal husbandry, grew grains, sailed in boats, and practiced religions. Civilizations arose earliest in the fertile river valleys of the Nile, Mesopotamia, the Indus, and the Hwang Ho.

There are four prerequisites of civilization:

- Use of metals rather than stone for tools and weapons,
- A system of writing,
- A calendar,
- And a territorial state organized on the basis of residence in the geographic region.

The earliest known civilizations developed in the Tigris-Euphrates valley of Mesopotamia (modern Iraq) and the Nile valley of Egypt between 4000 BCE and 3000 BCE. This area is known as the Fertile Crescent. Because these civilizations arose in river valleys, they are known as **fluvial civilizations**.

Geography and the physical environment played a critical role in the rise and the survival of both of these civilizations. First, the rivers provided a source of water that would sustain life, including animal life. The hunters of the society had ample access to a variety of animals, initially for hunting to provide food, as well as hides, bones, antlers, etc. from which clothing, tools and art could be made. Second, the proximity to water provided a natural attraction to animals that could be herded and husbanded to provide a stable supply of food and animal products. Third, the rivers of these regions overflowed their banks each year, leaving behind a deposit of very rich soil. As these early people began to experiment with growing crops rather than gathering food, the soil was fertile and water was readily available to produce sizeable harvests. In time, the people developed systems of irrigation that channeled water to the crops without significant human effort on a continuing basis.

The **Fertile Crescent** was bounded on the West by the Mediterranean, on the South by the Arabian Desert, on the north by the Taurus Mountains, and on the east by the Zagros Mountains. The designation "Fertile Crescent" was applied by the famous historian and Egyptologist James Breasted to the part of the Near East that extended from the Persian Gulf to the Sinai Peninsula. It included Mesopotamia, Syria and Palestine.

This region was marked by almost constant invasions and migrations. These invaders and migrants seemed to have destroyed the culture and civilization that existed. Upon taking a longer view, however, it becomes apparent that they actually absorbed and supplemented the civilization that existed before their arrival. This is one of the reasons the civilization developed so quickly and created so such an advanced culture.

Skill 6.2   Political, economic, religious, and cultural characteristics of the early civilizations of Egypt, the Middle East, India, and China

Ancient civilizations were those cultures that developed to a greater degree than others and were considered advanced. There are a number of ancient civilizations worth examining, each with its own major accomplishments.

The ancient civilization of the **Sumerians** invented the wheel, developed irrigation through use of canals, dikes, and devices for raising water, devised the system of cuneiform writing, learned to divide time, and built large boats for trade. The **Babylonians** devised the famous **Code of Hammurabi**, the first written code of laws, which would later form the basis for our modern laws. **Egypt** made numerous significant contributions including construction of the great pyramids, development of hieroglyphic writing, preservation of bodies after death, making paper from papyrus, the invention of the method of counting in groups of 1-10 (the decimal system), completion of a solar calendar; and laying the foundation for science and astronomy.

The civilizations of the Sumerians, Amorites, Hittites, Assyrians, Chaldeans, and Persians controlled various areas of the land we call Mesopotamia. The culture of **Mesopotamia** was definitely autocratic in nature. The various civilizations that crisscrossed the Fertile Crescent had a single ruler at the head of government and, in many cases, at the head of religion. The people followed his strict instructions or faced the dire, often life-threatening consequences.

For example, each Sumerian city-state (and there were a few) had its own god, with the city-state's leader doubling as the high priest of worship of that local god. Subsequent cultures had a handful of gods as well, although they had more of a national worship structure, with high priests centered in the capital city as advisers to the tyrant. With few exceptions, tyrants and military leaders controlled the vast majority of aspects of society, including trade, religions, and the laws.

Trade was vastly important to these civilizations, since they had access to some but not all of the things that they needed to survive. Some trading agreements led to occupation, as was the case with the Sumerians, who didn't bother to build walls to protect their wealth of knowledge. Egypt and the Phoenician cities were powerful and regular trading partners of the various Mesopotamian cultures.

Legacies handed down to us from these people include:

- The first use of writing, the wheel, and banking (Sumeria);
- The first epic story (*Gilgamesh*);
- The first library dedicated to preserving knowledge (instituted by the Assyrian leader Ashurbanipal);
- The Hanging Gardens of Babylon (built by the Chaldean Nebuchadnezzar)

One of the earliest civilizations to develop in the Nile River Valley, Kushite states rose to power before a period of Egyptian incursion into the area. The earliest historical record of **Kush** is in Egyptian sources. This civilization was characterized by a settled way of life in fortified mud-brick villages. They subsisted on hunting and fishing, herding cattle, and gathering grain. Skeletal remains suggest that the people were a blend of Negroid and Mediterranean peoples. This civilization appears to be the second oldest in Africa (after Egypt).

In government, the king ruled through a law of custom that was interpreted by priests. The king was elected from the royal family. As in Egypt, descent was determined through the mother's line, but unlike the Egyptians, the Kushites were ruled by a series of female monarchs. The Kushite religion was **polytheistic**, including all of the primary Egyptian gods. There were, however, regional gods which were the principal gods in their regions. Derived from other African cultures, there was also a lion warrior god. This civilization was vital through the last half of the first millennium BC, but it suffered about 300 years of gradual decline until it was eventually conquered by the Nuba people.

The **Phoenicians** were sea traders well known for their manufacturing skills in glass and metals and the development of their famous purple dye. They became so very proficient in the skill of navigation that they were able to sail by the stars at night. Further, they devised an alphabet using symbols to represent single sounds, which was an improved extension of the Egyptian principle and writing system. The ancient **Assyrians** were warlike and aggressive due to a highly organized military and used horse drawn chariots.

The **Minoans** had a system of writing using symbols to represent syllables in words. They built palaces with multiple levels containing many rooms, water and sewage systems with flush toilets, bathtubs, hot and cold running water, and bright paintings on the walls. The **Mycenaeans** later changed the Minoan writing system to aid their own language and used symbols to represent syllables.

The ancient **Persians** developed an alphabet, contributed the religions and/or philosophies of **Zoroastrianism**, **Mithraism**, and **Gnosticism**, and allowed conquered peoples to retain their own customs, laws, and religions. In **India**, the caste system was developed, the principle of **zero** in mathematics was discovered, and the major religion of Hinduism was begun.

China is considered by some historians to be the oldest uninterrupted civilization in the world and was in existence around the same time as the ancient civilizations founded in Egypt, Mesopotamia, and the Indus Valley. The Chinese studied nature and weather; stressed the importance of education, family, and a strong central government; followed the religions of Buddhism, Confucianism, and Taoism; and invented such things as gunpowder, paper, printing, and the magnetic compass.

China began building the Great Wall, practiced crop rotation and terrace farming, increased the importance of the silk industry, and developed caravan routes across Central Asia for extensive trade all while many of the nations of Europe were still in their infancy. They also increased proficiency in rice cultivation and developed a written language based on drawings or pictographs. The Chinese language has no alphabet symbolizing sounds; instead each word or character has its own form.

Skill 6.3 Fundamental ideas and beliefs of Hinduism, Buddhism, Confucianism, Taoism, and Shinto

Hinduism

Hinduism is unique among the major religions of the world in that it has no identifiable founder, no single theological system, no single code of ethics, and no central religious organization. Modern Hinduism evolved from an ancient religion called Vedism, which dates from around 1500 BCE. Hinduism is expressed in many forms, most of which are "henotheistic" – recognizing a single God that is manifested or expresses itself in other gods and goddesses.

Hinduism recognizes several sacred writings: the Vedas (the chants of the priestly class of the Aryan or "noble" people who introduced Vedism into the Indian subcontinent), with their four central texts – the **Rig Veda** ("hymn knowledge"), the **Yajur Veda** ("ceremonial knowledge"), the **Sama Veda** ("chant knowledge") and the **Atharva Veda** ("knowledge from Atharve," a Vedic teacher); the **Brahmana** and **Aranyakas**, which are ceremonial rules that were later added to the other Vedas; and the **Upanishads**, which is a collection of poetry and prose that explores the basic philosophical and spiritual concepts of Hinduism. The Upanishads teach that spiritual mastery is achievable by all who practice correct meditation and discipline. Two other important Hindu texts are the **Ramayana** and the **Mahabharata**, which includes the **Bahagavad Gita**. The Bhagavad Gita teaches that duty (dharma) and action are equal to prayer and sacrifice as paths to spiritual perfection.

Hinduism is a very complex and very diverse religion. Beliefs and practices vary from one school to another. Central beliefs are:

- Worship is an individual or family matter.
- **Atman** and **Brahman** are generally understood as "soul" and "divine spirit."
- Brahman is the course and substance of all existence; when it is understood as the "self" of humans, it is called Atman.
- The spiritual goal of Hinduism is to understand and experience that there is no difference between one's self and the rest of the universe.
- **Maya**, which is used to describe the world, comes from the concepts of magic and matter and is often translated as "illusion." This belief is that the world has a   single spiritual nature and is not divided into "things."
- **Karma** is the moral consequence of every act in the course of human life.
- **Samsara** is the cycle of birth and rebirth in life. The path of the soul through rebirth is determined by the individual's karma.
- **Moksha**, which means "liberation" or "freedom," refers to the soul breaking free of the endless cycle of rebirth in life. Moksha is attained by freeing oneself of egotism and anger and losing one's sense of individuality in Maya.

The ultimate goal of Hinduism is the achievement of recognition that one's self is indistinguishable from Brahman.

In addition, Hindus also believe in pursuing worldly goals, including religious and social duty, economic security and power, and pleasure, all of this according to one's place in society. The **caste** system provides the framework of society and this process. The society is divided into four major "castes" that are defined by social standing and occupation. These are the priestly class; the aristocratic protectors of society; the class of merchants, landowners and moneylenders; and the laborers. Those outside the caste system were the "Untouchables."

Yoga is an active path to spiritual perfection. Evolving around the cults of anthropomorphic gods, there are three major theistic traditions. Vishnu is the force of preservation, Shiva is a god of destruction, and Brahma is the creative force. Hindus honor a number of incarnations of these gods, including Rama and Krishna. Hindus believe that all living things share a common element of Brahman, and thus are to be respected. Some animals are understood to be manifestations of certain deities. The most honored animal is the cow.

Buddhism

Buddhism was developed and taught by Siddhartha Gautama in what is now Nepal around 563 BCE. Upon consideration of the suffering of people in the world, he traveled widely, studying and meditating. He experienced "enlightenment" and thus earned the name *Buddha*, which means "the awakened one" or "the enlightened one." He then created an order of monks and taught the Buddhist philosophy of escape from life's cycle of suffering through compassion, nonviolence, and moderate living.

The central written text of Buddhism is called the **Tipitaka**, the "three baskets" or collections of Buddhist thought. Although these were not written down until many years after the death of the Buddha, these texts are accepted as his exact words. The three baskets are: the **sutras**, which are the teachings in the form of dialogues and sermons; the **vinaya**, which are the rules for monastic life; and the **abhidharma**, a systematic ordering of the lessons of the sutras.

Buddism shared a number of beliefs and ideas with Hinduism. These include the cycle of birth and rebirth. The idea of **nirvana** is quite similar to moksha in the Hindu tradition, which is an escape from the cycle of rebirth. However, Buddhism teaches that nothing is permanent, including the universal spirit or the self. The Buddha taught that there is constant change in the universe and that all things will, in time, decay and disappear. Because nothing can endure unchanged forever, desire is infinite and insatiable. Peace and enlightenment are thus possible only by renouncing desire and accepting that existence is not permanent.

The **Three Jewels of Buddhism** are the three things that are the heart of Buddhist belief:

- the Buddha is the model of what all humans should aspire to be or become

- the overarching Buddhist worldview and way of life

- the community of Buddhist nuns and monks

The **Four Noble Truths** summarize the Buddhist worldview: All life involves suffering; suffering is caused by desire; desire can be overcome; the way to overcome desire is to follow the eightfold path.

The **Noble Eightfold Path** summarizes the steps one should practice simultaneously to understand the universe, to live compassionately, and to achieve peace and enlightenment: right views, right intentions, right speech, right conduct, right work, right effort, right meditation, and right contemplation.

There are three major schools or branches of Buddhism:

Theravada Buddhism (Doctrine of the Elders) adheres most closely to the earliest practices. The monastic life has special importance in this branch. The ideal is a person who has attained perfect enlightenment and the end of all desire.

Mahayana Buddhism (Greater Vehicle) focuses on compassion for others over personal progress toward enlightenment. The ideal of this branch is the "bodhisattva," an enlightened person who postpones entry into Nirvana to help others.

Vajrayana Buddhism (Tantric Buddhism) emphasizes ritual, including the use of mantras (chants), hand gestures, mandalas (icons of the universe), and prayer wheels.

Confucianism

This is a Chinese religion based on the teachings of the Chinese philosopher Kung Fu-Tzu (translated, Confucius). There is no clergy, no organization, and no belief in a deity or in life after death. Confucius took a code of ethics and the teaching of a scholarly tradition, and systematized it. The teachings of Confucius were written down in the *Analects*. These writings deal with individual morality, ethics, and the correct exercise of power by rulers.

Confucianism was primarily a philosophical and ethical system until about the first century CE, when Buddhism was introduced into China. It gradually began to take on aspects of a religion.

Confucianism is essentially a "humanitarian ethical system" built on five key values:

- **Ren**: reciprocal human feeling
- **Yi**: righteousness
- **Li**: propriety, which includes ritually correct behavior
- **Zhi**: knowledge
- **Xin**: trustworthiness

These five values enable one to exercise the virtues of *Xiao*, filial piety, and *Wen*, civilization.

Taoism

This is a native Chinese religion with worship of more deities than almost any other religion. It is believed to have been founded by Lao Tzu, who is believed to have been a contemporary of Confucius. The word Tao means path or way. The central writing of Taoism is the *Tao Te Ching* (*The Way and its Power*). The 81 brief chapters, in poetry, discuss the nature of the Tao, which is the source and essence of all being.

Primary Taoist concepts, practices and beliefs are: (1) Tao is the first cause of the universe and the force that flows through all life; (2) the goal of each believer is to develop harmony with the Tao; (3) there are many gods, which are manifestations of the one Tao; (4) answers to life's problems are to be sought through inner meditation and outward observation; (5) time is cyclical, not linear; (6) health and vitality are to be strengthened; (7) the five main organs and orifices of the body correspond to the five parts of the universe – fire, water, metal, earth, and wood; (8) the development of virtue is the chief goal of believers; (9) the three "Jewels" to be cultivated in life are moderation, humility, and compassion; (10) humans should allow nature to take its course; (11) one should carefully consider each action in advance; (12) one should be kind to others; and (13) people are compassionate by nature. A basic Taoist symbol is the Yin and Yang. It represents the balance and the essential unity of opposites in the universe.

Shinto

Shinto is a native religion of Japan that developed from native folk beliefs and involved the worship of spirits and demons in animals, trees, and mountains. According to its mythology, deities created Japan and its people, which resulted in worshipping the emperor as a god. Shinto was strongly influenced by Buddhism and Confucianism, but never had strong doctrines on salvation or life after death.

There are "Four Affirmations" in Shinto: (1) tradition and the family (the family is the primary mechanism for preserving traditions); (2) love of nature (nature is sacred. To be in contact with nature is to be close to the gods, who reside in natural objects); (3) physical cleanliness; and (4) "Matsuri" (the honor and worship of the Kami and the ancestral spirits). Morality in Shinto is defined by what is in the best interest of the group.

Skill 6.4   Institutions, culture, and legacies of Greek civilization

Ancient Greece is often called the "**Cradle of Western Civilization**" because of the enormous influence it had not only on the time in which it flourished, but on western culture ever since. Early Greek institutions have survived for thousands of years, and have influenced the entire world.

The **Athenian form of democracy**, with each citizen having an equal vote in his own government, is a philosophy upon which all modern democracies are based. In the United States, the Greek tradition of democracy was honored in the choice of **Greek architectural** styles for the nation's government buildings. The modern **Olympic Games** are a revival of an ancient Greek tradition and many of the events are recreations of original contests.

The works of the Greek epic poet **Homer** are considered the earliest in western literature, and are still read and taught today. The tradition of the theater was born in Greece, with the plays of Aristophanes and others. In philosophy, **Aristotle** developed an approach to learning that emphasized observation and thought, and **Socrates** and **Plato** contemplated the nature of being and the origins and ideals of government and political relations. Greek mythology, centered around a pantheon of gods and the mortals they interact with, has been the source of inspiration for literature into the present day.

In the field of mathematics, **Pythagoras** and **Euclid** laid the foundation of geometry and **Archimedes** calculated the value of pi. Herodotus and Thucydides were the first to apply research and interpretation to written history.

In the arts, Greek sensibilities were held as perfect forms to which others might strive. In sculpture, the Greeks achieved an idealistic aesthetic that had not been perfected before that time.

The Greek civilization served as an inspiration to the Roman Republic, which followed in its tradition of democracy, and was directly influenced by its achievements in art and science. Later, during the Renaissance, European scholars and artists would rediscover ancient Greece's love for dedicated inquiry and artistic expression, leading to a surge in scientific discoveries and advancements in the arts.

Alexander the Great and the spread of Greek culture

Alexander was a Macedonian who was tutored by the Greek philosopher Aristotle, and who became one of the greatest conquerors of history. Alexander lived in the fourth century BC.

Alexander was the son of Philip II of Macedon, who had united the various city-states of Greece into one kingdom. Upon Philip's death, these states again sought independence, but were conquered and reunited by Alexander. From there, Alexander expanded his empire to the east and south, reaching as far as Egypt and India. He founded the city of **Alexandria** in Egypt, which became a major center of learning. At its peak, Alexander's empire covered most of the known world.

As Alexander conquered and moved through foreign regions, he increased his forces by absorbing foreign officers and soldiers into his own army. He also encouraged his own soldiers to marry into local populations. This policy of inclusion and expansion had the effect of bringing Greek culture to the east with its ideals of learning and inquiry. For example, Alexander was apparently very affected by Persian culture after conquering a part of that region, and for a time took to wearing Persian style clothing and adopting some of their customs. This exemplified the spread of eastern culture to the west.

Alexander died mysteriously after a sudden illness at the age of 33 in 323 BC. Having left no heir, his empire was split into four kingdoms. His reputation did not die, however, and Greek culture in general and Alexander in particular served as the inspiration for the Roman leaders who would eventually recreate much of his empire in the following centuries.

Skill 6.5   Institutions, culture, decline, and legacies of the Roman Republic and Empire

The ancient civilization of Rome owed much to the Greeks. Romans admired Greek architecture and arts, and built upon these traditions to create a distinct tradition of their own that would influence the western world for centuries.

In government, the Romans took the Athenian concept of democracy and built it into a complex system of **representative government** that included executive, legislative and judicial functions. In the arts, Romans created a realistic approach to portraiture, in contrast to the more idealized form of the Greeks. In architecture, Rome borrowed directly from the Greek tradition, but also developed the dome and the arch, allowing for larger and more dramatic forms. The Romans continued the Greek tradition of learning, often employing Greeks to educate their children.

The Roman Republic flourished in the centuries leading up to the advent of the Christian era. An organized bureaucracy and active political population provided elite Roman citizens with the means to ascend to positions of considerable authority. During the first century BC, **Gaius Julius Caesar** ambitiously began to gather support among the ruling authorities of the Republic, eventually being named one of the two annually elected Consuls. Caesar was ultimately named dictator for life, and was the transitional leader between the Roman Republic and what would become the Roman Empire.

The Roman Empire extended through much of Europe and Roman culture extended with it. Everywhere the Romans went, they built roads, established cities, and left their mark on the local population. The Roman language, Latin, spread as well and was transformed into the Romance languages of French and Spanish. The Roman alphabet, which was based on the Greek transformation of Phoenician letters, was adopted throughout the empire and is still used today.

Like the Republic, the Roman Empire also looked to the east to Greece for inspiration. Now it was the Macedonian conqueror Alexander, who had unified Greece and introduced the culture throughout the eastern world who provided Roman emperors with a role model. The empire itself has served as a model for modern government, especially in federal systems such as that found in the United States. The eventual decline and fall of the empire has been a subject that has occupied historians for centuries.

The decline and fall of the Roman Empire

The causes of the decline and fall of the Roman Empire are widely debated even today. What is referred to as the fall of the empire is more properly described as the fall of the Western Roman Empire, as the eastern empire based in Constantinople continued on for a thousand years after Rome fell. The Roman Empire had gained dominion over the largest number of people of any empire in history at that time, stretching from the Atlantic Ocean in the west to Persia in the east, and from North Africa to the island of Britain. This vast empire stood for centuries, ruled by a series of emperors beginning in the first decades AD.

In the third century, the empire began experiencing an increase in civil unrest as well as increased invasions from outside. Internally, civil war became an almost constant factor as there were no clear rules for accession to the position of Emperor. Military factions battled for the position with Diocletian ascending to the role in 285 AD.

Diocletian realized that the vast empire was spread too wide to be governed effectively by one person in Rome. He divided the empire in half along a north-south line east of Italy and named his friend, Maximian, emperor of the eastern portion. Each emperor, who held the title **Augustus**, also named a kind of junior emperor, entitled Caesar. Thus the empire now had four emperors.

This system worked well for some time, as the four men were able to cooperate effectively. When Diocletian and Maximian withdrew, Augustus elevated their Caesars to the posts, and conflict soon followed. Constantius, who was Maximian's Caesar, died while in office and once the issue of succession was hotly contested with Constantius military backers installing his son, Constantine as Augustus in opposition to Severus, who had been Constantius' Caesar.

Several years of conflict ensued, with many pretenders to the position of Augustus. In the end, it was **Constantine** who won out as the sole Augustus. In 330 AD, he proclaimed the empire unified again and moved the capital from Rome to Byzantium, which was subsequently known as **Constantinople**. Constantine eventually converted to Christianity, and the Roman Empire was thenceforth officially a Christian state. Constantine divided the rule of the empire among his sons, but conflict over control of the empire continued for decades, with several emperors ascending the throne, all Christian.

The invasions by Germanic tribes continued to increase in their force and frequency. With power divided and the capital of the empire moved to the east, Rome became a prime target for these invading forces. The traditional "fall" of the Roman Empire is widely recognized as the defeat of Rome in 476 by Germanic invaders who deposed the western emperor and took control of the government. The eastern empire would continue to flourish for another thousand years, even regaining the Italian region from the Ostrogoths' various campaigns of conquest. It stood until it was conquered in 1453 by the Ottomans.

Skill 6.6   Origins, central teachings, and spread of Judaism, Christianity, and Islam

Judaism

Judaism is the oldest of the Western world's three monotheistic religions. It developed from the ancient religion of the Hebrews or Israelites. This early religion shared a number of common elements and primordial stories with neighboring peoples, especially the Mesopotamian and Babylonian cultures. Judaism's sacred writing, the Hebrew Scripture, is generally referred to as *Torah* or *Tannakh*. It consists of 24 books, which are divided into three sections: Law (*Torah*), Prophets (*Nevi'im*), and Writings (*Ketuvim*).

The word and law of God were transmitted orally for many generations prior to the writing of the Hebrew Scripture. The *Mishna* is the collection of the oral tradition. The *Gemara* is a collection of commentary by the rabbis (teachers). The tradition of living interpretation and commentary continued through the centuries. *Halakah* is the tradition of interpretation of law, history and practice. *Kabbalah* is a body of Jewish mystical literature. *Kabbalah* arose from a movement in France in the 11th Century that discovered an esoteric system of symbolic interpretation of scripture.

Judaism is centered in belief in a single, all-powerful, all-seeing, and all-knowing God. God chose the Hebrew people from all the people of the earth and entered into a covenant with them. "I will be your God, and you will be my people." This covenant implies special privileges, but it also implies certain obligations of the people. The life of the people is to be structured around the promises and commandments of God. The Law provides the structure of religious practice and daily life. The Law is the guide for making ethical choices that reflect and demonstrate their unique character as the chosen people of God. Failure to act in accordance with God's law is a willful act, called sin. Sin destroys the proper relationship between the person and God. It is, however, possible to return from willful rebellion and restore the broken relationship. Judaism is also marked by a strong sense of communal identity, and sin can be either individual or communal.

The Hebrew people, as the chosen people of God, are to remain separate or apart from other peoples in several ways. First, the Hebrews are to avoid marriage to persons outside the faith. Second, they are to observe certain dietary restrictions The rules for **kosher** (ritually correct) food preparation and consumption are quite detailed and include prohibitions against eating certain animals, including pork and shellfish, specifications for the slaughter and butchering of meat, and a prohibition against mixing meat and dairy products. Third, they shall not marry foreigners (this protects the faith of the community against other influences and conflicting ideas). Fourth is the circumcision of all males (this is both an act of obedience to the covenant and an indication of the separateness of the people).

Among devout Jews, special times for prayer are at dawn, noon, dusk and, for some, bedtime. The Jewish Sabbath is observed from sunset on Friday until sunset on Saturday. The Sabbath is a day of rest. Many observant Jews gather on the Sabbath for worship in synagogues, where a Rabbi leads them in readings from the Scriptures, prayer, and singing. The Jewish religious calendar is based on a lunar calendar, so the dates of religious holidays vary from year to year. With the exception of the New Year observance and the Day of Atonement, most holidays are based on either seasonal or historical events. The frequent prohibitions against idolatry in Hebrew Scripture reflect a deep and abiding concern that no limited entity or belief be mistaken for the one true God by God's chosen people.

The basic beliefs of Judaism are:

- There is one and only one God with whom each believer has direct personal experience and to whom prayers may be addressed.
- God is the ultimate authority and possesses final dominion over the universe, which God created.
- Life is holy.
- The **Torah** is a guide to correct living and a source of continued revelation of the word of God.
- Group worship and prayer are indispensable elements of a righteous life.
- Jews share a broad common diversity and a sense of collective purpose and responsibility to one another.

Today, there are three basic branches or schools of Jewish belief and practice. Each has various sects or groups within it.

Orthodox Judaism is the most rigorous and the smallest branch. This group conducts worship in Hebrew and interprets the Law very strictly and literally.

Reform Judaism, which originated in the 18th century, attempted to integrate Judaism into the mainstream European culture. Law, doctrine, and ritual are more liberally interpreted, and dietary laws generally are not observed.

Conservative Judaism combines doctrinal reform with traditional observance. This attempt to retain much of the old orthodoxy while also staying in touch with contemporary culture has made Conservatives slower in embracing most of the changes of Reform Judaism.

Christianity

Christianity grew out of Judaism and its belief that God would send a Messiah ("anointed one") who would establish the Kingdom of God on earth. Jesus of Nazareth appeared in the early years of the first century CE, preaching repentance in preparation for the arrival of the Kingdom of God. His brief (about three years) ministry of teaching, preaching, healing, and miracles gathered followers from among the common and the despised of his day, as well as non-Jews and the wealthy. This ministry was confined to the areas of Galilee and northwest Palestine.

According to Christian writings, Jesus eschewed the separatism of Judaism and reached out to the poor, the sick, and the social outcasts. He preached a Kingdom of God not of this world, which ran contrary to Jewish expectation of a political Messiah who would establish an earthly kingdom. As the movement grew, the teachings of Jesus were perceived as a danger to the political order by both the Jews and the Roman government. Jesus was handed over to the authorities by one of his closest followers, arrested, tried, and crucified. According to Christian belief, Jesus rose from the dead on the third day, appeared to his disciples, and then ascended to heaven.

Christians believe that Jesus is the Son of God; he died on the cross as an offering and sacrifice that saved humankind from sin. Those who believe in him will be saved. Christian scripture (**the Bible**) consists of two major parts: the Old Testament, which is an adaptation of the Hebrew Scripture, and the New Testament, which consists of 27 books. As an outgrowth of Judaism, Christianity accepts many of the beliefs—though not the practices—of Judaism.

Fundamental beliefs of Christianity are: (1) There is one God who is the creator and redeemer of humankind; God is all-knowing, all-powerful, and all-present. (2) Jesus Christ is the unique Son of God who is the savior of humankind. The doctrine of the Trinity teaches that the one God has three natures through/by which God is active in the world: God the Father, the creator and governor of creation, is the judge of humankind; God the Son (Jesus) is God in the flesh, who came among humankind to save them from sin; and God the Holy Spirit is the invisible presence of God that provides believers strength, faith, and guidance.

Christians observe Sunday as the Sabbath because Jesus was believed to have risen from the dead on a Sunday morning. Christian worship consists of the reading of scripture, the proclamation of the word of God, prayer, and the observance of the Sacraments. The Roman Catholic and Eastern Orthodox churches recognize seven sacraments: baptism, confirmation, marriage, ordination, anointing and absolution of the sick and dying, the confession of sins, and the Eucharist or Holy Communion. Protestant churches recognize only two sacraments: baptism and Holy Communion. Christians believe that each human being has an eternal soul that will be judged by God after death. The soul will then be "rewarded" or "punished" according to one's faith and actions in life. Roman Catholics and Eastern Orthodox also believe in the existence of a purgatory, which is a state in which some souls are purified for entry to heaven.

Christian ethics are based on the **Ten Commandments** of the Old Testament and the teachings of Jesus, which include the "Golden Rule" (Do unto others as you would have them do unto you") and a broader application of the commandments.

Until 1054, there was one Christian Church. In 1054, the Eastern Orthodox Church split from the Roman Catholic Church over several issues of belief and practice. In the 16th century, several reformers split from the Roman Catholic Church, again over issues of belief and practice, in what is known as the Protestant Reformation.

Islam

In about 610 CE, an orphan in Mecca named **Mohammed** began to preach Islam, a religion believed to have been revealed to him over a period of 23 years through the angel Gabriel. The word "Islam" is derived from an Arabic word meaning "peace." Literally meaning "submission to the will of God," Islam is considered by its followers as the final culmination and fulfillment of the same truths revealed through Moses, Jesus, and other chosen prophets of God. When Mohammed received his first revelation, it is believed that it was his cousin-in-law—a devout Christian of that time—who pronounced him prophet.

Like Judaism and Christianity, Islam traces its roots to Abraham. While Moses and Jesus descended from Abraham's son Isaac, Mohammed descended from his son Ishmael. When Mohammed began to preach, his followers suffered bitter persecution. So, in 622, the Muslim community left their city of Mecca for Medina, about 260 miles to the north. This migration event, called "hijrah," marks the beginning of the Muslim calendar. After several years of living in Medina, where Jews are believed to have been among the tribes that welcomed the Muslims, Mohammed returned to Mecca. Having learned that God loved patience and forgiveness, he forgave his enemies and succeeded in establishing Islam in Mecca as well.

- Islam is founded on these primary beliefs:
- There is one God for all. He is unique, incomparable and merciful.
- God has created angels.
- God has sent many prophets to humankind with his message. Prophet Mohammed, the last messenger, reconfirmed what was revealed prior to him.
- All people will be judged on the Day of Judgment. All individuals are accountable for their particular intentions and actions.
- God has complete authority over destiny, be it good or bad.
- This world is a temporary place; there's life after death.

Mohammed left behind a collection of divine revelations (*surahs*) he believed were delivered by the angel Gabriel. These revelations make up Islam's holy scripture, the *Koran* (reading). In addition, Muslims have access to the *Sunnah,* a record of the practices and traditions of Mohammed, and the *Hadith*, a record of Mohammed's sayings. While the *Koran* is the ultimate authority, the *Sunnah* and *Hadith* serve as guides in understanding the Koran in context.

The *Koran* mainly emphasizes the relationship between God and His creatures, but also addresses basic human concerns such as wisdom, worship, and law. It is considered a guide to a just society, proper human conduct, and equitable economic principles. As a guide to Muslim life, it sets forth five basic principles:

- There is one God (*Allah*). Mohammed, the last messenger of Allah, summed up the eternal truths revealed by previous prophets.
- One is obliged to pray five times a day at prescribed intervals, facing Mecca. Prayer is a direct link between the worshipper and God. All worshippers facing Mecca is symbolic of the idea that all are children of God and that there is one God for all. There are no distinctions of any kind.
- One should practice charity for the welfare of the community. It is believed that setting aside a proportion of personal wealth for those in need purifies possessions and encourages new and fair growth.
- Fasting is prescribed from sunrise to sunset every day during the holy month of Ramadan to cleanse the spirit. It is said that fasting helps a person focus on his or her real purpose in life by staying away from worldly pleasures. It makes one more considerate toward the poor and hungry.
- Pilgrimage to Mecca should be made if it is physically and financially possible. Mecca is where the "father" of monotheistic religion—Abraham—built the "Kaabah," a house of worship to the one God. Pilgrims wear simple garments that are said to remove all distinctions of class and culture so that all stand equal before God.

The moral principles of Islam are to practice charity, humility, and patience; forgive enemies; avoid avarice, lying, and malice; and stay away from drinking alcohol, eating pork, and gambling. According to the *Koran*, all souls will be judged on the Day of Judgment on the basis of their true and honest "intentions" in this world. Ultimately, God alone will determine who is faithful, just and honest. These people will see their rewards in heaven, while those who are swayed by worldly gain alone and engage in unjust and selfish practices will be given due punishment. Mohammed repeatedly instructed people to use their powers of intelligence and observation. He said God has bestowed humans with the ability to learn, so it is their obligation to seek knowledge. Islam, therefore, puts special emphasis on education.

The *Koran* also mentions the concept of "jihad," which literally means "struggle." This could be a personal and inner struggle against evil within oneself; a struggle for goodness and righteousness on the social level; or struggle on the battlefield, only if and when necessary for self defense. Even in combat, Muslims must follow strict rules. They are prohibited from harming civilians or destroying crops, trees and livestock.

The *Koran* elevates the level of women—although the treatment of women in many Muslim societies today is reflective of cultural practices rather than authentic Islamic teaching. In Islam, women are given the rights to earn their own living, choose their marriage partners, and own and dispose of their personal property and earnings as they wish. Roles of men and women are seen as complementary and collaborative. Their rights and responsibilities are to be equitable and balanced in society.

According to Islam, the family is the foundation of society. Marriage is encouraged as both a sacred act and a legal agreement between the partners. The groom is asked to give a marital gift to the bride for her own use, and she may keep her own family name instead of adopting her husband's. Although allowed as a last resort in troubled relationships, divorce is considered as "despised" by God and as a betrayal of a sacred relationship. Emphasis is placed on love, fairness, and harmony in the relationship.

Both men and women are expected to dress and act in a modest and dignified manner. However, specific traditions of dress that have evolved over time may once again reflect cultural practices.

Skill 6.7   The rise and achievements of Byzantine civilization

The **Byzantines** (who were Christians) made important contributions in art and the preservation of Greek and Roman achievements including architecture especially in eastern Europe and Russia, the Code of Justinian and Roman law. Byzantium was known for its exquisite artwork, including the famous church Hagia Sophia.

Bordering the east of Europe was the **Byzantine Empire**, which was the Eastern Roman Empire, after it was split into two by Emperor Diocletian. Diocletian's successor, Emperor Constantine renamed the capital Byzantium to **Constantinople**, after himself. With the fall of Western Rome in 476 CE, the Byzantine emperors, starting with Justinian, attempted to regain the lost western territories. Due to ineffective rulers between the seventh and ninth centuries CE, any gains were completely lost, reverting the territorial limits to the eastern Balkans of Ancient Greece and Asia Minor. The late ninth through eleventh centuries were considered the Golden Age of Byzantium.

Although Constantine had earlier made Christianity the official state religion of Rome, it left an unresolved conflict between Christian and classical (i.e., Greek and Roman) ideals. There were points of contention between the Pope in Rome and the Patriarch of Constantinople including celibacy of priests, language of the Liturgy (Latin in the west, Greek in the east), religious doctrine, and other un-reconciled issues. These issues led to the **Great Schism** which permanently split the church into the Roman Catholic and the Eastern Orthodox Churches. Perhaps the most wide-ranging success of the Byzantine Empire was in the area of trade. Uniquely situated at the gateway to both West and East, Byzantium could control trade going in both directions. Indeed, the Eastern Empire was much more centralized and rigid in its enforcement of its policies than the feudal West.

Skill 6.8 The relationship of Greek and Roman political concepts to modern government

Athenian democracy was a direct form of democracy, with every male citizen above the age of 20 able to vote in the legislative assembly. The assembly was made up of a minimum of 6,000 and voted on proposals made by a council of 500 citizens who were chosen by lot. Within the council of 500, one person was chosen each day to serve as the head of state. Trials were held by jury, without judges, with jurors being chosen from the pool of citizens. Athenian democracy differed from representative democracy in that each voter had the right to vote directly on public issues and no formal leaders were elected.

The concept of "**one person, one vote**," that was the basis of Greek democracy is still the primary ideal behind all modern democracies. **Direct democracy** after the Greek method has not survived as a national form of government, although smaller groups such as town meetings still practice a form of direct democracy over some matters. The Greeks provided the philosophy of democracy, but the modern form of national democratic government owes much to the Romans.

Democracy in the Roman Republic was an indirect form. Citizens were classified into groups based on economic status or tribal affiliation and were allowed to vote within that group. The majority vote of the group then determined how the group would vote in an assembly. There were three voting assemblies: The Curiate Assembly, made up of elite Romans, the Centuriate Assembly, made up of elite and common citizens, and the Tribal Assembly, which represented all citizens and conducted most trials. The Roman Republic also had a **Senate** made up of appointees who served for life. The Senate had no direct legislative power, but was nonetheless influential in its ability to recommend or oppose action by the assemblies.

The highest elected office in the Roman Republic was **consul**. Two consuls were elected by the Centuriate Assembly annually, each with veto power over the other's actions. The consuls held considerable administrative power, and were also expected to act as military leaders in times of war.

Nearly all modern democracies are formed in some fashion after the Roman model, with the legislative, executive and judicial functions placed in separate bodies. The framers of the US Constitution were well versed in the Roman system, and created counterparts in the new American government. Like the Roman Republic, the US system has an indirect form of democratic government with representative assemblies, including a Senate with six-year terms and the more "common" House of Representatives with two-year terms. Instead of consuls, the US has a President who oversees the executive function of the country and represents the nation to the world. The president is elected in a national election, however it is the Electoral College, overseen by the Senate, which formally elects the national leader.

Unlike the early Roman Republic, the US has established a permanent independent court system. The complex Roman system also had conflicting powers among the various political bodies, making it difficult for one body to gain complete control over the others. This was also built into the American system as a series of "checks and balances" that ensure that no one branch of the government becomes too dominant.

COMPETENCY 0700   **Understand major developments in world history from 600 to 1600**

Skill 7.1   **The development of Islam and the consequences of Islamic expansion**

As noted in Skill 6.6, Mohammed emerged around 610 as the founder of Islam. Islam slowly gained ground, and the persecutions became more severe around Mecca. In 622, Mohammed and his close followers fled the city and found refuge in **Medina** to the North. His flight is called the **Hegira**. This event marks the beginning of the Moslem calendar. Mohammed took advantage of the ongoing feuds between Jews and Arabs in the city and became the rulers of Medina, making it the capital of a rapidly growing state.

In the years that followed, Islam changed significantly. It became a fighting religion and Mohammed became a political leader. The group survived by raiding caravans on the road to Mecca and plundering nearby Jewish tribes. This was a victorious religion that promised plunder and profit in this world and the blessings of paradise after death. It attracted many converts from the Bedouin tribes. By 630, Mohammed was strong enough to conquer Mecca and make it the religious center of Islam, toward which all Moslems turned to pray, and the *Kaaba* the most sacred **Mosque** or temple. Medina remained the political capital.

By taking over the pilgrimage, the sacred city and the sanctuary from paganism, Mohammed made it easier for converts to join the religion. By the time of his death in 632, most of the people of Arabia had become at least nominal adherents of Islam.

Mohammed died without either a political or a religious succession plan. His cousin, Ali, who had married Mohammed's daughter Fatima, believed his kinship and his heroism as a warrior gave him a natural claim to leadership. But Moslems in Medina thought one of their own should succeed Mohammed. **Abu Bakr** was finally chosen. He took the title of **Caliph**. The title was retained throughout the duration of the Moslem Empire.

These Moslem Arabians immediately launched an amazing series of conquests that in time extended the empire from the Indus to Spain. It has often been said that these conquests were motivated by religious fanaticism and the determination to force Islam upon the infidel. In fact, however, the motives were economic and political.

During the period of expansion there was a brief civil war that occurred because Ali was proclaimed Caliph at Medina. He was opposed by an aristocratic family of Mecca called the **Umayyad**. Ali was assassinated in 661, and the Umayyads emerged supreme, handing the caliphate down in their family for nearly a century. Because their strongest support was in Syria, they moved the capital from Medina to Damascus.

Despite political divisions, the Moslem world maintained strong economic, religious and cultural unity throughout this period. Mohammed had taught that all Moslems are brothers, equal in the sight of God. Conversion to Islam erased the differences between peoples of different ethnic origin.

The converts to Islam, who brought their cultural traditions, probably contributed more to this emerging synthetic civilization than the Arabs. This blending of cultures, facilitated by a common language, a common religion, and a strong economy, created learning, literature, science, technology and art that surpassed anything found in the Western Christian world during the Early Middle Ages. Interestingly, the most brilliant period of Moslem culture was from the eighth century through the eleventh, coinciding with the West's darkest cultural period.

Reading and writing in Arabic, the study of the Koran, arithmetic and other elementary subjects were taught to children in schools attached to the mosques. In larger and wealthier cities, the mosques offered more advanced education in literature, logic, philosophy, law, algebra, astronomy, medicine, science, theology and the tradition of Islam. Books were produced for the large reading public. The wealthy collected private libraries and public libraries arose in large cities.

The most popular subjects were theology and the law. But the more important field of study was philosophy. The works of the Greek and Hellenistic philosophers were translated into Arabic and interpreted with commentaries. These were later passed on to the Western Christian societies and schools in the twelfth and thirteenth centuries. The basis of Moslem philosophy was Aristotelian and Neo-platonic ideas, which were essentially transmitted without creative modification.

The Moslems were also interested in natural science. They translated the works on Galen and Hippocrates into Arabic and added the results of their own experience in medicine. Avicenna was regarded in Western Europe as one of the great masters of medicine. They also adopted the work of the Greeks in the other sciences and modified and supplemented them with their own discoveries. Much of their work in chemistry was focused on alchemy (the attempt to transmute base metals into gold).

The **Muslim** culture outdistanced the Western world in the field of medicine, primarily because the people weren't constrained by the sort of superstitious fervor that had so embraced the West at this time. The Muslim doctor **Al-Razi** was one of the most well-known physicians in the world and was the author of a medical encyclopedia and a handbook for smallpox and measles

Adopting the heritage of Greek mathematics, the Moslems also borrowed a system of numerals from India. This laid the foundation for modern arithmetic, geometry, trigonometry and algebra.

Moslem art and architecture tended to be mostly uniform in style, allowing for some regional modification. They borrowed from Byzantine, Persian and other sources. The floor plan of the mosques was generally based on Mohammed's house at Medina. The notable unique elements were the tall **minarets** from which the faithful were called to prayer. Interior decoration was the style now called **arabesque**. Mohammed had banned paintings or other images of living creatures. These continued to be absent from mosques, although they occasionally appeared in book illustration and secular contexts. But their skilled craftsmen produced the finest art in jewelry, ceramics, carpets, and carved ivory.

The Moslems also produced sophisticated literature in both prose and poetry. Little, however, of their poetry or prose was carried down by Western culture. The best-known works of this period are the short stories known as the **Arabian Nights** and the poems of **Omar Khayyam**.

Skill 7.2   Medieval civilization in Europe and its influences

The political, economic and social structure of European feudalism and manorialism

During the Middle Ages, the system of **feudalism** became a dominant feature of the economic and social system in Europe. Feudalism began as a way to ensure that a king or nobleman could raise an army when needed. In exchange for the promise of loyalty and military service, **lords** would grant a section of land, called a **fief** to a **vassal**, as those who took this oath of loyalty were called. The vassal was then entitled to work the land and benefit from its proceeds or to grant it in turn as a fief to another. At the bottom of this ladder were **peasants** who actually worked the land. At the top was the king to whom all lands might legally belong. The king could ensure loyalty among his advisors by giving them use of large sections of land which they in turn could grant as fiefs.

Manorialism, which also arose during the Middle Ages, is similar to feudalism in structure, but consisted of self-contained manors that were often owned outright by a nobleman. Some manors were granted conditionally to their lords, and some were linked to the military service and oaths of loyalty found in feudalism, meaning that the two terms overlap somewhat. Manors usually consisted of a large house for the lord and his family, surrounded by fields and a small village that supported the activities of the manor. The lord of the manor was expected to provide certain services for the villagers and laborers associated with the manor including the support of a church.

Also coming into importance at this time was the era of **knighthood** and its code of **chivalry** as well as the tremendous influence of the Roman Catholic Church. Until the period of the Renaissance, the Church was the only place where people could be educated. The **Bible** and other books were hand-copied by monks in the monasteries. Cathedrals were built and were decorated with art depicting religious subjects.

Land is a finite resource, and as the population grew in the middle centuries of the Middle Ages, the manorial/feudal system became less and less effective as a system of economic organization. The end of the system was sealed by the outbreak and spread of the **Black Death**, which killed over one-third of the total population of Europe. Those who survived and were skilled in any job or occupation were in demand and many serfs and peasants found freedom and, for that time, a decidedly improved standard of living.

With the increase in trade and travel, cities sprang up and began to grow. Craft workers in the cities developed their skills to a high degree, eventually organizing **guilds** to protect the quality of the work and to regulate the buying and selling of their products. City government developed and flourished, centered around strong town councils. Active in city government and the town councils were the wealthy businessmen who made up the rising middle class. Strong nation-states became powerful and people developed a renewed interest in life and learning.

The significance of the Catholic Church, monasteries, and universities

The Medieval Catholic Church was the single most unifying organization in the West, exercising influence at every level of society. Catholic bishops and archbishops were named from the ranks of noblemen, and acted as advisors to royal leaders. Parish priests oversaw the indoctrination of peasants and the collection of church taxes, called tithes. The church was the central building of most medieval towns.

The Catholic Church was also the primary provider of formal education, establishing universities in Italy and France. The **university** tradition of higher learning was itself an extension of an interest in learning that grew out of the Catholic monasteries, which were isolated communities of religious monks devoted to service to the Church.

European government in the High Middle Ages

The **High Middle Ages** refers to the period in Europe between the Early and Late Middle Ages, spanning approximately the eleventh, twelfth and thirteenth centuries. The period is noted for a rapid increase in population that contributed to dramatic changes in society, culture, and political organization.

During this period, the concept of the nation state took hold as populations became more stable and people began to think of themselves as belonging to a larger group of ethnically similar cultures. In Italy, the independent nation states such as Venice, Pisa and Florence were established, providing a basis for the Renaissance. The concept of inherited nobility gained wide acceptance and knighthood and chivalry developed as virtuous codes of conduct.

The **Crusades** took place during the High Middle Ages, further strengthening the importance of these orders of knights, and solidifying the strength of the western Church throughout Europe. The routes opened by Crusaders marching to Jerusalem opened the way for an increase in trade, and contributed to the growth of many cities based on this trade.

A merchant class developed and began to exert its' influence on political and economic affairs. As the power and influence of the Church grew, it contributed to the growth of art and architecture, particularly in the development of the great gothic cathedrals, most of which were constructed during this era.

Crucial advances in thinking and technology occurred during the High Middle Ages. Improvements in shipbuilding and clock-making led to advances in navigation and cartography, setting the stage for the Age of Exploration. The field of printing, while not yet to the stage that Gutenberg was to take it in the fifteenth century, expanded the availability of texts, serving a growing educated class of people. The philosophy of Scholasticism, which emphasized empiricism and opposed mysticism in Christian education, was espoused by **Thomas Aquinas**.

The population increase that had brought these significant developments to Europe in the High Middle Ages was suddenly reversed in the mid-fourteenth century by the **Black Plague**, which decimated the region. As the concept of the nation state arose, so did the idea of national borders and national sovereignty, leading to numerous wars, which in turn had deleterious effects on the economy. These events are now used to mark the period of transition between the High Middle Ages and the Late Middle Ages.

The origins, course, and consequences of the Crusades

The **Crusades** were a series of military campaigns beginning in the eleventh century against the encroaching Muslim Empire, particularly in the holy land of Palestine and the city of Jerusalem. They continued into the thirteenth century as Jerusalem and other holy cities changed hands between Christian and Muslim forces. Several crusades took place within Europe, as well, such as the efforts to re-conquer portions of the Muslim-occupied Iberian Peninsula.

The Christian Byzantine Empire was centered in Constantinople. The empire was under attack from Seljuk Turk forces who had taken Palestine. The eastern emperor, Alexius I called on his western counterpart, **Pope Urban II** for assistance. Urban saw the situation as an opportunity to reunite Christendom, which was still in the throes of schism between the Eastern Orthodox and the Western Catholic sects, and to invest the papacy with religious authority.

In 1095, Urban called on all Christians to rally behind the campaign to drive the Turks out of the Holy Land. Participation in the crusade, Urban said, would count as full penance for sin in the eyes of the Church. A force of crusaders marched to Jerusalem and captured it, massacring the inhabitants. Along the way, several small Crusader states were established. A second crusade was led against Damascus in 1145, but was unsuccessful.

In 1187, **Saladin**, the Sultan of Egypt recaptured Jerusalem, and a third Crusade was called for by Pope Gregory VIII. This Crusade was joined by the combined forces of France, England and the Holy Roman Empire, but fell short of its goal to recapture Jerusalem. The fourth Crusade took place in 1202, under Pope Innocent III. The intention of the fourth Crusade was to enter the Holy Land through Egypt. The plan was changed, however, and forces diverted to Constantinople.

One result of the Crusades was to establish and reinforce the political and military authority of the Catholic Church and the Roman pope. The religious fervor spurred on by the Crusades would eventually culminate in such movements as the **Inquisition** in Spain and the expulsion of the **Moors** from Europe. The marches of the crusaders also opened new routes between Europe and the East along which culture, learning and trade could travel.

Skill 7.3   Major civilizations of Asia

The Mongol Empire was founded by Genghis Khan and during the height of the empire covered a majority of the territory from Southeast Asia to central Europe. One of the primary military tactics of conquest was to annihilate any cities that refused to surrender.

Government was by decree on the basis on a code of laws developed by Genghis Khan. It is interesting that one of the tenets of this code was that the nobility and the commoners shared the same hardship. The society, and the opportunity to advance within the society, was based on a system of **meritocracy**. The carefully structured and controlled society was efficient and safe for the people. Religious tolerance was guaranteed. Theft and vandalism were strictly forbidden. Trade routes and an extensive postal system were created linking the various parts of the empire. Taxes were quite onerous, but teachers, artists and lawyers were exempted from the taxes. Mongol rule, however, was absolute. The response to all resistance was collective punishment in the form of destruction of cities and slaughter of the inhabitants.

The lasting achievements of the Mongol Empire include:

- Reunification of China and expansions of its borders
- Unification of the Central Asian Republics that later formed part of the USSR
- Expansion of Europe's knowledge of the world

The Ming Dynasty in China followed the Mongol-led Yuan Dynasty. In addition to its expansion of trade and exploration of surrounding regions, the period is well known for its highly talented artists and craftsmen. The Hongwu emperor rose from peasant origins. He distributed land to small farmers in an effort to help them support their families. To further protect these family farms, he proclaimed title of the land non-transferable. He also issued an edict by which anyone who cultivated wasteland could keep the land as their property and would never be taxed. One of the major developments of the time was the development of systems of irrigation for farms throughout the empire. Hongwu maintained a strong army by creating military settlements. During peacetime, each soldier was given land to farm and, if he could not afford to purchase equipment, it was provided by the government.

The legal code created during the period is generally considered one of the greatest achievements of the dynasty. The laws were written in understandable language and in enough detail to prevent misinterpretation. The law reversed previous policy toward slaves, and promised them the same protection as free citizens. Great emphasis was placed on family relations. It was clearly based on Confucian ideas. The other major accomplishment of this dynasty was the decision to begin building the **Great Wall of China** to provide protection from northern horsemen.

The Mogul Empire reached its height during the reign of **Akbar**. In the administration of the empire, Akbar initiated two approaches that are notable. First, he studied local revenue statistics for the various provinces within the empire. He then developed a revenue plan that matched the revenue needs of the empire with the ability of the people to pay the taxes. Although the taxes were heavy, one third to one half of the crop, it was possible to collect the taxes and meet the financial needs of the empire. Second, he created a rank and pay structure for the warrior aristocracy that was based on number of troops and obligations.

Akbar introduced a policy of acceptance and assimilation of Hindus, allowed temples to be built, and abolished the poll tax on non-Muslims. He devised a theory of "ruler-ship as a divine illumination" and accepted all religions and sects. He encouraged widows to remarry, discouraged marriage of children, outlawed the practice of sati, and persuaded the merchants in Delhi to recognize special market days for women who were otherwise required to remain secluded at home. The empire supported a strong cultural and intellectual life. He sponsored regular debates among religious and scholarly individuals with different points of view.

The unique style of architecture of the Mogul Empire was its primary contribution to South Asia. The **Taj Mahal** was one of many monuments built during this period. The cultural was a blend of Indian, Iranian and Central Asian traditions. Other major accomplishments were:

- Centralized government,
- Blending of traditions in art and culture,
- Development of new trade routs to Arab and Turkish lands,
- A unique style of architecture,
- Landscape gardening,
- A unique cuisine,
- And the creation of two languages (Urdu and Hindi) for the common people.

From its beginnings, **Japan** morphed into an imperial form of government, with the divine emperor being able to do no wrong and, therefore, serving for life. **Kyoto**, the capital, became one of the largest and most powerful cities in the world. The rich and powerful landowners, the nobles, grew powerful. Eventually, the nobles had more power than the emperor, which required an attitude change in the minds of the Japanese people.

The nobles were lords of great lands and were called **Daimyos**. They were of the highest social class and people of lower social classes worked for them The Daimyos had warriors serving them, known as **Samurai**, who were answerable only to the Daimyo. The Samurai code of honor was an exemplification of the overall Japanese belief that every man was a soldier and a gentleman.

The main economic difference between imperial and feudal Japan was that the money that continued to flow into the country from trade with China, Korea, and other Asian countries and from plunder on the high seas, made its way into the pockets of the Daimyos rather than the emperor's coffers.

Feudalism developed in Japan later than it did in Europe and lasted longer. Japan deflected Mongol invasion because of the famed **kamikaze**, or "divine wind," in the 12th century. Japan was thus free to continue to develop on its own terms and to refrain from interacting with the West. This isolation continued until the 19th century.

Skill 7.4   The development of African civilizations

The conquest of **Ghana** by Muslim Berbers in 1076 permitted rule to devolve to a series of lesser successor states. By the thirteenth century, the successor state of Kangaba established the Kingdom of Mali. This vast trading state extended from the Atlantic coast of Africa to beyond Gao on the Niger River in the east. The government of the Mali kingdom was held together by military power and trade. The kingdom was organized into a series of feudal states that were ruled by a king. Most of the kings used the surname "Mansa" (meaning, "sultan"). The most powerful and effective of the kings was Mansa Musa.

Much of the history of **Mali** was preserved by Islamic scholars because the Mali rulers converted to Islam and were responsible for the spread of Islam throughout Africa. The expansion of the Mali kingdom began from the city of Timbuktu and gradually moved downstream along the Niger River. This provided increasing control of the river and the cities along its banks, which were critical for both travel and trade. The Niger River was a central link in trade for both west and north African trade routes.

The religion and culture of the kingdom of Mali was a blend of Islamic faith and traditional African belief. The influence of the Islamic Empire provided the basis of a large and very structured government which allowed the king to expand both territory and influence. The people, however, did not follow strict Islamic law. The king was thought of in traditional African fashion as a divine ruler removed from the people. A strong military and control of the Niger River and the trade that flourished along the river enabled Mali to build a strong feudal empire.

Farther to the east, the king of the **Songhai** people had earlier converted to Islam in the eleventh century. Songhai was at one time a province of Mali. By the fifteenth century, Songhai was stronger than Mali and it emerged as the next great power in western Africa. Songhai was situated on the great bend of the Niger River. From the early fifteenth to the late sixteenth centuries, the Songhai Empire stood, one of the largest empires in the history of Africa. The first king Sonni Ali conquered many neighboring states, including the Mali Empire. This gave him control of the trade routes and cities like Timbuktu. He was succeeded by Askia Mohammad who initiated political reform and revitalization. He also created religious schools, built mosques, and opened his court to scholars and poets from all parts of the Muslim world.

During the same period, the **Zimbabwe** kingdom was built. "Great Zimbabwe" was the largest of about 300 stone structures in the area. This capital city and trading center of the Kingdom of Makaranga was built between the twelfth and fifteenth centuries. It was believed to have housed as many as 20,000 people. The structures are built entirely of stone, without mortar. The scanty evidence that is available suggests that the kingdom was a trading center that was believed to be part of a trading network that reached as far as China.

The area known today as the Republic of **Benin** was the site of an early African kingdom known as Dahomey. By the seventeenth century, the kingdom included a large part of West Africa. The kingdom was economically prosperous because of slave trading relations with Europeans, primarily the Dutch and Portuguese, who arrived in the fifteenth century. The coastal part of the kingdom was known as "**the Slave Coast**." This kingdom was known for a very distinct culture and some very unusual traditions. In 1729 the kingdom started a female army system. A law was passed stating that females would be inspected at the age of 15. Those thought beautiful were sent to the Palace to become wives of the king. Those who were sick or were considered unattractive were executed. The rest were trained as soldiers for two years. Human sacrifice was practiced on holidays and special occasions. Slaves and prisoners of war were sacrificed to gods and ancestors.

The slave trade provided economic stability for the kingdom for almost three hundred years. The continuing need for human sacrifices caused a decrease in the number of slaves available for export. As many colonial countries declared the trade of slaves illegal, demand for slaves subsided steadily until 1885 when the last Portuguese slave ship left the coast. With the decline of the slave trade, the kingdom began a slow disintegration. The French took over in 1892.

Skill 7.5   The civilizations in the Americas

See Skill 1.1 for information about the native civilizations of North America.

The empires of Central and South America include the Aztec, Inca, and Maya. However, people lived in South America before the advent of these empires. One of the earliest people of record was the **Olmecs**, who left behind little to prove their existence except a series of huge carved figures.

The **Aztecs** dominated Mexico and Central America. They weren't the only people living in these areas, just the most powerful. The Aztecs had many enemies, some of whom were only too happy to help Hernando Cortes precipitate the downfall of the Aztec society. The Aztecs had access to large numbers of metals and jewels, and they used the metals to make weapons and the jewels to trade for items they didn't already possess.

Though in practice the Aztecs didn't do a lot of trading; rather, they conquered neighboring tribes and demanded tribute from them. This is the source of much of Aztec riches. They also believed in a handful of gods and believed that these gods demanded human sacrifice in order to continue to smile on the Aztecs. The center of Aztec society was the great city of **Tenochtitlan**, which was built on an island so as to be easier to defend and boasted a population of 300,000 at the time of the arrival of the conquistadors. Tenochtitlan was known for its canals and its pyramids, none of which survive today.

The **Inca** Empire stretched across a vast period of territory down the western coast of South America and was connected by a series of roads. A series of messengers ran along these roads, carrying news and instructions from the capital, Cusco, another large city along the lines of but not as spectacular as Tenochtitlan. The Incas are known for inventing the *quipu*, a string-based device that provided them with a method of keeping records. The Inca Empire, like the Aztec Empire, was very much a centralized state, with all income going to the state coffers and all trade going through the emperor as well. The Incas worshiped the dead, their ancestors, and nature and often took part in what we could consider strange rituals.

The most advanced Native American civilization was the **Maya**, who lived primarily in Central America. They were the only Native American civilization to develop writing, which consisted of a series of symbols that has still not been deciphered. The Mayas also built huge pyramids and other stone figures and sculptures, mostly of the gods they worshiped. The Mayas are most famous, however, for their **calendars** and for their mathematics. The Mayan calendars were the most accurate on the planet until the 16th Century. The Mayas also invented the idea of zero, which might sound like a small thing except that no other culture had thought of such a thing. Maya worship resembled the practices of the Aztec and Inca, although human sacrifices were rare. The Mayas also traded heavily with their neighbors.

Skill 7.6   The origins, principal figures, and influence of the Renaissance

The word "**Renaissance**" literally means "rebirth" and signaled the rekindling of interest in the glory of ancient classical Greece and Rome civilizations. It was the period in human history marking the start of many ideas and innovations leading to our modern age. It began in the late 1300s and continued through the 1600s. It marks the end of the Middle Ages and a resurgence in many areas of human endeavor.

The **Renaissance** began in Italy with many of its ideas starting in Florence, controlled by the famous Medici family. Education flourished, especially for some of the merchants. This new openness to ideas and learning involved the study of reading, writing, math, law, and the writings of classical Greece and Rome. Contributions of the Italian Renaissance period occurred in many disciplines, and gradually spread throughout Europe.

Art - The more important artists were Giotto and his development of perspective in paintings; Leonardo da Vinci who was not only an artist but also a scientist and inventor; Michelangelo who was a sculptor, painter, and architect; and others including Raphael, Donatello, Titian, and Tintoretto.

Political philosophy – specifically the writings of Machiavelli on the machinations of power.

Literature - the writings of Boccaccio and the poet Petrarch.

Science – Galileo's contributions to both astronomy and physics changed the way people viewed the world around them and the heavens above.

Medicine - the work of Brussels-born Andrea Vesalius earned him the title of "father of anatomy" and had a profound influence on the Spaniard Michael Servetus and the Englishman William Harvey.

In Germany, Gutenberg's invention of the **printing press** with movable type facilitated the rapid spread of Renaissance ideas, writings and innovations, thus ensuring the enlightenment of most of Western Europe. Contributions were also made by **Durer** and **Holbein** in art and by **Paracelsus** in science and medicine.

The effects of the Renaissance in the Low Countries can be seen in the literature and philosophy of **Erasmus** and the art of **van Eyck** and **Breughel the Elder**, as well as many others. **Rabelais** and **de Montaigne** in France also contributed to literature and philosophy. In Spain, the art of **El Greco** and **de Morales** flourished, as did the writings of **Cervantes** and **De Vega**.

In England, **Sir Thomas More** and **Sir Francis Bacon** wrote and taught philosophy and were inspired by Vesalius. **William Harvey** made important contributions in medicine. Talents in literature and drama were contributed by **Chaucer, Spenser, Marlowe, Jonson,** and the incomparable **Shakespeare.**

Skill 7.7   Significant ideas, leaders and events of the Reformation

The **Reformation** period consisted of two phases: the Protestant Revolution and the Catholic Reformation. The Protestant Revolution came about because of religious, political, and economic reasons. The religious reasons stemmed from abuses in the Catholic Church including fraudulent clergy with their scandalous immoral lifestyles; the sale of religious offices, indulgences, and dispensations; different theologies within the Church; and frauds involving sacred relics.

The political reasons for the **Protestant Revolution** involved the increase in the power of rulers who were considered "absolute monarchs" wanting all power and control, especially over the Church; and the growth of "nationalism" or patriotic pride in one's own country. Economic reasons included the greedy desire of ruling monarchs to possess and control all lands and wealth of the Church, deep animosity against the burdensome papal taxation, the rise of the affluent middle class and its clash with medieval Church ideals, and the increase of an active system of "intense" capitalism.

The Protestant Revolution began in Germany with the revolt of **Martin Luther** against Church abuses. It spread to Switzerland where it was led by Calvin. It began in England with the efforts of King Henry VIII to have his marriage to Catherine of Aragon annulled so he could wed another and have a male heir. The results were the increasing support given not only by the people but also by nobles and some rulers, and of course, the attempts of the Church to stop it.

The **Catholic Reformation** was undertaken by the Church to "clean up its act" and to slow or stop the Protestant Revolution. The major efforts to this end were supplied by the Council of Trent and the Jesuits. Six major results of the Reformation included:

- Religious freedom,
- Religious tolerance,
- More opportunities for education,
- Power and control of rulers limited,
- Increase in religious wars, and
- An increase in fanaticism and persecution.

COMPETENCY 0800   **Understand major developments in world history during the Era of Global Expansion and Encounter (1450 TO 1750)**

Skill 8.1   Major elements of the Age of Exploration

The **Age of Exploration** actually had its beginnings centuries before exploration actually took place. The rise and spread of Islam in the seventh century and its subsequent control over the holy city of Jerusalem led to the European holy wars, the Crusades, to free Jerusalem and the Holy Land from this control. Even though the Crusades were not a success, those who survived and returned to their homes and countries in Western Europe brought back with them new products such as silks, spices, perfumes, new and different foods. Luxuries that were unheard of that gave new meaning to colorless, drab, dull lives.

New ideas, new inventions, and new methods also went to Western Europe with the returning Crusaders and from these new influences was the intellectual stimulation which led to the period known as the Renaissance. The revival of interest in classical Greek art, architecture, literature, science, astronomy, medicine and increased trade between Europe and Asia and the invention of the printing press helped to push the spread of knowledge and start exploring.

The Renaissance had ushered in a time of curiosity, learning, and incredible energy sparking the desire for trade to procure these new, exotic products and to find better, faster, cheaper trade routes to get to them. The work of geographers, astronomers and mapmakers made important contributions and many studied and applied the work of such men as **Hipparchus** of Greece, **Ptolemy** of Egypt, **Tycho Brahe** of Denmark, and **Fra Mauro** of Italy.

For many centuries, various mapmakers made many maps and charts, which in turn stimulated curiosity and the seeking of more knowledge. At the same time, the Chinese were using the magnetic compass in their ships. Pacific islanders were going from island to island, covering thousands of miles in open canoes navigating by sun and stars. Arab traders were sailing all over the Indian Ocean in their **dhows**.

The trade routes between Europe and Asia were slow, difficult, dangerous, and very expensive. Between sea voyages on the Indian Ocean and Mediterranean Sea, and the camel caravans in central Asia and the Arabian Desert, trade was still controlled by the Italian merchants in **Genoa** and **Venice**. It would take months and even years for the exotic luxuries of Asia to reach the markets of Western Europe. A faster, cheaper way had to be found. A way had to be found which would bypass traditional routes and end the control of the Italian merchants.

Prince Henry of Portugal (also called the Navigator) encouraged, supported, and financed the Portuguese seamen who led in the search for an all-water route to Asia. A shipyard was built along with a school teaching navigation. New types of sailing ships were built which would carry the seamen safely through the ocean waters. Experiments were conducted in newer maps, newer navigational methods, and newer instruments. These included the astrolabe and the compass enabling sailors to determine direction as well as latitude and longitude for exact location. Although Prince Henry died in 1460, the Portuguese kept on, sailing along and exploring Africa's west coastline.

In 1488, **Bartholomew Diaz** and his men sailed around Africa's southern tip and headed toward Asia. Diaz wanted to push on but turned back because his men were discouraged and weary from the long months at sea, extremely fearful of the unknown, and just refusing to travel any further.

However, the Portuguese were finally successful ten years later in 1498 when **Vasco da Gama** and his men, continuing the route of Diaz, rounded Africa's Cape of Good Hope, sailing across the Indian Ocean, reaching India's port of Calicut (Calcutta). Although, six years earlier, Columbus had reached the New World and an entire hemisphere, da Gama had proved Asia could be reached from Europe by sea.

With the increase in trade and travel, cities sprang up and began to grow. Craft workers in the cities developed their skills to a high degree, eventually organizing guilds to protect the quality of the work and to regulate the buying and selling of their products. City government developed and flourished centered on strong town councils. Active in city government and the town councils were the wealthy businessmen who made up the growing middle class.

In addition, there were a number of individuals and events during the time of exploration and discoveries. The **Vivaldo brothers** and **Marco Polo** wrote of their travels and experiences, which signaled the early beginnings. From the Crusades, the survivors made their way home to different places in Europe bringing with them fascinating, new information about exotic lands, people, customs, and desired foods and goods such as spices and silks.

The first Europeans in the New World were Norsemen led by **Eric the Red** and later, his son Leif the Lucky. However, before any of these, the ancestors of today's Native Americans and Latin American Indians crossed a land bridge across the Bering Strait from Asia to Alaska, eventually settling in all parts of the Americas.

Christopher Columbus, sailing for Spain, is credited with the discovery of America although he never set foot on its soil. **Magellan** is credited with the first circumnavigation of the earth. Other Spanish explorers made their marks in parts of what are now the United States, Mexico, and South America.

For France, claims to various parts of North America were the result of the efforts of such men as **Champlain, Cartier, LaSalle, Father Marquette** and **Joliet.** Dutch claims were based on the work of one **Henry Hudson.** **John Cabot** gave England its stake in North America along with **John Hawkins, Sir Francis Drake,** and the half-brothers **Sir Walter Raleigh and Sir Humphrey Gilbert.**

Skill 8.2   The rise of absolute monarchies and constitutional governments in Europe

The most familiar form of government throughout history was the **monarchy**. We can include dictatorships or authoritarian governments in this description because the basic idea—that one person was in charge of the government—applies to all. In this kind of government, the head of state was responsible for governing his or her subjects. In earlier times, this meant laws that weren't exactly written down, though written laws have increasingly been the standard as the centuries have progressed. Monarchies and one-person governments still exist today, although they are rare. In these states, the emphasis is on keeping the monarch in power, and many laws of the country have been written with that purpose in mind.

An **absolute monarchy** is a form of government where a king or queen rules with complete authority without any legal opposition. The absolute monarch arose out of the concept of the **divine right of kings**. This ideal held that monarchs received authority to rule from God. It arose during the late Middle Ages as feudalism increased the relative wealth and power of kings compared to other nobles. In theory an absolute monarch has total power over his or her subjects. In practice, absolute monarchs were expected to act wisely and to seek counsel on important decisions from advisors and church leaders, and in some cases were restricted by public agreements.

This increased power of monarchy combined with the relative weakness of the Church during the Reformation in the sixteenth century led to monarchs exercising influence over religious matters. This was the case of **Henry VIII of England**, who seized all Catholic Church property in his dominion, claiming responsibility only to God. **Louis XIV** of France was another absolute monarch who believed that the monarch was the embodiment of the state. In Russia, **Peter the Great** and his successors ruled as absolute monarchs until the early twentieth century.

Peter the Great of Russia was named **Czar** (sometimes spelled **Tsar**) in 1682, when he was ten years old, with his mother, Sophia, as regent. During his reign, Peter suppressed revolt and dissent with violence, eventually being named Emperor of Russia. Peter was a reformer who brought Western culture to Russia and traveled to Europe to learn about the newest military technology. Peter also laid the foundations of a legislative body by creating a Governing Senate made up of his appointees, and introduced a system of ranking based on merit and service rather than heredity.

In the 1640s, England saw a series of civil wars between the Royalist supporters of the **King Charles I** and the Parliamentarian army led by Oliver Cromwell. Prior to the civil wars, Parliament was called only at the king's will, and then mainly to levy taxes. Dispute over Charles' autocratic rule, his taking of a Catholic wife, his desire to engage in war in Europe, and what some took to be illegal attempts at taxation led to armed conflict. After extended fighting, the forces of Parliament succeeded, naming Cromwell "Protector." Charles I was tried for treason and beheaded. Cromwell's rule was short-lived, however, and after his death in 1658 the regime collapsed. By 1660 the monarchy had been restored.

In contrast to absolute monarchy based on religious right, constitutional governments derive their authority from written documents that lay out a form of government and define its powers and limitations. Beginning with the Magna Carta in England, the practice in many European countries has been to mix the two forms into a "**constitutional monarchy**." This form of government recognizes a monarch as leader, but invests most of the legal authority in a legislative body such as a Parliament. Great Britain still operates as a constitutional monarchy, as do many other European countries. European monarchs have been reduced to mainly ceremonial figures in modern government, however.

Skill 8.3   Contributions of the scientific revolution

The Scientific Revolution was, above all, a shift in focus from **belief to evidence**. Scientists and philosophers wanted to see proof not just believe what other people told them. It was an exciting time, if you were a forward-looking thinker.

A Polish astronomer, **Nicolaus Copernicus**, began the Scientific Revolution. He crystallized a lifetime of observations into a book that was published about the time of his death; in this book, Copernicus argued that the Sun, not the Earth, was the center of a solar system and that other planets revolved around the Sun, not the Earth. This flew in the face of established, i.e. Church-mandated, doctrine. The Church still wielded tremendous power at this time, including the power to banish people or sentence them to prison or even death.

The Danish astronomer **Tycho Brahe** was the first to catalog his observations of the night sky, of which he made thousands. Building on Brahe's data, German scientist **Johannes Kepler** instituted his theory of planetary movement, embodied in his famous Laws of Planetary Movement. Using Brahe's data, Kepler also confirmed Copernicus's observations and argument that the Earth revolved around the Sun.

The most famous defender of this idea was **Galileo Galilei**, an Italian scientist who conducted many famous experiments in the pursuit of science. He is most well known, however, for his defense of the **heliocentric** (sun-centered) idea. He wrote a book comparing the two theories, but most readers could tell easily that he favored the new one. He was convinced of this mainly because of what he had seen with his own eyes. He had used the relatively new invention of the telescope to see four moons of Jupiter. They certainly did not revolve around the Earth, so why should everything else? His ideas were not at all favored with the Church, which continued to assert its authority in this and many other matters. The Church was still powerful enough at this time, especially in Italy, to order Galileo to be placed under house arrest. Galileo died under house arrest, but his ideas did not die with him.

Picking up the baton was an English scientist named **Isaac Newton**, who became perhaps the most famous scientist of all. He is known as the discoverer of gravity and a pioneering voice in the study of optics (light), calculus, and physics. More than any other scientist, Newton argued for (and proved) the idea of a mechanistic view of the world: You can see how the world works and prove how the world works through observation. Up to this time, people believed what other people told them. Newton, following in the footsteps of Copernicus and Galileo, changed this in a significant way.

COMPETENCY 0900   **Understand major developments in world history during the Age of revolutions (1750 to 1914)**

Skill 9.1   **The influence of Enlightenment thinkers on political and economic development**

The Scientific Revolution led to the **Enlightenment**, a period of intense self-study that focused on ethics and logic. More so than at any time before, scientists and philosophers questioned cherished truths, widely held beliefs, and their own sanity in an attempt to discover why the world worked—from within. "I think, therefore I am" was one of the famous sayings of that or any day, uttered by **Rene Descartes**, a French scientist-philosopher whose dedication to logic and the rigid rules of observation were a blueprint for the thinkers who came after him.

One of the giants of the era was England's **David Hume**, a pioneer of the doctrine of empiricism: believing things only when you've seen the proof for yourself. Hume was a prime believer in the value of skepticism; in other words, he was naturally suspicious of things that other people told him to be true and constantly set out to discover the truth for himself. These two related ideas influenced many great thinkers after Hume, and his writings, of which there are many, continue to inspire philosophers to this day.

Perhaps the most famous Enlightenment thinker is **Immanuel Kant** of Germany. Both a philosopher and a scientist, he took a definitely scientific view of the world. He wrote the movement's most famous essay, "Answering the Question: What Is Enlightenment?" and he answered his famous question with the motto "Dare to Know." For Kant, the human being was a rational being capable of hugely creative thought and intense self-evaluation. He encouraged all to examine themselves and the world around them. He believed that the source of morality lay not in nature of in the grace of God but in the human soul itself. He believed that man believed in God for practical, not religious or mystical, reasons.

During the Enlightenment, the idea of the "**social contract**" confirmed the belief that government existed because people wanted it to, that the people had an agreement with the government that they would submit to it as long as it protected them and didn't encroach on their basic human rights. This idea was first made famous by the Frenchman **Jean-Jacques Rousseau** but was also adopted by England's John Locke and America's Thomas Jefferson.

Thomas Hobbes (1588-1679*)* Author of the book ***Leviathan** (l651)* which was actually written as a reaction to the disorders caused by the English civil wars which had culminated with the execution of King Charles I. Hobbes perceived people as rational beings, but unlike Locke and Jefferson, he had no faith in their abilities to live in harmony with one another without a government. The trouble was, as Hobbes saw it, people were selfish and the strong would take from the weak. However, the weak being rational would in turn band together against the strong. For Hobbes, the state of nature became a chaotic state in which every person becomes the enemy of every other. It became a war of all against all, with terrible consequences for all.

John Locke (1632-1704) was an important thinker on the nature of democracy. He regarded the mind of man at birth as a tabula rasa, a blank slate upon which experience imprints knowledge and behavior. He did not believe in the idea of intuition or theories of innate knowledge. Locke also believed that all men are born good, independent and equal, that it is their actions that will determine their fate. Locke's views, espoused in his most important work, ***Two Treatises of Civil Government*** (1690) attacked the theory of the divine right of kings and the nature of the state as conceived by Thomas Hobbes. Locke argued that sovereignty did not reside in the state, but with the people. The state is supreme, but only if it is bound by civil and what he called "**natural'** law.

Many of Locke's political ideas, such as those relating to natural rights, property rights, the duty of the government to protect these rights and the rule of the majority, were embodied in the Constitution of the United States. He further held that revolution was not only a right, but also often an obligation and advocated a system of checks and balances in government. A government comprised of three branches of which the legislative is more powerful than either the executive or the judicial. He also believed in the separation of the church and state. All of these ideas were to be incorporated in the Constitution of the United States. As such Locke is considered in many ways the true founding father of our Constitution and government system. He remains one of history's most influential political thinkers to this day.

Jean-Jacques Rousseau (1712-1778) was one of the most famous and influential political theorists before the French Revolution. His most important and most studied work is **The Social Contract** (1762). He was concerned with what should be the proper form of society and government. However, unlike Hobbes, Rousseau did not view the state of nature as one of absolute chaos.

The problem as Rousseau saw it was that the natural harmony of the state of nature was due to people's intuitive goodness not to their actual reason. Reason only developed once a civilized society was established. The intuitive goodness was easily overwhelmed however by arguments for institutions of social control, which likened rulers to father figures and extolled the virtues of obedience to such figures. To a remarkable extent, strong leaders have, in Rousseau's judgment, already succeeded not only in extracting obedience from the citizens that they ruled, but also more importantly, have managed to justify such obedience as necessary.

Rousseau's most direct influence was upon the **French Revolution** (1789-1815*)*. In the *Declaration of the Rights of Man and The Citizen* (1789), it explicitly recognized the sovereignty of the general will as expressed in the law. In contrast to the American **Declaration of Independence***,* it contains explicit mention of the obligations and duties of the citizen, such as assenting to taxes in support of the military or police forces for the common good. In modern times, ideas such as Rousseau's have often been used to justify the ideas of authoritarian and totalitarian systems.

Karl Marx (1818-1883), was perhaps the most influential theorist of the 19th century and his influence has continued in various forms until this day. Contrary to popular belief, he was not the first to believe in socialist ideas, many of which had been around for some time and in various forms. Nevertheless, he was the first to call his system truly "scientific" or "**Scientific Socialism**". (Also called Marxian Socialism or as it is more widely known Marxism). It was opposed to other forms of socialism that had been called, (with some derision), "**Utopian Socialism**." These were socialist ideas which though they sounded good, nevertheless, would never really work in the real world. In fact, it is the very idea of Marxism being "scientific" that has appealed to so many thinkers in modern history. This and the underlying aspect of prophecy and redemption that is inherent, though seldom acknowledged, in Marxist ideology, has made it that much more attractive to those looking for something to believe in. Marx expounded his ideas in two major theoretical works, *The Communist Manifesto* (1848*)* and *Das Capital*, (Volume 1 1867*)*.

Skill 9.2   **The origins and consequences of the American and French Revolutions**

The period from the 1700s to the 1800s was characterized in Western countries by opposing political ideas of democracy and nationalism. This resulted in strong nationalistic feelings and people of common cultures asserting their belief in the right to have a part in their government.

The **American Revolution** resulted in the successful efforts of the English colonists in America to win their freedom from Great Britain. After more than one hundred years of mostly self-government, the colonists resented the increased British meddling and control, they declared their freedom, won the Revolutionary War with aid from France, and formed a new independent nation. (See Skills 1.7 and 1.8 for more information.)

The **French Revolution** was the revolt of the middle and lower classes against the gross political and economic excesses of the rulers and the supporting nobility. It ended with the establishment of the first in a series of French Republics. Conditions leading to revolt included extreme taxation, inflation, lack of food, and the total disregard for the impossible, degrading, and unacceptable condition of the people on the part of the rulers, nobility, and the Church.

The American Revolution and the French Revolution were similar yet different, liberating their people from unwanted government interference and installing a different kind of government. They were both fought for the liberty of the common people, and they both were built on writings and ideas that embraced such an outcome; yet there is where the similarities end. Both Revolutions proved that people could expect more from their government and that such rights as self-determination were worth fighting - and dying - for.

Several important differences need to be emphasized:

- The British colonists were striking back against unwanted taxation and other sorts of "government interference." The French people were starving and, in many cases, destitute and were striking back against an autocratic regime that cared more for high fashion and courtly love than bread and circuses.
- The American Revolution involved a years-long campaign, of often bloody battles, skirmishes, and stalemates. The French Revolution was bloody to a degree but mainly an overthrow of society and its outdated traditions.
- The American Revolution resulted in a representative government, which marketed itself as a beacon of democracy for the rest of the world. The French Revolution resulted in a consulship, a generalship, and then an emperor—probably not what the perpetrators of the Revolution had in mind when they first struck back at the king and queen.

Still, both Revolutions are looked back on as turning points in history, as times when the governed stood up to the governors and said, "Enough."

Skill 9.3   The spread of democratic ideas beyond Europe and the United States

The major turning point for Latin America, already unhappy with Spanish restrictions on trade, agriculture, and the manufacture of goods, was Napoleon's move into Spain and Portugal. Napoleon's imprisonment of King Ferdinand VII, made the local agents of the Spanish authorities feel that they were in fact agents of the French. Conservative and liberal locals joined forces, declared their loyalty to King Ferdinand, and formed committees (*juntas*). Between May of 1810 and July of 1811, the *juntas* in Argentina, Chile, Paraguay, Venezuela, Bolivia and Colombia all declared independence. Fighting erupted between Spanish authorities in Latin America and the members and followers of the *juntas*. In Mexico City another *junta* declared loyalty to Ferdinand and independence.

Society in Latin America was sharply distinguished according to race and the purity of Spanish blood. **Miguel Hidalgo**, a 60-year-old priest and enlightened intellectual, disregarded the racial distinctions of the society. He had been fighting for the interests of the Indians and part Indian/part white citizens of Mexico, including a call for the return of land stolen from the Indians. He called for an uprising in 1810.

Simon Bolivar had been born into Venezuela's wealthy society and educated in Europe. With Francisco de Miranda, he declared Venezuela and Columbia to be republics and removed all Spanish trading restrictions. They removed taxes on the sale of food, ended payment of tribute to the government by the local Indians, and prohibited slavery. In March 1812 Caracas was devastated by an earthquake. When the Spanish clergy in Caracas proclaimed the earthquake God's act of vengeance against the rebel government, they provided support for the Spanish government officials, who quickly regained control.

When Ferdinand was returned to power in 1814, it was no longer possible for the rebel groups to claim to act in his name. Bolivar was driven to Colombia, where he gathered a small army that returned to Venezuela in 1817. As his army grew, Spain became concerned and the military moved into the interior of Venezuela. This action aroused the local people to active rebellion. As he freed slaves, he gained support and strength. Realizing that he did not have the strength to take Caracas, Bolivar moved his people to Colombia. Bolivar's forces defeated the Spanish and organized "Gran Colombia" (which included present-day Ecuador, Colombia and Panama), and became president in 1819. When Ferdinand encountered difficulties in Spain, soldiers assembled to be transported to the Americas revolted. Several groups in Spain joined the revolt and, together, drove Ferdinand from power. Bolivar took advantage of the opportunity and took his army back into Venezuela. In 1821, Bolivar defeated the Spanish, took Caracas, and established Venezuelan freedom from Spanish rule.

In Peru, **San Martin** took his force into Lima amid celebration. Bolivar provided assistance in winning Peru's independence in 1822. Bolivar now controlled Peru. By 1824, Bolivar had combined forces with local groups and rid South America of Spanish control.

In 1807, Queen Maria of Portugal fled to escape Napoleon. The royal family sailed to Brazil, where they were welcomed by the local people. Rio de Janeiro became the temporary capital of Portugal's empire. Maria's son **Joao** ruled as regent. He opened Brazil's trade with other nations, gave the British favorable tax rates in gratitude for their assistance against Napoleon, and opened Brazil to foreign scholars, visitors and immigrants. In 1815, he made Brazil a kingdom that was united with Portugal. By 1817 there was economic trouble in Brazil and some unrest over repression (such as censorship). This discontent became a rebellion that was repressed by Joao's military.

When Napoleon's forces withdrew from Portugal, the British asked Joao to return. Liberals took power in Portugal and in Spain and both drafted liberal constitutions. By 1821, Joao decided to return to Portugal as a constitutional monarch. He left his oldest son **Pedro** on the throne in Brazil. When Portugal tried to reinstate economic advantages for Portugal and restrict Brazil, resistance began to grow. Pedro did not want to be controlled by Portugal and was labeled a rebel. When he learned that Portuguese troops had been sent to arrest him, he prohibited the landing of the ship, sent them back to Portugal and declared independence in 1822. In a little more than a month he was declared Emperor of Brazil.

Skill 9.4   The causes and consequences of the agricultural and industrial revolutions

The **Agricultural Revolution** occurred first in England. It was marked by experimentation that resulted in increased production of crops from the land and a new and more technical approach to the management of agriculture. The revolution in agricultural management and production was hugely enhanced by the Industrial Revolution and the invention of the steam engine. The introduction of steam-powered tractors greatly increased crop production and significantly decreased labor costs. Developments in agriculture were also enhanced by the Scientific Revolution and the learning from experimentation that led to philosophies of crop rotation and soil enrichment. Improved system of irrigation and harvesting also contributed to the growth of agricultural production.

The **Industrial Revolution**, which began in Great Britain and spread elsewhere, was the development of power-driven machinery, fueled by coal and steam, leading to the accelerated growth of industry with large factories replacing homes and small workshops as work centers. The lives of people changed drastically and a largely agricultural society changed to an industrial one. In Western Europe, the period of empire and colonialism began. The industrialized nations seized and claimed parts of Africa and Asia in an effort to control and provide the raw materials needed to feed the industries and machines in the "mother country." Later developments included power based on electricity and internal combustion, replacing coal and steam.

(See Skill 3.2 for additional information.)

Skill 9.5   Major developments in the arts and literature of this period

Baroque painters of the seventeenth and eighteenth centuries across Europe shared similar traits in their works. Italy's Caravaggio and Flanders' **Rubens** and **Rembrandt van Rijn** used dramatic chiaroscuro (the interplay of light and dark) and strong diagonals to illustrate the climax of well known myths and stories, while their portraiture often gave insight in to the minds of their sitters.

Baroque architecture was often ornamental, with emphasis on light and dark, movement, emotion and affluence. The large scale of Baroque buildings lent a feeling of drama to the architecture, as evidenced by Louis XIV's **Palace of Versailles.**

Some of the most spectacular Baroque achievements were in the field of music. Opera incorporated the Baroque characteristics of dramatic storytelling and sensational shifts from soft to loud, joy to suffering. **Bach**'s cantatas powerfully express the profound religious faith of the Reformation, usually in a contrapuntal mode for four voices. His music for keyboard, in the form of **fugues**, also reflects the Baroque penchant for ornamentation, dramatic shifts, and large-scale performance. Oratorios and sonatas also tended toward the dramatic, with an emphasis on contrasting passages and tempos, as well as instrumental experimentation.

The reign of England's Elizabeth I ushered in an era of splendor for English literature. **Shakespeare**'s plays focused on the drama of human psychology, dealing with the turbulent and often contradictory emotions experienced in life. In the process, he vastly enriched the English language with original vocabulary and eloquent phrasing. Elsewhere in Europe, lyric poetry and sonnets took on new, more dramatic characteristics, while the novel developed into a more popular, easy-to-read format, as exemplified by **Cervantes**' *Don Quixote.*

The eighteenth century spawned several artistic styles, the first of which was an offshoot of Baroque, known as **Rococo** (rocks and shells) which utilized decorative motifs. In architecture, it referred generally to a style of interior design featuring a light, delicate feeling, enhanced with curvilinear furniture and gilt tracery, often based on a shell motif. In exterior design, it featured undulating walls, reliance on light and shadow for dramatic effect, and caryatid ornamentation. In painting, rococo exuded sentimentality, love of pleasure, and delight in love. Rococo musicians improvised pretty "ornaments" or additions to the musical scores, and composers included delicate and artificial passages in their works.

The classical **symphony** grew out of the eighteenth century Italian overture, which usually had three separate movements and was played as a prelude to an operatic or vocal concert. Early symphonies were short and were included on musical programs with other works, mainly vocal. In the early years of the nineteenth century, **Ludwig von Beethoven** began to experiment with the form of the symphony, expanding it into an extended orchestral work that is usually the main piece in a program.

Simultaneously with rococo, a style known as Expressive developed in music. This style was original and uncomplicated, yet well-proportioned and logical as evidenced in many works by C.P.E. Bach. The classical style also rose which was based on classical ideals. A highly defined structure, a predominant melody, and an increase in contrasts of rhythm marked the classical style, as evidenced by many of the works by **Mozart**. Many musical forms such as opera and sonata changed to accommodate these classical requirements. Haydn, Mozart and Beethoven all composed in their own manner within the classical constraints.

Other painting styles of the eighteenth century included Humanitarianism, the chief characteristic of which was social commentary, and **Neo-classicism**, the works of which not only detail historical subject matter, but strive to embrace the classical ideals of proportion, harmony, and rationalism. Neo-classicism in architecture reflected the idea that while ancient architectural styles enhance present buildings, architects are free to mix elements from various periods with their own creative expressions to produce unique architecture, thus producing a kind of eclecticism.

The Industrial Age brought with it a myriad of changes as Europe dealt with the every-quickening pace of modern life. This was mirrored by the multiplicity of styles that surfaced during the century.

Romanticism in the visual arts implied a variety of sub-styles, most of which were characterized by a sense of melancholy, love of nature, emotionalism, and a sense of the exotic. Romanticism was often regarded as a reaction against the cool restraint of neo-classicism. Romantic music was an extension of classical music. Romantic authors emphasized love of nature, emotionalism and the exotic and bizarre in their works, as evidenced by **Wordsworth, Byron** and **Shelley**. **Realism** in the visual arts emerged during the second half of the century. Realistic authors such as **Balzac** wrote novels which depict human beings caught in an uncompromising society.

The painting style known as **Impressionism** was inspired by scientific studies of light and the philosophy that the universe is constantly changing. Artists attempted to capture the transitory aspect of the world by recording a particular moment or "impression" usually working out-of-doors and fairly quickly. Many of the impressionist paintings have a candid quality to them, probably a direct influence of the new medium of photography. Post-impressionism in art refers to a collection of personal styles, all inspired in some way by impressionism. The styles were as diverse as the artists, ranging from the emotional intensity of **Van Gogh**, to the precision of **Seurat**, to the allegory of **Gaugin**.

Literature also underwent a profound change in the period between the 18th and early 20th Century. The idea of the "popular" novel came into its own as ordinary citizens began to have the time and interest in reading poems, stories, and books. American authors like **James Fenimore Cooper** and later **Mark Twain** embraced both a "frontier spirit" and, especially in Twain's case, reflected the life of the common man. **Charles Dickens** became one of the first modern novelists, with best-sellers and serial installments of his stories that took a harsh look at real life. Others turned inwards, resulting in the works of **Sigmund Freud** and **Henry David Thoreau**, as well as the novels of **Joseph Conrad. Melville, Dickenson, Poe, Bronte**, and a host of other writers helped literature become a major art form that remained accessible to the masses.

Skill 9.6   Causes, key events, and consequences of the new imperialism

Imperialism emerged during the 19th century is significant ways, following various revolutions, mergers and divisions among countries. In Europe, Italy and Germany each were totally united into one nation from many smaller states. There were revolutions in Austria and Hungary, the Franco-Prussian War, the dividing of Africa among the strong European nations, interference and intervention of Western nations in Asia, and the breakup of Turkish dominance in the Balkans.

Africa was divided among France, Great Britain, Italy, Portugal, Spain, Germany, and Belgium who controlled the entire continent except for the nations of Liberia and Ethiopia. In Asia and the Pacific Islands, only China, Japan, and present-day Thailand (Siam) kept their independence. The others were controlled by the strong European nations.

An additional reason for **European imperialism** was the harsh, urgent demand for the raw materials needed to fuel and feed the great Industrial Revolution. These resources were not available in the huge quantity so desperately needed which both necessitated and rationalized the partitioning of the continent of Africa and parts of Asia. In turn, these colonial areas would purchase the finished manufactured goods. Europe in the 19th Century was a crowded place. Populations were growing but resources were not. The peoples of many European countries were also agitating for rights as never before. To address these concerns, European powers began to look elsewhere for relief.

One of the main places for European imperialist expansion was Africa. Britain, France, Germany, and Belgium took over countries in Africa and claimed them as their own. The resources (including people) were then shipped back to the mainland and claimed as colonial gains. The Europeans made a big deal about "civilizing the savages," reasoning that their technological superiority gave them the right to rule and "educate" the peoples of Africa.

Southeast Asia was another area of European expansion at this time, mainly by France. So, too, was India, colonized by Great Britain. These two nations combined with Spain to occupy countries in Latin America. Spain also seized the rich lands of the Philippines.

As a result of all this activity, a whole new flood of goods, people, and ideas began to come back to Europe and a whole group of people began to travel to these colonies, to oversee the colonization and to "help bring the people up" to the European level. European leaders could also assert their authority in these colonies as they could not back home.

In the United States, **territorial expansion** occurred in the expansion westward under the banner of **"Manifest Destiny."** In addition, the U.S. was involved in the War with Mexico, the Spanish-American War, and support of the Latin American colonies of Spain in their revolt for independence. In Latin America, the Spanish colonies were successful in their fight for independence and self-government.

The time from 1830 to 1914 is characterized by the extraordinary growth and spread of patriotic pride in a nation along with intense, widespread imperialism. Loyalty to one's nation included national pride; extension and maintenance of sovereign political boundaries; unification of smaller states with common language, history, and culture into a more powerful nation; or smaller national groups who, as part of a larger multi-cultural empire, wished to separate into smaller, political, cultural nations.

COMPETENCY 0100   **Understand major developments in world history during the modern era (1914 to the present)**

Skill 10.1   Causes and results of the World War I (1914-1918)

Emotions ran high in early 20th Century Europe, and minor disputes magnified into major ones and sometimes quickly led to threats of war. Especially sensitive to these conditions was the area of the states on the Balkan Peninsula. Along with the imperialistic colonization for industrial raw materials, military build-up (especially by Germany), and diplomatic and military alliances, the conditions for one tiny spark to set off the explosion were in place. In July 1914, a Serbian national assassinated **Archduke Ferdinand**, the Austrian heir to the throne, and his wife as they visited Sarajevo. War began a few weeks later. There were a few attempts to keep war from starting, but these efforts were futile. Eventually nearly 30 nations were involved, and the war didn't end until 1918.

One of the major causes of the war was the tremendous surge of **nationalism** during the 1800s and early 1900s. People of the same nationality or ethnic group sharing a common history, language or culture began uniting or demanding the right of unification, especially in the empires of Eastern Europe, such as Russian Ottoman and Austrian-Hungarian Empires. Getting stronger and more intense were the beliefs of these peoples in loyalty to common political, social, and economic goals considered to be before any loyalty to the controlling nation or empire. Other causes were the increasing strength of military capabilities, massive colonization for raw materials needed for industrialization and manufacturing, and military and diplomatic alliances.

World War I saw the introduction of such warfare as use of tanks, airplanes, machine guns, submarines, poison gas, and flame throwers. Fighting on the Western front was characterized by a series of **trenches** that were used throughout the war until 1918. The atrocities of war took everyone by surprise, and led to much of the animosity that marked the terms of the end of the war. It would lead to ban on certain weapons, particularly poison gas, and leave the nations of Europe unwilling to go to war again.

In 1918, when Germany agreed to an armistice, it assumed that the peace settlement would be drawn up on the basis of US President Woodrow Wilson's Fourteen Points, which it considered equitable and without recrimination. Instead, at the Paris Peace Conference, Germany was subjected to harsh reparations, being asked to pay the other countries for damages during the war. Heavy restrictions were placed on Germany as well, taking away arms and territories, losses that weighed heavily on the German psyche. The European powers even went so far as the force Germany to assume responsibility for causing the war.

Pre-war empires lost tremendous amounts of territories as well as the wealth of natural resources in them. New, independent nations were formed and some predominately ethnic areas came under control of nations of different cultural backgrounds. Some national boundary changes overlapped and created tensions and hard feelings as well as political and economic confusion. The wishes and desires of every national or cultural group could not possibly be realized and satisfied, resulting in disappointments for both; those who were victorious and those who were defeated. Germany received harsher terms than expected from the treaty which weakened its post-war government and, along with the world-wide depression of the 1930s, set the stage for the rise of Adolf Hitler and his Nationalist Socialist Party and World War II.

Skill 10.2 Lenin, the Russian Revolution and emergence of Communist totalitarianism

Until the early years of the twentieth century Russia was ruled by a succession of **Czars**. The Czars ruled as autocrats or, sometimes, despots. Society was essentially feudalistic and was structured in three levels. The top level was held by the Czar. The second level was composed of the rich nobles who held government positions and owned vast tracts of land. The third level of the society was composed of the remaining people who lived in poverty as peasants or serfs. There were several unsuccessful attempts to revolt during the nineteenth century, caused largely by discontent among these three levels, especially the peasant, but they were quickly suppressed. The two revolutions of the early 20th Century, in 1905 and 1917, however, were quite different.

Discontent with the social structure, the living conditions of peasants, and working conditions despite industrialization were among the causes of the **1905 Revolution**. This general discontent was aggravated by the **Russo-Japanese War** (1904-1905) with inflation, rising prices, etc. Peasants who had been able to eke out a living began to starve. Many of the fighting troops were killed in battles Russia lost to Japan because of poor leadership, lack of training, and inferior weaponry. Czar Nicholas II refused to end the war despite setbacks, and, in January 1905, Port Arthur fell.

A trade union leader (Father Gapon) organized a protest to demand an end to the war, industrial reform, more civil liberties, and a constituent assembly. Over 150,000 peasants joined a demonstration outside the Czar's **Winter Palace**. Before the demonstrators even spoke, the palace guard opened fire on the crowd. This destroyed the people's trust in the Czar. Illegal trade unions and political parties formed and organized strikes to gain power.

The strikes eventually brought the Russian economy to a halt. This led Czar Nicholas II to sign the **October Manifesto** which created a constitutional monarchy, extended some civil rights, and gave the parliament limited legislative power. In a very short period of time, the Czar disbanded the parliament and violated the promised civil liberties.

The violation of the October Manifesto would help foment the **1917 Revolution**. There were other factors as well. Defeats on the battlefields during WWI caused discontent, loss of life, and a popular desire to withdraw from the war. The war had also caused another surge in prices and scarcity of many items. Most of the peasants could not afford to buy bread. In addition, the Czar's behavior triggered more unrest. The Czar continued to appoint unqualified people to government posts and handle the situation with general incompetence. The Czar also listened to his wife's (Alexandra) advice. She was strongly influenced by Rasputin. This caused increased discontent among all level of the social structure.

Workers in Petrograd went on strike in 1917 over the need for food. The Czar again ordered troops to suppress the strike. This time, however, the troops sided with the workers. The revolution then took a unique direction. The parliament created a provisional government to rule the country. The military and the workers also created their own governments called **soviets** (popularly elected local councils). The parliament was composed of nobles who soon lost control of the country when they failed to comply with the wishes of the populace. The result was chaos.

The most significant differences between the 1905 and 1917 revolutions were the formation of political parties and their use of propaganda and the support of the military and some of the nobles in 1917. The political leaders who had previously been driven into exile returned. **Lenin**, Stalin and Trotsky won the support of the peasants with the promise of "Peace, Land, and Bread." The parliament, on the other hand, continued the country's involvement in the war. Lenin and the Bolshevik party gained the support of the **Red Guard** and together overthrew the provisional government. In short order they had complete control of Russia and established a new communist state.

Skill 10.3   Events, issues and effects of the emergence of Fascism

The effects of the Depression were very strong throughout Europe, which was still rebuilding after the devastation of World War I. Germany was especially hard hit, as US reconstruction loans dried up. Unemployment skyrocketed in Germany, leaving millions out of work.

During the Depression in Germany, large numbers of urban workers found themselves unemployed and dissatisfied with the government. Communist and Fascist paramilitary organizations arose, promising dramatic action and economic restructuring. These organizations found a receptive audience among the disgruntled German workers. It was out of this climate that the **Nazi Party** emerged.

After a failed attempt at a coup, many of the Nazi leaders, including **Adolf Hitler**, were jailed. Upon his release, Hitler was able to take leadership again and built the fascist Nazi party into a political organization with seats in the German parliament. Hitler was eventually named Chancellor of Germany, from which position he implemented his policies of military expansion and aggression which culminated in the Second World War.

Fascist movements often had socialists' origins. For example, in Italy, where fascism first arose in place of socialism, **Benito Mussolini**, sought to impose what he called **corporativism**. A fascist "corporate" state would, in theory, run the economy for the benefit of the whole country like a corporation. It would be centrally controlled and managed by an elite who would see that its benefits would go to everyone.

Fascism has always declared itself the uncompromising enemy of communism, with which, however, fascist actions have much in common. (In fact, many of the methods of organization and propaganda used by fascists were taken from the experience of the early Russian communists, along with the belief in a single strong political party, secret police, etc.) The propertied interests and the upper classes, fearful of revolution, often gave their support to fascism on the basis of promises by the fascist leaders to maintain the status quo and safeguard property. In effect, accomplishing a revolution from above with their help as opposed from below against them. However, fascism did consider itself a revolutionary movement of a different type.

Once established, a fascist regime ruthlessly crushes communist and socialist parties as well as all democratic opposition. It regiments the propertied interests to its national goals and wins the potentially revolutionary masses to fascist programs by substituting a rabid nationalism for class conflict. Thus fascism may be regarded as an extreme defensive expedient adopted by a nation faced with the sometimes illusionary threat of communist subversion or revolution. Under fascism, capital is regulated as much as labor and fascist contempt for legal or constitutional guarantees effectively destroyed whatever security the capitalistic system had enjoyed under pre-fascist governments.

In addition, fascist or similar regimes are at times anti-Communist. This is evidenced by the Soviet-German treaty of 1939. During the period of alliance created by the treaty, Italy and Germany and their satellite countries ceased their anti-Communist propaganda. They emphasized their own revolutionary and proletarian origins and attacked the so-called plutocratic western democracies.

The fact that fascist countries sought to control national life by methods identical to those of communist governments make such nations vulnerable to communism after the fascist regime is destroyed.

Skill 10.4   Origins, key events and issues of World War II

The World War I had seriously damaged the economies of the European countries, both the victors and the defeated, leaving them deeply in debt. There was difficulty on both sides paying off war debts and loans. It was difficult to find jobs and some countries like Japan and Italy found themselves without enough resources and more than enough people. Solving these problems by expanding the territory merely set up conditions for war later.

Germany suffered horribly with runaway inflation ruining the value of its money and wiping out the savings of millions. Even though the U.S. made loans to Germany, which helped the government to restore some order and which provided a short existence of some economic stability in Europe, the Great Depression only served to undo any good that had been done. Mass unemployment, poverty, and despair greatly weakened the democratic governments that had been formed and greatly strengthened the increasing power and influence of extreme political movements, such as communism, fascism, and national-socialism. These ideologies promised to put an end to the economic problems.

The extreme form of patriotism called nationalism that had been the chief cause of World War I grew even stronger after the war ended in 1918. The political, social, and economic unrest fueled nationalism and it became an effective tool enabling dictators to gain and maintain power from the 1930s to the end of World War II in 1945. In the Soviet Union, **Joseph Stalin** succeeded in gaining political control and establishing a strong harsh dictatorship. **Benito Mussolini** and the Fascist party, promising prosperity and order in Italy, gained national support and set up a strong government. In Japan, although the ruler was considered Emperor **Hirohito,** actual control and administration of government came under military officers. In Germany, the results of war, harsh treaty terms, loss of territory, great economic chaos and collapse all enabled **Adolf Hitler** and his National Socialist, or **Nazi,** party to gain complete power and control.

Germany, Italy, and Japan initiated a policy of aggressive territorial expansion with Japan being the first to conquer. In 1931, Japanese forces seized control of **Manchuria**, a part of China containing rich natural resources, and in 1937 began an attack on the rest of China, occupying most of its eastern part by 1938. Italy invaded **Ethiopia** in Africa in 1935, having complete control by 1936. The Soviet Union did not invade or take over any territory but along with Italy and Germany, actively participated in the **Spanish Civil War**, using it as a proving ground to test tactics and weapons setting the stage for World War II.

In Germany, almost immediately after taking power, in direct violation of the World War I peace treaty, Hitler began the buildup of the armed forces. He sent troops into the Rhineland in 1936, then invaded Austria in 1938 and united it with Germany. In 1938, he seized control of the Sudetenland, part of western Czechoslovakia and containing mostly Germans, followed by the rest of Czechoslovakia in March 1939. Despite his territorial designs, the other nations of Europe made no moves to stop Hitler.

Preferring not to embark on another costly war, the European powers opted for a policy of **Appeasement**, believing that once Hitler had satisfied his desire for land he would be satisfied, and war could be averted. Then, on September 1, 1939, Hitler began World War II in Europe by invading **Poland**.

By 1940, Germany had invaded and controlled Norway, Denmark, Belgium, Luxembourg, the Netherlands, and France. Germany military forces struck in what came to be known as the **blitzkrieg**, or "lightning war." A shock attack, it relied on the use of surprise, speed, and superiority in firepower. The German blitzkrieg coordinated land and air attacks to paralyze the enemy by disabling its communications and coordination capacities.

When France fell in June 1940, the Franco-German armistice divided France into two zones: one under German military occupation and one under nominal French control (the southeastern two-fifths of the country). The National Assembly, summoned at Vichy, France ratified the armistice and granted **Philippe Pétain** control of the French State. The **Vichy** government then collaborated with the Germans, eventually becoming little more than a rubber stamp for German policies. Germany would occupy the whole of France in 1942, and by early 1944 a **Resistance** movement created a period of civil war in France. The Vichy regime was abolished after the liberation of Paris.

With Europe safely conquered, Hitler turned his sights to England. The **Battle of Britain** (June 1940 – April 1941) was a series of intense raids directed against Britain by the **Luftwaffe**, Germany's air force. Intended to prepare the way for invasion, the air raids were directed against British ports and Royal Air Force (**RAF**) bases. In September 1940, London and other cities were attacked in the "**blitz**," a series of bombings that lasted for 57 consecutive nights. Sporadic raids until April 1941. The RAF was outnumbered but succeeded in blocking the German air force, and eventually Hitler was forced to abandon his plans for invasion, Germany's first major setback in the war.

After success in North Africa and Italy, and following the D-Day Invasion, the Allied forces faced a protracted campaign across Europe. Each gain was hard won, and both the weather and local terrain at times worked against them. The **Battle of the Bulge**, also known as Battle of the Ardennes (December 16, 1944-January 28, 1945) was the largest World War II land battle on the Western Front, and the last major German counteroffensive of the war. Launched by Adolf Hitler himself, the German army's goal was to cut Allied forces in half and to retake the crucial port of Antwerp. Secretly massed Panzer tank-led units launched their assault into the thinnest part of the Allied forces.

Though surprised and suffering tremendous losses, Allied forces still managed to slow the Germans. American tanks moved swiftly to counterattack and cut German supply lines. The attack resulted in a bulge seventy miles deep into Allied lines, but all forward momentum for the Germans was essentially stopped by Christmas. It took another month before the Allies could push back to the original line. Both sides suffered great casualties, but the Germans' losses were a crushing blow, as the troops and equipment lost were irreplaceable.

During the war, Allied forces flew extensive bombing raids deep into German territory. Launched from bases in England, both American and RAF bomber squadrons proceeded to massively bomb German factories and cities. Although the raids were dangerous, with many planes and lives lost both to the Luftwaffe and anti-aircraft artillery, the raids continued throughout the war. German cities were reduced to virtual rubble by war's end, and the impact on Germany's production capacity and transportation lines helped swing the tide of war.

Before war in Europe had ended, the Allies had agreed on a military occupation of Germany. It was divided into four zones each one occupied by Great Britain, France, the Soviet Union, and the United States with the four powers jointly administering Berlin. After the war, the Allies agreed that Germany's armed forces would be abolished, the Nazi Party outlawed, and the territory east of the Oder and Neisse Rivers taken away. Nazi leaders were accused of war crimes and brought to trial at **Nuremburg**.

Major consequences of the war included horrendous death and destruction, millions of displaced persons, the gaining of strength and spread of Communism and Cold War tensions as a result of the beginning of the nuclear age. World War II ended more lives and caused more devastation than any other war. Besides the losses of millions of military personnel, the devastation and destruction directly affected civilians, reducing cities, houses, and factories to ruin and rubble and totally wrecking communication and transportation systems. Millions of civilian deaths, especially in China and the Soviet Union, were the results of famine. More than 12 million people were uprooted by wars end and had no place to live. Included in those numbers were prisoners of war, those that survived Nazi concentration camps and slave labor camps, orphans, and people who escaped war-torn areas and invading armies. Changing national boundary lines also caused the mass movement of displaced persons.

Germany and Japan were completely defeated; Great Britain and France were seriously weakened; and the Soviet Union and the United States became the world's leading powers. Although allied during the war, the alliance fell apart as the Soviets pushed Communism in Europe and Asia. In spite of the tremendous destruction it suffered, the Soviet Union was stronger than ever. During the war, it took control of Lithuania, Estonia, and Latvia and by mid-1945 parts of Poland, Czechoslovakia, Finland, and Romania. It helped Communist governments gain power in Bulgaria, Romania, Hungary, Czechoslovakia, Poland, and North Korea. China fell to Mao Zedong's Communist forces in 1949. Until the fall of the Berlin Wall in 1989 and the dissolution of Communist governments in Eastern Europe and the Soviet Union, the United States and the Soviet Union faced off in what was called a Cold War. The possibility of the terrifying destruction by nuclear weapons loomed over both nations.

Decolonization refers to the period after World War II when many African and Asian colonies and protectorates gained independence from the powers that had colonized them. The independence of India and Pakistan from Britain in 1945 marked the beginning of an especially important period of decolonization that lasted through 1960. Several British colonies in eastern Africa and French colonies in western Africa and Asia also formed as independent countries during this period.

Colonial powers had found it efficient to draw political boundaries across traditional ethnic and national lines, thereby dividing local populations and making them easier to control. With the yoke of colonialism removed, many new nations found themselves trying to reorganize into politically stable and economically viable units. The role of nationalism was important in this reorganization, as formerly divided peoples had opportunity to reunite.

Skill 10.5   Causes, key events, and consequences of the Cold War, and the fall of the Soviet Union

The major thrust of U.S. foreign policy from the end of World War II to 1990 was the post-war struggle between non-Communist nations, led by the United States, and the Soviet Union and the Communist nations who were its allies. It was referred to as a **Cold War** because its conflicts did not lead to a major war of fighting, or a "hot war." Both the Soviet Union and the United States embarked on an arsenal buildup of atomic and hydrogen bombs as well as other nuclear weapons. Both nations had the capability of destroying each other but because of the continuous threat of nuclear war and accidents, extreme caution was practiced on both sides. The efforts of both sides to serve and protect their political philosophies and to support and assist their allies resulted in a number of events during this 45-year period.

After 1945, social and economic chaos continued in Western Europe, especially in Germany. Secretary of State George C. Marshall came to realize that Europe's problems were serious and could affect the U.S. To aid in the recovery, he proposed a program known as the European Recovery Program or the **Marshall Plan**. Although the Soviet Union withdrew from any participation, the U.S. continued the work of assisting Europe in regaining its economic stability. In Germany in particular the situation was critical, with the American Army shouldering the staggering burden of relieving the serious problems of the German economy. In February 1948, Britain and the U.S. combined their two zones, with France joining in June.

In 1946, Josef Stalin stated publicly that the presence of capitalism and its development of the world's economy made international peace impossible. This led an American diplomat in Moscow named **George F. Kennan** to propose the idea of **containment**, as a response to Stalin and as a statement of U.S. foreign policy. The goal of the U.S. would be to limit the extension or expansion of Soviet Communist policies and activities. After Soviet efforts to make trouble in Iran, Greece, and Turkey, U.S. President Harry Truman stated what is known as the **Truman Doctrine** which committed the U.S. to a policy of intervention in order to contain or stop the spread of communism throughout the world.

The Soviets were opposed to German unification and in April 1948 took serious action to either stop it or to force the Allies to give up control of West Berlin to the Soviets. The Soviets blocked all road traffic access from West Germany to West Berlin, which lay wholly within Soviet-controlled East German,. To avoid any armed conflict, it was decided to airlift into West Berlin the needed food and supplies. During the **Berlin Airlift**, from June 1948 to mid-May 1949 Allied air forces flew in all that was needed for the West Berliners, forcing the Soviets to lift the blockade and permit vehicular traffic access to the city.

The Cold War was, more than anything else, an ideological struggle between proponents of democracy and those of communism. The two major players were the United States and the Soviet Union, but other countries were involved as well. It was a "cold" war because no large-scale fighting took place directly between the two big protagonists. It wasn't just differing forms of government that was driving this war, either. Economics were a main concern as well. A concern in both countries was that the precious resources (such as oil and food) from other like-minded countries wouldn't be allowed to flow to "the other side." These resources didn't much flow between the U.S. and Soviet Union, either.

The Soviet Union kept much more of a tight leash on its supporting countries, including all of Eastern Europe, which made up a military organization called the Warsaw Pact. The Western nations responded with a military organization of their own, **NATO or North Atlantic Treaty Organization**. Another prime battleground was Asia, where the Soviet Union had allies in China, North Korea, and North Vietnam, and the U.S. had allies in Japan, South Korea, Taiwan, and South Vietnam. The Korean War and Vietnam War were major conflicts in which both big protagonists played big roles but didn't directly fight each other.

The main symbol of the Cold War was the **arms race**, a continual buildup of missiles, tanks, and other weapons that became ever more technologically advanced and increasingly more deadly. The ultimate weapon, which both sides had in abundance, was the nuclear bomb. Spending on weapons and defensive systems eventually occupied great percentages of the budgets of the U.S. and the USSR, and some historians argue that this high level of spending played a large part in the end of the latter.

The war was a cultural struggle as well. Adults brought up their children to hate "the Americans" or "the Communists." Cold War tensions spilled over into many parts of life in countries around the world. The ways of life in countries on either side of the divide were so different that they served entirely foreign to outside observers.

The Cold War continued to varying degrees from 1947 to 1991, when the Soviet Union collapsed. The "**Iron Curtain**" referred to the ideological, symbolic and physical separation of Europe between East and West. The **Berlin Wall** fell in 1989, and this set in motion the collapse of the Soviet system of government in Eastern Europe. By 1991 communist regimes in Eastern European countries had been largely overthrown, marking the shredding of the "Iron Curtain." None of this would have been possible without the presence of change in the Soviet Union itself.

Mikhail Gorbachev was elected leader by the Politburo in 1984, bringing with him a program of reform intended to bolster the flagging Soviet economy. As part of his plan, Gorbachev instituted a policy of economic freedoms called **perestroika**, which allowed private ownership of some businesses. He relaxed the government's control over the media in a policy of openness, called **glasnost**. Gorbachev also instituted free, multi-party elections.

Gorbachev felt these new policies were required to apply pressure to more conservative members of the government, thereby increasing his support. The media seized upon their new freedom, however and began reporting on the corruption and economic problems of the Soviet Union, which had been largely hidden from the public by the previous state-controlled news services. Meanwhile, the United States, under President Ronald Reagan, had rapidly increased its military spending, outpacing the Soviet Union and increasing economic pressure.

Faced with growing independence movements in many of the Eastern Bloc countries, the government under Gorbachev reversed Brezhnev's policies of tight control via the Communist Party. Unlike previous efforts, protestors and advocates for democracy were not met with tanks and repression, but rather allowed to take hold. As the countries of Eastern Europe and Soviet states began pulling away from Russia, there were certain hard-line factions who opposed the new policy. A coup was launched in 1991 to overthrow Gorbachev. Ironically, the defeat of the coup through peaceful means proved the final nail in the old Soviet coffin.

When the Soviet Union finally collapsed it was replaced by a Russian Federation led by **Boris Yeltsin**. The fifteen republics of the former USSR became independent nations with varying degrees of freedom and democracy in government and together formed the Commonwealth of Independent States (CIS). The former Communist nations of Eastern Europe also emphasized their independence with democratic forms of government.

Skill 10.6   Nationalism and conflict in the post-Cold War world

Nationalism is most simply defined as the belief that the nation is the basic unit of human association, and that a nation is a well-defined group of people sharing a common identity. This process of organizing new nations out of the remains of former colonies was called nation building.

Nation building in this fashion did not always result in the desired stability. Pakistan, for example, eventually split into Bangladesh and Pakistan along geographic and religious lines. Ethnic conflicts in newly formed African nations arose, and are still flaring in some areas. As the United States and the Soviet Union emerged as the dominant world powers, these countries encouraged dissent in post-colonial nations such as Cuba, Vietnam and Korea, which became arenas for Cold War conflict.

With the emergence of so many new independent nations, the role of **international organizations** such as the newly formed United Nations grew in importance. The **United Nations** was formed after World War II to establish peaceful ties between countries. Dismayed by the failure of the former League of Nations to prevent war, the organizers of the United Nations provided for the ability to deploy peacekeeping troops and to impose sanctions and restrictions on member states. Other international organizations arose to take the place of former colonial connections. The British Commonwealth and the French Union, for example, maintained connections between Britain and France and their former colonies.

Global migration saw an increase in the years during and following World War II. During the war years, many Jews left the hostile climate under Nazi Germany for the United States and Palestine and the newly established state of **Israel**. Following the war, the Allied countries agreed to force German people living in Eastern Europe to return to Germany, affecting over 16 million people. In other parts of the world, instability in post-colonial areas often led to migration. Colonial settlers who had enjoyed the protection of a colonial power sometimes found themselves in hostile situations as native peoples gained independence and ascended to power, spurring migration to more friendly nations. Economic instability in newly forming countries created incentive for people to seek opportunity in other countries.

Individuals and societies have divided the earth's surface through conflict for a number of reasons:

- The domination of peoples or societies, e.g., nationalism, religious or colonialism
- The control of valuable resources, e.g., oil
- The control of strategic routes, e.g., the Panama Canal

Religion, political ideology, national origin, language, and race can spur conflicts. Conflicts can result from disagreement over how land, ocean or natural resources will be developed, shared, and used. Conflicts have resulted from trade, migration, and settlement rights. Conflicts can occur between small groups of people, between cities, between nations, between religious groups, and between multi-national alliances.

Today, the world is primarily divided by political/administrative interests into state sovereignties. A particular region is recognized to be controlled by a particular government, including its territory, population and natural resources. The only area of the earth's surface that today is not defined by state or national sovereignty is Antarctica.

Alliances are developed among nations on the basis of political philosophy, economic concerns, cultural similarities, religious interests, or for military defense. Some of the most notable alliances today are:

- The United Nations
- The North Atlantic Treaty Organization
- The Caribbean Community
- The Common Market
- The Council of Arab Economic Unity
- The European Union

Throughout human history there have been conflicts on virtually every scale over the right to divide the Earth according to differing perceptions, needs and values. These conflicts have ranged from tribal conflicts to urban riots, to civil wars, to regional wars, to world wars. While these conflicts have traditionally centered on control of land surfaces, new disputes are beginning to arise over the resources of the oceans and space. International organizations such as the UN and the World Bank have programs to assist developing nations with loans and education so they might join the international economy. Many countries are taking steps to regulate immigration.

Ethnic cleansing in Yugoslavia occurred in Kosovo in the 1990s. The Serbian government expelled ethnic Albanians from the province. The Serbian officials also confiscated all identity documentation from those who were expelled so that any attempt to return could be refused by claiming that without documents to prove Serbian citizenship the people must be native Albanians. The effort even went so far as to destroy archival documents that proved citizenship.

In 1989 the Serbian president, **Slobodan Milosevic**, abrogated the constitutional autonomy of Kosovo. He and the minority of Serbs in Kosovo had long bristled at the fact that Muslim Albanians were in control of an area considered sacred to Serbs Growing tensions led in 1998 to armed clashes between Serbs and the Kosovo Liberation Army (**KLA**), which had begun killing Serbian police and politicians. The Serbs responded with a ruthless counteroffensive, inducing the UN Security Council to condemn the Serbs' excessive use of force, including ethnic cleansing (killing and expulsion), and to impose an arms embargo, but the violence continued. After diplomatic efforts broke down, **NATO** responded with an 11-week bombing campaign that extended to Belgrade and significantly damaged Serbia's infrastructure. NATO and Yugoslavia signed an accord in June 1999 outlining Serbian troop withdrawal and the return of nearly 1,000,000 ethnic Albanian refugees as well as 500,000 displaced within the province.

Rwandan Genocide was the 1994 mass extermination of hundreds of thousands of ethnic **Tutsis** and moderate **Hutu** sympathizers in Rwanda and was the largest atrocity during the Rwandan Civil War. This genocide was mostly carried out by two extremist Hutu militia groups April 6 through mid-July 1994. Hundreds of thousands of people were slaughtered.

In the wake of the Rwandan Genocide, the United Nations and the international community drew severe criticism for its inaction. Despite international news media coverage of the violence as it unfolded, most countries, including France, Belgium, and the United States, declined to intervene or speak out against the massacres. Canada continued to lead the UN peacekeeping force in Rwanda. However, the UN Security Council did not authorize direct intervention or the use force to prevent or halt the killing.

The genocide ended when a Tutsi-dominated expatriate rebel overthrew the Hutu government and seized power. Fearing reprisals, hundreds of thousands of Hutu and other refugees fled into eastern Zaire (now the Democratic Republic of the Congo). People who had actively participated in the genocide hid among the refugees, fueling the First and Second Congo Wars. Rivalry between Hutu and Tutsi tribal factions is also a major factor in the Burundi Civil War.

In **South Africa** in the early 1990s, the system of racial segregation, called **apartheid** was abolished. The system of racial segregation was an institutionalized discriminatory system of restricted contact between races. The population was separated and defined by law into 'whites', 'blacks', 'colored', and 'mixed racial'. The long-term aim of this policy was to restrict the majority African population to small 'homelands', which were to be governed and developed separately from white South Africa. With the election of South Africa's first democratic government in 1994, the last vestiges of apartheid were officially removed, but the policy continues to have consequences on the South African landscape and its society years afterward.

The **Iranian Revolution** in 1979 transformed a constitutional monarchy, led by the Shah, into an Islamic populist theocratic republic. The new ruler was Ayatollah Ruhollah Khomeini. This revolution occurred in two essential stages. In the first, religious, liberal and leftist groups cooperated to oust the **Shah** (king). In the second stage, the Ayatollah rose to power and created an Islamic state.

The Shah had faced intermittent opposition from the middle classes in the cities and from Islamic figures. These groups sought a limitation of the Shah's power and a constitutional democracy. The Shah enforced censorship laws and imprisoned political enemies. At the same time, living conditions of the people improved greatly and several important democratic rights were given to the people. Islamic **Mullahs** fiercely opposed giving women the right to vote.

The Shah was said to be a puppet of the U.S. government. A series of protests in 1978 escalated until December of that year when more than two million people gathered in Tehran in protest against the Shah. In a very short period of time, the Ayatollah Khomeini had gathered his revolutionaries and completed the overthrow of the monarchy.

The revolution accomplished certain goals: reduction of foreign influence and a more even distribution of the nation's wealth. It did not change repressive policies or levels of government brutality. It reversed policies toward women, restoring ancient policies of repression. Religious repression became rife, particularly against members of the Bahai Faith. The revolution has also isolated Iran from the rest of the world, being rejected by both capitalist and communist nations. This isolation, however, allowed the country to develop its own internal political system, rather than having a system imposed by foreign powers.

The countries of the Middle East, despite their economic similarities, have important differences in their government, belief systems, and global outlooks. Iran and Iraq fought a devastating war in the 1980s. **Iraq** invaded **Kuwait** in the late 1990s. It is not outside the realm of possibility that other conflicts will arise in the future.

Another large factor of the instability in the Middle East is ethnic strife. It's not just Muslims who occupy these countries. Each country has its own ethnic mix. A good example of this is Iraq, which has a huge minority of **Kurdish** people. Saddam Hussein, the former dictator of Iraq, made a habit of persecuting Kurds just because of who they were. Iraq is an also an example of a religious conflict, with the minority Shiites now in power and Hussein's Sunnis out of power. These two people agree very little outside the basics of Islamic faith The prospect of a civil war in Iraq looms large, as it does in other neighboring countries, which have their own ethnic problems.

Religious conflict is very strong in Israel as well, as **Israelis** and **Palestinians** continue a centuries-old fight over religion and geography. This conflict goes back to the beginnings of Islam in the seventh century. Muslims claimed Jerusalem, capital of the ancient civilization of Israel, as a holy city, in the same way that Jews and Christians did. Muslims seized control of Palestine and Jerusalem and held it for a great many years, prompting Christian armies from Europe to muster for the Crusades, in a series of attempts to "regain the Holy Land." For hundreds of years after Christendom's failure, these lands were ruled by Muslim leaders and armies. In recent centuries, Palestine was made a British colony and then eliminated in favor of the modern state of Israel. Since that last event, in 1948, the conflict has escalated to varying degrees.

The addition of Israel to the Middle East equation presents a religious conflict not only with the Palestinians but also with the Arab peoples of neighboring Egypt and Syria. The armed forces of all of these countries have so many advanced weapons that they would seem to be a deterrent to further bloodshed, yet the attacks continue. In the last 40 years, Israel has won two major wars with its neighbors. Nearly daily conflict continues, much as it has for thousands of years. This conflict is not so much an economic one, but a full-blown war in this region would certainly involve Israel's neighbors and, by extension, other large countries in the world, most notably the United States.

Skill 10.7 Global economic developments in the 20th century

Globalism is defined as the principle of the interdependence of all the world's nations and their peoples. Within this global community, every nation, in some way to a certain degree, is dependent on other nations. Since no one nation has all of the resources needed for production, trade with other nations is required to obtain what is needed for production, to sell what is produced or to buy finished products, to earn money to maintain and strengthen the nation's economic system.

Developing nations receive technical assistance and financial aid from developed nations. Many international organizations have been set up to promote and encourage cooperation and economic progress among member nations. Through the elimination of such barriers to trade as tariffs, trade is stimulated resulting in increased productivity, economic progress, increased cooperation and understanding on diplomatic levels.

Those nations not part of an international trade organization not only must make those economic decisions of what to produce, how and for whom, but must also deal with the problem of tariffs and quotas on imports. Regardless of international trade memberships, economic growth and development are vital and affect all trading nations. Businesses, labor, and governments share common interests and goals in a nation's economic status. International systems of banking and finance have been devised to assist governments and businesses in setting the policy and guidelines for the exchange of currencies.

See Skill 4.6 for further information.

DOMAIN III.   **SOCIAL STUDIES CONCEPTS AND SKILLS**

COMPETENCY 0011   **Understand and apply social studies terms, concepts, and perspectives**

Skill 11.1   Key social science terms and concepts

The disciplines within the social sciences, sometimes referred to as social studies, include anthropology, geography, history, sociology, economics, and political science. Some programs include psychology, archaeology, philosophy, religion, law, and criminology. Also, the subjects of civics and government may be a part of an educational curriculum as separate from political science.

ANTHROPOLOGY is the scientific study of human culture, the relationship between people and culture. Anthropologists study different groups, how they relate to other cultures, and patterns of behavior, similarities and differences. Their research is two-fold: cross-cultural and comparative. The major method of study is referred to as "participant observation." The anthropologist studies and learns about the people being studied by living among them and participating with them in their daily lives. Other methods may be used but this is the most characteristic method used.

ARCHAEOLOGY is the scientific study of past human cultures by studying the remains they left behind--objects such as pottery, bones, buildings, tools, and artwork. Archaeologists locate and examine any evidence to help understand the way people lived in past times. They use special equipment and techniques to gather the evidence and make special effort to keep detailed records of their findings because a lot of their research results in destruction of the remains being studied. The first step is to locate an archaeological site using various methods. Next, archaeologists survey the site by making detailed descriptions of it using notes, maps, photographs, and collecting artifacts from the surface. Excavating comes next, either by digging for buried objects or by diving and working in submersible decompression chambers, when underwater. Archaeologists record and preserve the evidence for eventual classification, dating, and evaluation.

CIVICS is the study of the responsibilities and rights of citizens with emphasis on such subjects as freedom, democracy, and individual rights. Students study local, state, national, and international government structures, functions, and problems. Related to this are other social, political, and economic institutions. As a method of study, students gain experience and understanding through direct participation in student government, school publications, and other organizations. They also participate in community activities such as conservation projects and voter registration drives.

ECONOMICS generally is the study of the ways goods and services are produced and the ways they are distributed. It also includes the ways people and nations choose what they buy from what they want. Some of the methods of study include research, case studies, analysis, statistics, and mathematics.

GEOGRAPHY involves studying location and how living things and earth's features are distributed throughout the earth. It includes where animals, people, and plants live and the effects of their relationship with earth's physical features. Geographers also explore the locations of earth's features, how they got there, and why it is so important.

Geographers study four areas:

- **location** (the exact site of something on the earth)
- **spatial relations** (the earth's features and places as well as groups of people)
- **regional characteristics** (landform, climate, plants and animals, how people use the land)
- **forces**(changes on the earth, including human activities)

Special research methods used by geographers include mapping, interviewing, field studies, mathematics, statistics, and scientific instruments.

HISTORY is the study of the past, especially the aspects of the human past, political and economic events as well as cultural and social conditions. Students study history through textbooks, research, field trips to museums and historical sights, and other methods. Most nations set the requirements in history to study the country's heritage, usually to develop an awareness and feeling of loyalty and patriotism. History is generally divided into the three main divisions: **(a) time periods, (b) nations, and (c) specialized topics.** Study is accomplished through research, reading, and writing. Specialized fields of historical study include the following:

- Social history – the approach to the study of history that views a period of time through the eyes of everyday people and is focused on emerging trends.
- Archaeology: study of prehistoric and historic human cultures through the recovery, documentation and analysis of material remains and environmental data.
- Art History: the study of changes in social context through art.
- Big History: study of history on a large scale across long time frames (since the Big Bang and up to the future) through a multi-disciplinary approach.
- Chronology: science of localizing historical events in time.
- Cultural history: the study of culture in the past.

- Diplomatic history: the study of international relations in the past.
- Economic History: the study of economies in the past.
- Military History: the study of warfare and wars in history and what is sometimes considered to be a sub-branch of military history, Naval History.
- Paleography: study of ancient texts.
- Political history: the study of politics in the past.
- Psychohistory: study of the psychological motivations of historical events.
- Historiography of science: study of the structure and development of science.
- Social History: the study of societies in the past.
- World History: the study of history from a global perspective.

POLITICAL SCIENCE is the study of political life, different forms of government including elections, political parties, and public administration. In addition, political science studies include values such as justice, freedom, power, and equality. There are six main fields of political-study in the United States:

1 Political theory and philosophy
2 Comparative governments
3 International relations
4 Political behavior
5 Public administration
6 American government and politics

PSYCHOLOGY involves scientifically studying behavior and mental processes. The ways people and animals relate to each other are observed and recorded. Psychologists scrutinize specific patterns, which enables them to discern and predict certain behaviors, using scientific methods to verify their ideas. In this way, they are able to learn how to help people fulfill their individual human potential and strengthen understanding between individuals, as well as groups, nations and cultures. The results of the research of psychologists have deepened our understanding of the reasons for people's behavior.

Psychology is not only closely connected to the natural science of biology and the medical field of psychiatry, it is also connected to the social sciences of anthropology, and sociology which study people in society. Along with sociologists and anthropologists, psychologists also study humans in their social settings, analyzing their attitudes and relationships. The disciplines of anthropology, psychology, and sociology often research the same kinds of problems but from different points of view, with the emphasis in psychology on individual behavior, and how an individual's actions are influenced by feelings and beliefs.

In their research, psychologists develop hypotheses, and then test them using the scientific method. The methods used in psychological research include:

1. **Naturalistic Observation** which includes observing the behavior of animals and humans in their natural surroundings or environment
2. **Systematic Assessment,** which describes assorted ways to measure the feelings, thoughts, and personality traits of people using case histories, public opinion polls or surveys, and standardized tests. These three types of assessments enable psychologists to acquire information not available through naturalistic observations
3. **Experimentation** enables psychologists to find and corroborate the cause-and-effect relationships in behavior, usually by randomly dividing the subjects into two groups: experimental group and control group

SOCIOLOGY is the study of the individuals, groups, and institutions making up human society. It includes every feature of human social conditions. It deals with the predominant behaviors, attitudes, and types of relationships within a society, which is defined as a group of people with a similar cultural background living in a specific geographical area.

Sociology is divided into five major areas of study: **Population studies:** General social patterns of groups of people living in a certain geographical area; **Social behaviors**: Changes in attitudes, morale, leadership, conformity, and others; **Social institutions**: Organized groups of people performing specific functions within a society such as churches, schools, hospitals, business organizations, and governments; **Cultural influences**: Including customs, knowledge, arts, religious beliefs, and language; and **Social change**: Including wars, revolutions, inventions, fashions, and other events or activities

Sociologists use three major methods to test and verify theories:

1. Surveys
2. Controlled experiments
3. Field observation

History is without doubt an integral part of every other discipline in the social sciences. Historical knowledge goes a long way towards explaining that what happened in the past leads up to and explains the present.

Concepts Utilized in Social Studies

The following concepts are often addressed in the study of history and other social sciences.

Bias: A prejudice or a predisposition, either toward or against something. In the study of history, bias can refer to the persons or groups studied, in terms of a society's bias toward a particular political system, or it can refer to the historian's predisposition to evaluate events in a particular way.

Causality: Understanding the reason something happens – its cause – is a basic category of human thinking. We want to know the causes of major events in our lives. Within the study of history, causality is the analysis of the reasons for change. The question we are asking is why and how a particular society or event developed in the particular way it did, given the context in which it occurred.

City-state: A particular type of political entity that provides a sovereign territory for a specific city and its surrounds where other factors also unite the citizens (e.g., language, race, ancestry, etc.).

Conflict: Conflict within history is opposition of ideas, principles, values or claims. Conflict may take the form of internal clashes of principles or ideas or claims within a society or group, or it may take the form of opposition between groups or societies.

Culture: the civilization, achievements, and customs of the people of a particular time and place.

Identity: The state or perception of being a particular thing or person. Identity can also refer to the understanding or self-understanding of groups, nations, etc.

Interdependence: A condition in which two things or groups rely upon one another; as opposed to independence, in which each thing or group relies only upon itself.

Nationalism: The division of land and resources based on political ideology, religion, race, or ethnic group; a striving for a sense of group identity that is tied to a specific territory.

Nation-state: A particular type of political entity that provides a sovereign territory for a specific nation in which other factors also unite the citizens (e.g., language, race, ancestry, etc.).

Skill 11.2   Historical periods and epochs

The practice of dividing history into a number of discrete periods or blocks of time is called "periodization." Because history is continuous, all systems of periodization are arbitrary to some extent. However, dividing time into segments facilitates understanding of changes that occur over time and helps identify similarities of events, knowledge, and experience within the defined period. Further, some divisions of time into these periods apply only under specific circumstances.

Divisions of time may be determined by date, cultural advances or changes, historical events, the influence of particular individuals or groups, or geography. Speaking of the World War II era defines a particular period of time in which key historical, political, social, and economic events occurred. Speaking of the Jacksonian Era, however, has meaning only in terms of American history. Defining the "Romantic Period" makes sense only in England, Europe, and countries under their direct influence.

Many of the divisions of time that are commonly used are open to some controversy and discussion. The use of BC and AD dating, for example, has clear reference only in societies that account time according to the Christian calendar. Similarly, speaking of "the year of the pig" has greatest meaning in China.

An example of the kind of questions that can be raised about designations of time periods can be seen in the use of "Victorian." Is it possible to speak of a Victorian era beyond England? Is literature written in the style of the English poets and writers "Victorian" if it is written beyond the borders of England?

Some designations also carry both positive and negative connotations. "Victorian" is an example of potential negative connotations, as well. The term is often used to refer to class conflict, sexual repression, and heavy industry. These might be negative connotations. In contrast, the term "Renaissance" is generally read with positive connotations.

Sometimes, several designations can be applied to the same period. The period known as the "Elizabethan Period" in English history is also called "the English Renaissance." In some cases, the differences in designation refer primarily to the specific aspect of history that is being considered. For example, one designation may be applied to a specific period of time when one is analyzing cultural history, while a different designation is applied to the same period of time when considering military history.

Skill 11.3   Alternate perspectives on historical experience and various interpretations of historical movements and events

Varying perspectives on the study of history may be summarized by one of three definitions:

1. History is the study of what persons have done, said, and thought in the past.
2. History is a creative attempt to reconstruct the lives and thoughts of particular persons who lived at specific times (biography).
3. History is the study of the social aspects of humans, both past and present.

The first definition essentially applies to the *narrative school of history.* This approach attempts to provide a general account of the most important things people have said, done, written, etc. in the past. Several schools fall within this category:

- The political-institutional school believes that what has occurred in government and law is the most important.
- The school of intellectual history (the history of ideas) finds greatest importance in the emergence of higher thought and feeling (including philosophy, art, science, literature).
- Economic historians are most concerned with the way humans have controlled the environment and made a living.
- Cultural historians focus on the development of ideas within the total context of a social, economic, and political situation.

The second definition understands history as a biography of important persons. These historians fall into one of two schools:

- Psychologizing approaches – historians who believe the motivations and actions of people in the past can be understood and explained in terms of modern psychological theories.
- Non-psychologizing approaches – historians who believe it is impossible to psychoanalyze people who are dead and that people of the past must be understood in terms of the theories of personality and motivation that were accepted at the time.

The third definition essentially equates history with sociology. This approach believes it is possible to study history to observe forms of social change that are relevant to current social problems. This group is also divided:

- One group uses the Marxist doctrine of dialectical materialism to explain social change.
- Another group believes that each society is unique and distinctive.
- Comparative sociological historians study history to identify consistent patterns that run through all or several societies.

COMPETENCY 0012 **Understand how to locate social studies information.**

Skill 12.1 **Key research concepts and the scientific method**

Formulating meaningful questions is a primary part of any research process, and providing students with a wide variety of resources promotes this ability by making them aware of a wide array of social studies issues. Encouraging the use of multiple resources also introduces diverse viewpoints and different methods of communicating research results. This promotes the ability to judge the value of a resource and the appropriate ways to interpret it, which supports the development of meaningful inquiry skills.

There are many different ways to find ideas for **research problems**. One of the most common ways is through experiencing and assessing relevant problems in a specific field. Researchers are often involved in the fields in which they choose to study, and thus encounter practical problems related to their areas of expertise on a daily basis. They can use their knowledge, expertise, and research ability to examine their selected research problem.

For students, all that this entails is being curious about the world around them. Research ideas can come from one's background, culture, education, readings, or experiences. Another way to get research ideas is by exploring literature in a specific field and coming up with a question that extends or refines previous research.

Once a **topic** is decided, a research question must be formulated. A research question is a relevant, researchable, feasible statement that identifies the information to be studied. Once this initial question is formulated, it is a good idea to think of specific issues related to the topic. This will help to create a hypothesis.

A research **hypothesis** is a statement of the researcher's expectations for the outcome of the research problem. It is a summary statement of the problem to be addressed in any research document. A good hypothesis states, clearly and concisely, the researcher's expected relationship between the variables that he or she is investigating. Once a hypothesis is decided, the rest of the research paper should focus on analyzing a set of information or arguing a specific point. Thus, there are two types of research papers: analytical and argumentative.

Analytical papers focus on examining and understanding the various parts of a research topic and reformulating them in a new way to support your initial statement. In this type of research paper, the research question is used as both a basis for investigation as well as a topic for the paper. Once a variety of information is collected on the given topic, it is coalesced into a clear discussion.

Argumentative papers focus on supporting the question or claim with evidence or reasoning. Instead of presenting research to provide information, an argumentative paper presents research in order to prove a debatable statement and interpretation.

The scientific method is the process by which researchers over time endeavor to construct an accurate (that is, reliable, consistent and non-arbitrary) representation of the world. Recognizing that personal and cultural beliefs influence both our perceptions and our interpretations of natural phenomena, standard procedures and criteria minimize those influences when developing a theory.

The scientific method has four steps:

1. Observation and description of a phenomenon or group of phenomena.
2. Formulation of a hypothesis to explain the phenomena.
3. Use of the hypothesis to predict the existence of other phenomena or to predict quantitatively the results of new observations.
4. Performance of experimental tests of the predictions by several independent experimenters and properly performed experiments.

While the researcher may bring certain biases to the study, it's important that bias not be permitted to enter into the interpretation. It's also important that data that does not fit the hypothesis not be ruled out. This is unlikely to happen if the researcher is open to the possibility that the hypothesis might turn out to be null. Another important caution is to be certain that the methods for analyzing and interpreting are flawless. Abiding by these mandates is important if the discovery is to make a contribution to human understanding.

Skill 12.2   Locating reference materials

Reference materials in the 21st century are often sought initially on the Internet, as many historical documents have been uploaded to a digital format to improve access for researchers and historians. Keyword searches on the computer are generally the first step to identifying possible sources of historical data. As with all Internet searches, care must be taken to explore and ensure the reliability and authenticity of the information uncovered.

Often, computer-based searches are just the starting point. Many historians find it is important to go to source documents and do field research. This may involve traveling to specific museums and archives, sites of historical importance, and special libraries, as well as reading a variety of literature, both fiction and nonfiction, to uncover key information and leads.

Common documents utilized in historical research include governmental records, archeological and anthropological artifacts, diaries and journals from the time period being studied, corporate and union archival materials, photographs and other visual records, pamphlets, newspapers and magazines, deeds and other legal documentation, letters, and local government meeting minutes. Statistics may also be explored, although it may be difficult to ascertain the research methodologies and therefore the accuracy of the information.

Persistence and creativity allow the historical researcher to gather a comprehensive picture of the era or event under study. It is not appropriate to rely on one or two sources, or make generalizations based on limited information. In substantive research, it is crucial to include primary source data.

Skill 12.3 The characteristics, uses, advantages, and limitations of primary and secondary source materials

The resources used in the study of history can be divided into two major groups: primary sources and secondary sources. Primary sources are works, records, and other documents and artifacts that were created during the period being studied or immediately after it. Secondary sources are works written significantly after the period being studied and are based upon primary sources. In other words, primary sources provide raw data, while secondary sources offer conceptualizations, explanations and ideas that an historian or other writer has developed based on his or her understanding of the raw materials.

Primary sources include the following kinds of materials:

- Documents that reflect the immediate, everyday concerns of people: memoranda, bills, deeds, charters, newspaper reports, pamphlets, graffiti, popular writings, journals or diaries, records of decision-making bodies, letters, receipts, snapshots, etc.
- Theoretical writings that reflect care and consideration in composition and an attempt to convince or persuade. The topic is generally deeper and has more pervasive values than is the case with "immediate" documents. These may include newspaper or magazine editorials, sermons, political speeches, philosophical writings, etc.
- Narrative accounts of events, ideas, trends, etc. written with intentionality by someone who has contemporary knowledge of the events described. Statistical data (although statistics may be inaccurate or incomplete)
- Literature and non-verbal materials, including novels, stories, poetry, and essays from the period, as well as coins, archaeological artifacts, and art produced during the period.

Guidelines for the use of primary resources:

1. Be certain that you understand how language was used at the time the document was written and that you understand the context in which it was produced.
2. Do not read history blindly; be certain that you comprehend both explicit and implicit references in the material.
3. Read the entire text you are reviewing; do not simply extract a few sentences to read.
4. Although anthologies of materials may help you identify primary source materials, the full original text should be consulted before completing a research project.

Secondary sources include the following kinds of materials:

- Books written on the basis of primary materials about the period of time
- Books written on the basis of primary materials about persons who played a major role in the events under consideration
- Books and articles written on the basis of primary materials about the culture, the social norms, the language, and the values of the period
- Quotations from primary sources
- Statistical data on the period
- The conclusions and inferences of other historians
- Multiple interpretations of the ethos of the time

Guidelines for the use of secondary sources:

1. Do not rely upon only a single secondary source.
2. Check facts and interpretations against primary sources whenever possible.
3. Do not accept the conclusions of other historians uncritically.
4. Place greatest reliance on secondary sources created by the best and most respected scholars.
5. Do not use the inferences of other scholars as if they were facts.
6. Ensure that you recognize any bias the writer brings to his/her interpretation of history.
7. Understand the primary point of the book as a basis for evaluating the value of the material presented in it to your questions.

COMPETENCY 0013   **Understand methods for analyzing and interpreting social studies information and applying critical reasoning to evaluate presentations of social studies data**

Skill 13.1   **Multiple points of view and frames of reference relating to social studies issues**

Social studies provide an opportunity for students to broaden their general academic skills in many areas. By encouraging students to ask and investigate questions, they gain skill in making meaningful inquiries into social issues. Providing them with a range of resources requires students to make judgments about the best sources for investigating a line of inquiry and helps them to develop the ability to determine authenticity among those sources. Collaboration develops the ability to work as part of a team and to respect the viewpoints of others.

Historic events and social issues cannot be considered only in isolation. People and their actions are connected in many ways, and events are linked through cause and effect over time. Identifying and analyzing these social and historic links is a primary goal of the social sciences. The methods used to analyze social phenomena borrow from several of the social sciences. Interviews, statistical evaluation, observation and experimentation are just some of the ways that people's opinions and motivations can be measured. From these opinions, larger social beliefs and movements can be interpreted, and events, issues and social problems can be placed in context to provide a fuller view of their importance.

Analyzing an event or issue from multiple perspectives involves seeking out sources that advocate or express those perspectives and comparing them with one another. Listening to the speeches of Martin Luther King, Jr., provides insight into the perspective of one group of people concerning the issue of civil rights in the U.S. in the 1950s and 1960s. Public statements of George Wallace (an American governor initially opposed to integration) provide another perspective from the same time period. Looking at the legislation that was proposed at the time and how it came into effect offers a window into the thinking of the day.

One way to analyze historical events, patterns, and relationships is to focus on historical themes. There are many themes repeating throughout human history, and they can be used to make comparisons between different historical times as well as between nations and peoples. While new themes are always being explored, a few of the widely recognized historical themes are as follows:

Politics and political institutions can provide information of prevailing opinions and beliefs of a group of people and how they change over time. For example, in some regions and states, one political party has maintained influence and control for many years. In other areas, there have been gradual shifts over the last thirty years to a different political party, or pockets of ideological change. Exploring these patterns can reveal the popular social ideals that developed in a given state or region and how they impact historical perspectives and writings.

Race and ethnicity is another historical theme that runs through the history of our nation. For example, in the state of Washington, there are thirty recognized Indian tribes and seven other tribes not officially recognized but of distinct cultural difference. Various tribes have occupied the state for over 10,000 years. Significant numbers of Caucasian and Hispanic settlers did not come to Washington until after the 1850s, less than 200 years ago. Therefore, the ethnicity of the people of the state of Washington (like many other states in the U.S.) contributes to a range of differences and similarities in their experiences as citizens. Researching the history of how peoples of different races treated one another reflects on many other social aspects of a society, and can be a fruitful line of historical interpretation.

Skill 13.2 Reasoning and critical thinking

Helping students become critical thinkers is an important objective of the social studies curriculum. History, geography, and political science classes provide many opportunities to teach students to recognize and understand reasoning errors. Errors tend to fall into two categories: a) inadequate reasoning; and b) misleading reasoning. Following are examples of each:

Inadequate reasoning:

1. Faulty analogies: The two things being compared must be similar in all significant aspects if the reasoning is to be relied upon. If there is a major difference between the two, then the argument falls apart.
2. False cause (*Post Hoc Ergo Propter Hoc*): after this, therefore because of this. There must be a factual tie between the effect and its declared cause.
3. *Ad Hominem*: Attacking the person instead of addressing the issues.
4. Slippery Slope: The domino effect. This is usually prophetic in nature— predicting what will follow if a certain event occurs. This is only reliable when it is used in hindsight—not in predicting the future.
5. Hasty Conclusions: Leaping to conclusions when not enough evidence has been collected. A good example is the accusations made in the 1996 bombing at the summer Olympics in Atlanta. Not enough evidence had been collected and the wrong man was arrested.

Misleading reasoning:

1. The Red Herring: often used in politics—getting your opponent on the defensive about a different issue other than the one under discussion.
2. *Ad Populum* or Jumping on the Bandwagon: "Everybody's doing it, so it must be right." Biggest is not necessarily best when it comes to following a crowd.
3. Appeal to Tradition: "We've always done it this way." Often used to squelch innovation.
4. The False Dilemma or the Either/Or Fallacy: No other alternative is possible except the extremes at each end. Used in politics a lot. The creative statesman finds other alternatives.

Making a decision based on a set of given information requires a careful interpretation of the information to decide the strength of the evidence supplied and what it means. Acknowledging the limitations of the information is also important when expressing "facts" or conclusions.

For example, a chart showing that the number of people of foreign birth living in the U.S. has increased annually over the last ten years might allow one to make conclusions about population growth and changes in the relative sizes of ethnic groups in the U.S. However, such a chart would not give information about the reason the number of foreign-born citizens increased, nor would it address matters of immigration status. Conclusions in these areas would be invalid based on this information.

Skill 13.3   Analysis of social studies data using basic mathematical and statistical concepts and other analytical methods

Demography is the branch of science of statistics most concerned with the social well being of people. **Demographic tables** may include:

- Analysis of the population on the basis of age, parentage, physical condition, race, occupation, and civil position, giving the actual size and the density of each separate area.
- Changes in the population as a result of birth, marriage, and death.
- Statistics on population movements and their effects and their relations to given economic, social and political conditions.
- Statistics of crime, illegitimacy, and suicide.
- Levels of education and economic and social statistics.

Such information is also similar to that area of science known as **vital statistics** and is indispensable in studying social trends and making important legislative, economic, and social decisions. Such demographic information is gathered from census and registrar reports. By state laws such information is kept by physicians, attorneys, funeral directors, members of the clergy, and similar professional people.

Social scientists analyze data in a variety of ways from simple construction of charts to complex analysis requiring knowledge of advanced calculus and statistics. Social scientists use statistics to describe a variety of observations that might include the characteristics of a population, the result of a survey, and the testing of a hypothesis.

Measures of central tendency include the common average or **mean** routinely calculated by summing the value of observations and dividing by the number of observations; the **median** or middle score of observations; or the **mode** that is the most repeated observation.

It is typically not possible to secure data on a full **population**. Social scientists routinely collect data on **samples** that are based on measurements or observations of a portion of a population. The samples are described using measures of central tendencies but also by the range from the low score to the high score. Samples ideally are collected **randomly** meaning that each observation in a population had an equal chance of being selected.

Hypothesis testing involves analyzing the results of a sample to show support for a particular position. A social scientist will establish a hypothesis regarding some pattern in the world. This may be that a particular counseling approach is better than another or that the President has greater support than other candidates running for office.

The scientist will collect data and analyze it against a **null hypothesis** that there is no difference in counseling strategies or no preferred presidential candidate. Using the standard normal curve, the scientist is able to evaluate if there is a **significant difference** allowing the acceptance or rejection of the null hypothesis. More advanced forms of analysis include regression analysis, modeling, and game theory.

Social scientists need to be concerned about **bias** in a sample. Bias can be caused by sample selection problems, ambiguous questions, or simply some people refusing to answer some or all of the questions. An **asymmetrical** distribution is one that is skewed because of some factor in the distribution.

Skill 13.4 Utilizing and interpreting visual representations of historical information

We use **illustrations** of various sorts because it is often easier to demonstrate a given idea visually instead of orally. This is especially true in the areas of education and research because humans are visually stimulated. Among the more common illustrations used in the social sciences are various types of **maps, graphs and charts.** Further, **posters** and **cartoons** are also both expressions and sources of historical information. **Photographs** and **globes** are also useful, particularly as primary sources of research information. As always, care must be taken about the generalizations or conclusions reached from all illustrations.

Although **maps** can be very useful, they do have a major disadvantage. The major problem with all maps comes about because most maps are flat and the Earth is a sphere. It is impossible to reproduce exactly on a flat surface an object shaped like a sphere. In order to put the earth's features onto a map they must be stretched in some way. This stretching is called **distortion.**

Distortion does not mean that maps are wrong, it simply means that they are not perfect representations of the Earth or its parts. **Cartographers,** or mapmakers, understand the problems of distortion. They try to design them so that there is as little distortion as possible in the maps.

The process of putting the features of the Earth onto a flat surface is called **projection**. All maps are really map projections. There are many different types. Each one deals in a different way with the problem of distortion. Map projections are made in a number of ways. Some are done using complicated mathematics.

However, the basic ideas behind map projections can be understood by looking at the three most common types:

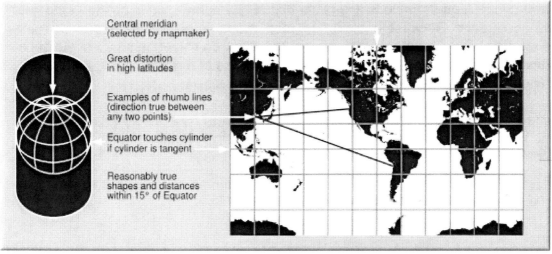

(1) **Cylindrical Projections** - These are done by taking a cylinder of paper and wrapping it around a globe. A light is used to project the globe's features onto the paper. Distortion is least where the paper touches the globe. For example, suppose that the paper was wrapped so that it touched the globe at the equator, the map from this projection would have just a little distortion near the equator. However, in moving north or south of the equator, the distortion would increase as you moved further away from the equator. The best-known and most widely used cylindrical projection is the **Mercator Projection.** Gerard's Mercator, a Flemish mapmaker, first developed it in 1569.

(2) **Conical Projections** - The name for these maps comes from the fact that the projection is made onto a cone of paper. The cone is made so that it touches a globe at the base of the cone only. It can also be made so that it cuts through part of the globe in two different places. Again, there is the least distortion where the paper touches the globe. If the cone touches at two different points, there is some distortion at both of them. Conical projections are most often used to map areas in the **middle latitudes**. Maps of the United States are most often conical projections. This is because most of the country lies within these latitudes.

(3) **Flat-Plane Projections** - These are made with a flat piece of paper. It touches the globe at one point only. Areas near this point show little distortion. Flat-plane projections are often used to show the areas of the north and south poles. One such flat projection is called a **Gnomonic Projection**. On this kind of map, all meridians appear as straight lines, Gnomonic projections are useful because any straight line drawn between points on it forms a **Great-Circle Route**.

Great-Circle Routes can best be described by thinking of a globe and when using the globe the shortest route between two points on it can be found by simply stretching a string from one point to the other. However, if the string was extended in reality, so that it took into effect the globe's curvature, it would then make a great-circle. A great-circle is any circle that cuts a sphere, such as the globe, into two equal parts. Because of distortion, most maps do not show great-circle routes as straight lines, Gnomonic projections, however, do show the shortest distance between the two places as a straight line, because of this they are valuable for navigation. They are called **Great-Circle Sailing Maps.**

Different maps reflect the great variety of knowledge covered by social sciences, and it is important to develop adequate map reading skills to gain this wealth of information

Graphs are another kind of visual representation of information, and they may be used for two purposes:

1. To present a <u>model</u> or <u>theory</u> visually, in order to show how two or more variables interrelate.
2. To present <u>real world</u> data visually, in order to show how two or more variables interrelate.

Graphs are most useful in demonstrating the sequential increase or decrease of a variable ,or to show specific correlations between two or more variables in a given circumstance.

Bar graphs are the most commonly used graphs, as they show differences between given sets of variables, and they are easy to understand. However, bar graphs cannot show the actual proportional increase, or decrease, of each given variable to each other. They may only show information at a specific point in time.

To make a **bar graph** or a **pictograph**, determine the scale to be used for the graph. Then determine the length of each bar on the graph or determine the number of pictures needed to represent each item of information. Be sure to include an explanation of the scale in the legend.

Example: A class had the following grades:
4 As, 9 Bs, 8 Cs, 1 D, 3 Fs.
Graph these on a bar graph and a pictograph.

Pictograph

Grade	Number of Students
A	☺☺☺☺
B	☺☺☺☺☺☺☺☺☺
C	☺☺☺☺☺☺☺☺
D	☺
F	☺☺☺

Bar graph

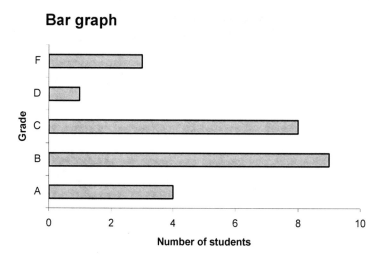

To make a **line graph**, determine appropriate scales for both the vertical and horizontal axes (based on the information to be graphed). Describe what each axis represents, and mark the scale periodically on each axis. Graph the individual points of the graph and connect the points on the graph from left to right.

Example: Graph the following information using a line graph.

The number of National Merit finalists/school year

	90-91	91-92	92-93	93-94	94-95	95-96
Central	3	5	1	4	6	8
Wilson	4	2	3	2	3	2

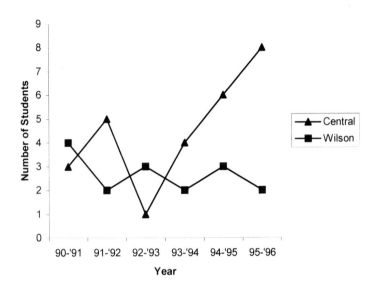

To make a **circle graph**, total all the information that is to be included on the graph. Determine the central angle to be used for each sector of the graph using the following formula:

$$\frac{\text{information}}{\text{total information}} \times 360° = \text{degrees in central} \measuredangle$$

Lay out the central angles to these sizes, label each section and include its percent. A circle graph is also known as a **pie chart**.

Example: Graph this information on a circle graph:

Monthly expenses:

Rent	$400
Food	$150
Utilities	$75
Clothes	$75
Church	$100
Misc-	$200

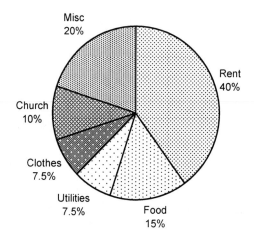

Scatter plots compare two characteristics of the same group of things or people and usually consist of a large body of data. They show how much one variable is affected by another. The relationship between the two variables is their **correlation**. The closer the data points come to making a straight line when plotted, the closer the correlation.

Stem and leaf plots are visually similar to line plots. The **stems** are the digits in the greatest place value of the data values, and the **leaves** are the digits in the next greatest place values. Stem and leaf plots are best suited for small sets of data and are especially useful for comparing two sets of data. The following is an example using test scores:

4	9
5	4 9
6	1 2 3 4 6 7 8 8
7	0 3 4 6 6 6 7 7 7 8 8 8 8
8	3 5 5 7 8
9	0 0 3 4 5
10	0 0

Histograms are used to summarize information from large sets of data that can be naturally grouped into intervals. The vertical axis indicates **frequency** (the number of times any particular data value occurs), and the horizontal axis indicates data values or ranges of data values. The number of data values in any interval is the **frequency of the interval**.

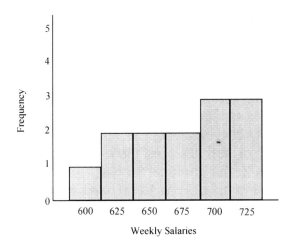

In all graphs, an upward sloping line represents a direct relationship between the two variables. A downward slope represents an inverse relationship between the two variables. In reading any graph, one must always be very careful to understand what is being measured, what can be deduced and what cannot be deduced from the given graph.

In addition to maps, graphs and charts, there are other forms of illustration that are particularly relevant to historical research and information. These are **posters, cartoons, photographs, illustrations in newsletter and newspapers** and other visual representations. All of these may be generated to display information but more commonly they are primary sources of information in historical research.

Posters: The power of the political poster in the 21st century seems trivial considering the barrage of electronic campaigning, mudslinging, and reporting that seems to have taken over the video and audio media in election season. Even so, the political poster has long been a powerful propaganda tool. For example, in the 1st century AD, a poster that calls for the election of a Satrius as quinquennial has survived to this day. Nowhere have political posters been used more powerfully or effectively than in Russia in the 1920s in the campaign to promote communism. Many of the greatest Russian writers of that era were the poster writers. Those posters can only be understood in light of what was going on in the country at the time.

Today we see posters primarily at rallies and protests where they are usually hand-lettered and hand-drawn. The message is rarely subtle. Understanding the messages of posters is easy when placed in the context it is being used. For example, a poster reading "Camp Democracy" can only be understood in the context of the protests of the Iraq War near President George W. Bush's home near Crawford, Texas in the first decade of the 21st century. Similarly, "Impeach" posters are understood in 2006 to be directed at President Bush, not a local mayor or representative.

Cartoons: The political cartoon (or editorial cartoon) presents a message or point of view concerning people, events, or situations using caricature and symbolism to convey the cartoonist's ideas, sometimes subtly, sometimes brashly, but always quickly. A good political cartoon will have wit and humor, which is usually obtained by exaggeration that is slick and not used merely for comic effect. It will also have a foundation in truth; that is, the characters must be recognizable to the viewer and the point of the drawing must have some basis in fact, even if it has a philosophical bias. The third requirement is a moral purpose.

Using political cartoons as a teaching tool enlivens lectures, prompts classroom discussions, promotes critical thinking, develops multiple talents and learning styles, and helps prepare students for standardized tests. It also provides humor. However, it may be the most difficult form of literature to teach. Many teachers who choose to include cartoons in their social studies curricula caution that, while students may enjoy them, it is doubtful whether they are actually getting the cartoonists' messages.

The best strategy for using cartoons in teaching is a sub skills approach that leads students step-by-step to higher orders of critical thinking. For example, the teacher can introduce caricature and use cartoons to illustrate the principles. Students are able to identify and interpret symbols if they are given the principles for doing so and they get plenty of practice. Political cartoons exist everywhere and are more readily available to teachers and educators than ever before.

A popular example of an editorial cartoon that provides a way to analyze current events in politics has been demonstrated by the popular comic strip "Doonesbury" by Gary Trudeau. In the time period prior to the 2004 presidential election (in which Howard Dean and Ralph Nader were contenders for the Democratic ticket), Alex, the media savvy teenager does her best for political participation. In January she rallies her middle school classmates to the phones for a Deanathon and by August she is luring Ralph Nader supporters into discussions on Internet chat rooms. Knowledgeable about government, active in the political process, and willing to enlist others, Alex has many traits sought by the proponents of civics education.

Skill 13.5   How social movements and other concepts impact the interpretation of social studies information

Movements, belief systems, or other phenomena can be identified and examined as a particular pathway to better understand historical data. Capitalism, communism, democracy, racism, and globalization are all examples of social science concepts that inform the reader and writer of history. These concepts can be interpreted as part of other, larger historical themes and provide insight into past events by placing them in a broader historical context.

For example, the study of **gender** issues is a theme that focuses on the relative places men and women ch as politics and economics. In the United States, women were not allowed to vote until 1920, for example. In economic matters, married women were expected not to hold jobs. For women who did work, a limited number of types of work were available. Investigating the historical theme of gender can reveal changes in public attitudes, economic changes, and shifting political attitudes, among other things.

Economic factors drive many social activities such as where people live and work and the relative wealth of nations. As an historical theme, economic history can connect events to their economic causes and explore the results. For example, immigration is a current national political issue connected to both foreign policy and economics. A range of issues cause people to look for work or seek asylum in the United States. Consideration of these issues from an historical perspective is an important part of interpreting social studies information and understanding current political, economic and social situations.

Seeking information from varied sources men hold in a society, and is connected to many other themes so regarding any specific historical theme or issue is one way to help identify bias, stereotype and propaganda, and bring a larger understanding to historical events. If a specific situation or event is highly charged with people lining up on either side of an issue, good researchers try to draw on multiple sources to help them better understand the dimensions of the event. Such attention to detail and a comprehensive assessment of a situation can help the researcher or user of historical data develop a more accurate picture.

COMPETENCY 0014 **Understand methods for presenting social studies information, communicating about social studies topics, and deliberating effectively with others**

Skill 14.1 **Reporting research and synthesizing information**

The phenomena that interest social scientists are usually complex. Capturing that complexity more fully requires the assessment of simultaneous co-variations along the following dimensions: the units of observation, their characteristics, and time. This is how behavior occurs. For example, obtaining a richer and more accurate picture of the progress of school children means measuring changes in their knowledge attainment over time together with changes in the school over time. This acknowledges that changes in one area of behavior are usually contingent on changes in other areas. While descriptions of a research project and presentation of outcomes along with analysis must be a part of every report, graphs, charts, and sometimes maps are necessary to make the results clearly understandable.

A synthesis of information from multiple sources requires an understanding of the content chosen for the synthesis, first of all. The writer of the synthesis generally wishes to incorporate his/her own ideas, particularly in any conclusions that are drawn, and show relationships to those of the chosen sources. This can only happen if the writer has a firm grip on what others have said or written. The focus is not so much on documentary methods but on techniques of critically examining and evaluating the ideas of others.

Even so, careful documentation is extremely important in this type of presentation, particularly with regard to which particular edition is being read in the case of written sources; and date, location, etc., of online sources. The phrase "downloaded from such-and-such a website on such-and-such a date" is useful. If the conversation, interview, or speech is live, then the date, circumstances, and location must be indicated.

The purpose of a synthesis is to understand the works of others and to use that work in shaping a conclusion. The writer or speaker must clearly differentiate between the ideas that come from a source and his/her own.

Skill 14.2 **Graphic formats for conveying social studies information**

Various graphical formats are useful in communicating social science and historical information. Visual aids can be great teaching tools and often convey complex data in a succinct and clear manner. However, simply placing bulleted lists on slides for a Powerpoint presentation or adding a picture is not enough. Choosing the best graphic or visual option requires thought and planning. Some questions the presenter should ask include:

- Does this graphic enhance what I am trying to communicate?
- Is this line graph easy to read?
- How does this map capture the points I am making?
- Does this image carry any connotation other than the one I intend?
- Could this image be offensive in some way? How and why?
- Does this chart clearly identify the key data?
- Am I infringing on any copyright law by using this photo?

For more information about using visual information (maps, charts, graphs, cartoons, etc.) to present social science data, see Skill 13.4.

Skill 14.3   Effective communication of social studies information

There are some basic communication skills that are relevant to all disciplines. Good communication practices (which focuses primarily on the oral presentation of information) and tips on report writing are detailed here.

Summary of Good Communication Practices

- Think first. This means preparing for a formal written, or oral presentation and it means pausing to gather your thoughts before impromptu speaking.
- Stay informed. Never speak or write off-the-cuff or attempt to discuss matters beyond your scope of knowledge. Stay abreast of social studies issues in general, especially those related to the area of history or other social science about which you are speaking or writing.
- Assess your audience. Know the audience's interests and attitudes. Show respect for their points-of-view by your tone and pace as well as by your volume and posture when speaking. Demonstrate a genuine liking for people by a willingness to share your ideas and solicit their responses.
- Focus attention on your message, not on yourself. A little nervousness is normal even for practiced writers/speakers. Familiarity with your topic, the ability to develop clear, complete sentences, and the use of concrete examples will enhance delivery.
- Speak/write correctly. Use of proper grammar, word-choice, and sentence structure will allow listeners/readers to concentrate on what you say, rather than on distracting language errors.
- Be concise. Get to the point and then quit. Use words and sentences economically. Being unnecessarily long-winded is a sure way to lose your audience.

- Use delivery techniques to your advantage. In written communication, be sure to state the main idea, give examples or explanations, and link the ideas in a logical manner. In oral communication, use eye contact to establish sincerity and hold listener attention. Use body language to add enthusiasm and conviction to your words, but avoid expansive or repetitive movements that can distract. Modulate the pitch and volume of your voice for emphasis.

Listen thoughtfully to feedback. In face-to-face communication, be aware of nonverbal cues that suggest either active listening or boredom.

Report Writing

When writing a report that involves data analysis and interpretation, care needs to be given to think through precisely what needs to be communicated and how this can best be achieved. The intended audience needs to be considered, as different groups and individuals will have varying knowledge bases from which to understand the report. Tone and style can vary depending upon the topic and the writer's personality, but the goal should always be to write in a way that is succinct, clear, free of jargon as much as possible, and limited in personal judgments and opinions.

The format of the report and any accompanying charts or graphs should be chosen thoughtfully. The goal is to ensure that the format and visual depictions clarify and explicate the information, thus enhancing the reader's ability to understand the content. Similarly, direct quotes should only be included when they increase the clarity of the report or provide information that cannot be stated in any other way. References should be available but not interrupt the flow of the text.

The following guidelines provide a basic structure for a report.

- Introduction: Introduce the topic or main idea, state a point a view when relevant, and tell the reader briefly what the main points are.
- Main Points (3 or more): Each paragraph or section should include a lead-in sentence that states the main point. This sentence is followed by supporting detail and evidence regarding the point. Information about the source of data, methodologies and results may be reported in this section. At times, questions may be posed regarding the data to identify gaps in information or the need for further data-gathering or review.
- Summary: Restate the main idea and sum up the main points addressed in the report. Add any comments about future action that may be relevant.

Some key concepts to consider when presenting an analysis and interpretation of data are:

- Analyze: examine the parts
- Compare: look at similarities
- Contrast: look at differences
- Discuss: examine in detail
- Explain: provide reasons or examples, or clarify meaning

Skill 14.4 Key concepts in conflict resolution and collaborative problem-solving approaches

As in many areas of academic study, people reach different conclusions about the same event or situation. People interpret data differently and weight certain information in different ways. The capacity to recognize these differences without animosity or judgment is valuable in working to better understand historical events. Sometimes compromise is needed; other times differing viewpoints can comfortably co-exist.

In order to be prepared for such situations, students and teachers of history would do well to understand basic concepts about conflict resolution and collaborative problem-solving. Whether or not a formal conflict resolution process is involved, the underlying concepts are useful guidelines when working with others about potentially charged and strongly held beliefs or ideas.

Some ideas that can encourage dialogue between and among people who disagree with each other:

- Be willing to suspend judgment about the other person's ideas and just listen.
- Share your ideas without putting down anyone else's.
- Don't assume you know what another person's viewpoint is. Again, listen, and when necessary, ask questions for clarification.
- Agree to disagree respectfully, and see what you can learn from the other person.
- Keep a sense of humor and perspective; generally the topic is not a life-and-death issue.
- Find common values or beliefs that you share with the other person or people and acknowledge these commonalities.
- Figure out when a compromise is really needed, and when you can simply accept the differences between or among you.
- Approach the discussion as a chance to explore ideas, rather than an argument or a debate.
- Do not be attacking or hostile; display curiosity and respect.
- Do not bring personal issues into the discussion; address the social science topic at hand, not the person expressing the idea.

Sample Test

1. Which of the following is not a native North American tribe?
(Average) (Skill 1.1)

   A. Algonquian

   B. Inca

   C. Iroquois

   D. Hopi

2. Which one of the following is not a reason why Europeans came to the New World?
(Average) (Skill 1.2)

   A. To find resources in order to increase wealth

   B. To establish trade

   C. To increase a ruler's power and importance

   D. To spread Christianity

3. The only colony not founded and settled for religious, political, or business reasons was:
(Average) (Skill 1.2)

   A. Delaware

   B. Virginia

   C. Georgia

   D. New York

4. After 1783, the largest "land owner" in the Americas was:
(Rigorous) (Skill 1.2)

   A. Spain

   B. Britain

   C. France

   D. United States

5. The Navigation Acts of 1650 and 1661 reflected Britain's efforts to control which of the following:
(Easy) (Skill 1.4)

   A. The number of colonists who left for America

   B. The number of ships sailing for America

   C. Trade

   D. The way captains ran their ships

6. During the period of Spanish colonialism, which of the following was not fundamental to the goal of exploiting, transforming and including the native people? (Average) (Skill 1.5)

A. Missions

B. Ranchos

C. Presidios

D. Pueblos

7. Which of the following was not one of the events leading to the Revolutionary War?
(Average) (Skill 1.6)

A. Stamp Act

B. Quartering Act

C. Sugar Act

D. Monroe Doctrine

8. France decided in 1777 to help the American colonies in their war against Britain. This decision was based on: (Rigorous) (Skill 1.6)

A. The naval victory of John Paul Jones over the British ship "Serapis"

B. The survival of the terrible winter at Valley Forge

C. The success of colonial guerilla fighters in the South

D. The defeat of the British at Saratoga

9. There is no doubt of the vast improvement of the U.S. Constitution over the weak Articles of Confederation. Which one of the four statements below is not a description of the document? (Rigorous) (Skill 1.7)

   A. The establishment of a strong central government in no way lessened or weakened the individual states

   B. Individual rights were protected and secured

   C. The Constitution demands unquestioned respect and subservience to the federal government by all states and citizens

   D. Its flexibility and adaptation to change gives it a sense of timelessness

10. The Federalists: (Rigorous) (Skill 2.1)

    A. Favored state's rights

    B. Favored a weak central government

    C. Favored a strong federal government

    D. Supported the British

11. Under the brand new Constitution, the most urgent of the many problems facing the new federal government was that of: (Average) (Skill 2.2)

    A. Maintaining a strong army and navy

    B. Establishing a strong foreign policy

    C. Raising money to pay salaries and war debts

    D. Setting up courts, passing federal laws, and providing for law enforcement officers

12. Which one of the following was not a reason why the United States went to war with Great Britain in 1812? (Rigorous) (Skill 2.2)

    A. Resentment by Spain over the sale, exploration, and settlement of the Louisiana Territory

    B. The westward movement of farmers because of the need for more land

    C. Canadian fur traders were agitating the northwestern Indians to fight American expansion

    D. Britain continued to seize American ships on the high seas and force American seamen to serve aboard British ships

13. Which one of the following events did not occur during the period known as the "Era of Good Feeling"? (Average) (Skill 2.2)

A. President Monroe issued the Monroe Doctrine

B. Spain ceded Florida to the United States

C. The building of the National Road

D. The charter of the second Bank of the United States

14. From about 1870 to 1900, the last settlement of America's "last frontier", the West, was completed. One attraction for settlers was free land but it would have been to no avail without: (Easy) (Skill 2.3)

A. Better farming methods and technology

B. Surveying to set boundaries

C. Immigrants and others to see new lands

D. The railroad to get them there

15, The belief that the United States should control all of North America was called: (Easy) (Skill 2.3)

A. Westward Expansion

B. Manifest Destiny

C. Pan Americanism

D. Nationalism

16. As a result of the Missouri Compromise: (Average) (Skill 2.4)

A. Slavery was not allowed in the Louisiana Purchase

B. The Louisiana Purchase was nullified

C. Louisiana separated from the Union

D. The Embargo Act was repealed

17. Which Supreme Court ruling dealt with the issue of civil rights? (Average) (Skill 2.6)

A. Jefferson v. Madison

B. Lincoln v. Douglas

C. Dred Scott v. Sanford

D. Marbury v. Madison

18. The term "sectionalism" refers to: (Easy) (Skill 2.6)

A. Different regions of the continent

B. Issues between the North and South

C. Different regions of the country

D. Different groups of countries

19. The principle of "popular sovereignty," allowing people in any Territory to make their own decision concerning slavery was stated by:
(Average) (Skill 2.7)

A. Henry Clay

B. Daniel Webster

C. John C. Calhoun

D. Stephen A. Douglas

20. The Radical Republicans who pushed the harsh Reconstruction measures through Congress after Lincoln's death lost public and moderate Republican support when they went too far:
(Rigorous) (Skill 2.8)

A. In their efforts to impeach the President

B. By dividing ten southern states into military-controlled districts

C. By making the ten southern states give freed African-Americans the right to vote

D. Sending carpetbaggers into the South to build up support for Congressional legislation

21. The post-Civil War years were a time of low public morality, a time of greed, graft, and dishonesty. Which one of the reasons listed would not be accurate?
(Rigorous) (Skill 2.8)

A. The war itself because of the money and materials needed to carry on war

B. The very rapid growth of industry and big business after the war

C. The personal example set by President Grant

D. Unscrupulous heads of large impersonal corporations

22. The American labor union movement started gaining new momentum:
(Average) (Skill 3.2)

A. During the building of the railroads

B. After 1865 with the growth of cities

C. With the rise of industrial giants such as Carnegie and Vanderbilt

D. During the war years of 1861-1865

23. In the 1800s, the era of industrialization and growth were characterized by:
(Average) (Skill 3.2)

A. Small firms

B. Public ownership

C. Worker owned enterprises

D. Monopolies and trusts

24. Historians state that the West helped to speed up the Industrial Revolution. Which one of the following statements was not a reason for this?
(Rigorous) (Skill 3.3)

A. Food supplies for the ever-increasing urban populations came from farms in the West.

B. A tremendous supply of gold and silver from western mines provided the capital needed to build industries.

C. Descendants of western settlers, educated as engineers, geologists, and metallurgists in the East, returned to the West to mine the mineral resources needed for industry.

D. Iron, copper, and other minerals from western mines were important resources in manufacturing products.

25. **What event triggered World War I?**
(Average) (Skill 3.4)

A. The fall of the Weimar Republic

B. The resignation of the Czar

C. The assassination of Austrian Archduke Ferdinand

D. The assassination of the Czar

26. **The Great Depression resulted from all of the following except: (Rigorous) (Skill 3.6):**

A. Speculative investments on the stock market

B. Uneven distribution of wealth

C. Economic conditions in Europe

D. Individual spending and saving patterns such as hoarding

27. **The New Deal was: (Average) (Skill 3.6)**

A. A trade deal with England

B. A series of programs to provide relief during the Great Depression

C. A new exchange rate regime

D. A plan for tax relief

28. **Which country was not a part of the Axis in World War II? (Easy) (Skill 3.7)**

A. Germany

B. Italy

C. Japan

D. United States

29. **After World War II, the United States: (Average) (Skill 3.7)**

A. Limited its involvement in European affairs

B. Shifted foreign policy emphasis from Europe to Asia

C. Passed significant legislation pertaining to aid to farmers and tariffs on imports

D. Entered the greatest period of economic growth in its history

30. **Which country was a Cold War foe?**
(Easy) (Skill 4.1)

   A. Russia

   B. Brazil

   C. Canada

   D. Argentina

31. **Which one of the following was not a post World War II organization?**
(Average) (Skill 4.2)

   A. Monroe Doctrine

   B. Marshall Plan

   C. Warsaw Pact

   D. North Atlantic Treaty Organization

32. **Which of the following is not a name associated with the Civil Rights movement?**
(Average) (Skill 4.3)

   A. Rosa Parks

   B. Emmett Till

   C. Tom Dewey

   D. Martin Luther King, Jr.

33. **Which of the following women was not a part of the women's rights movement?**
(Easy) (Skill 4.3)

   A. Elizabeth Cady Stanton

   B. Lucretia Borgia

   C. Lucretia Mott

   D. Susan B. Anthony

34. **What conflict brought the United States and the Soviet Union to the brink of war in 1962?**
(Average) (Skill 4.4)

   A. Cuban Missile Crisis

   B. Viet Nam war

   C. Crisis in Brazil

   D. Crisis in India

35. **On the spectrum of American politics the label that most accurately describes voters to the "right of center" is:**
(Easy) (Skill 4.4)

   A. Moderates

   B. Liberals

   C. Conservatives

   D. Socialists

36. **A major factor that contributed to the technological growth of the last 50 years is:**
(Average) (Skill 4.5)

A. The development of the microchip

B. The accessibility of personal computers

C. The increased infrastructure of electrical power plants

D. The global satellite system

37. **Globalization:**
(Average) (Skill 4.6)

A. Is inherently good for the U.S. economy overall in spite of recent downturns

B. Has resulted from U.S. technological developments

C. Refers to the complex interaction and interdependence of nations around the world

D. Has been negative for the U.S. during the recent 2008-2009 recession

38. **Which of the following best characterizes the native people of the state of Washington?**
(Rigorous) (Skill 5.1)

A. They came from two main tribes, divided by the Cascade Mountains

B. They were primarily fishers living in longhouses in the west, and hunter-gathers who traveled a large territory in the eastern part of the state

C. They consisted of 35-40 different tribes, each of whom had quite different lifestyles and cultures

D. They were unique to the state of Washington, sharing little similarity to other tribes in the northwest

39. **By the 1880s, which of the following statements is most accurate: (Rigorous) (Skill 5.2)**

    A. Most Indian tribes were living in peaceful settlements amidst the growing numbers of white and Asian settlers.

    B. Chinese and Scandinavian immigrants constituted the largest ethnic groups in the area due to the need for unskilled labor for building railroads.

    C. There was very little discrimination in early Washington, as the state was a mix of people from all over, as well as having large numbers of Indians.

    D. Most of the Indians land had been taken by white settlers, and most tribes were living on reservations.

40. **The Grand Coulee Dam, a New Deal Project, contributed to which of the following industries during and after World War II: (Average) (Skill 5.3)**

    A. Agriculture, aluminum processing, and airplane building

    B. Agriculture

    C. Aluminum processing

    D. Airplane building

41. **The Hanford Nuclear Plant: (Average) (Skill 5.4)**

    A. Was originally built to make plutonium during World War II and was never shut down

    B. Closed in 1988, and was found to have leaked hazardous waste

    C. Was built in 1966 as a nuclear power plant to make electricity

    D. Is one of the cleanest nuclear power plants operating today

42. The Fertile Crescent was bounded by all of the following except:
(Rigorous) (Skill 6.1)

A. Mediterranean Sea

B. Arabian Desert

C. Taurus Mountains

D. Ural Mountains

43. The end to hunting, gathering, and fishing of prehistoric people was due to:
(Average) (Skill 6.1)

A. Domestication of animals

B. Building crude huts and houses

C. Development of agriculture

D. Organized government in villages

44. Bathtubs, hot and cold running water, and sewage systems with flush toilets were developed by the:
(Average) (Skill 6.2)

A. Minoans

B. Mycenaeans

C. Phoenicians

D. Greeks

45. The principle of zero in mathematics is the discovery of the ancient civilization found in:
(Rigorous) (Skill 6.2)

A. Egypt

B. Persia

C. India

D. Babylon

46. Development of a solar calendar, invention of the decimal system, and contributions to the development of geometry and astronomy are all the legacy of:
(Rigorous) (Skill 6.2)

A. The Babylonians

B. The Persians

C. The Sumerians

D. The Egyptians

47. The world religion which includes a caste system, is:
(Average) (Skill 6.3)

A. Buddhism

B. Hinduism

C. Sikhism

D. Jainism

48. The Roman Empire gave so much to the world, especially the Western world. Which of the legacies below has been most influential and had the most lasting effect: (Average) (Skill 6.5)

A. The language of Latin

B. Roman law, justice, and political system

C. Engineering and building

D. The writings of its poets and historians

49. The first ancient civilization to introduce and practice monotheism was that of the: (Rigorous) (Skill 6.6)

A. Sumerians

B. Minoans

C. Phoenicians

D. Hebrews

50. Which one of the following is not an important legacy of the Byzantine Empire? (Rigorous) (Skill 6.7)

A. It protected Western Europe from various attacks from the East by such groups as the Persians, Ottoman Turks, and Barbarians

B. It played a part in preserving the literature, philosophy, and language of ancient Greece

C. Its military organization was the foundation for modern armies

D. It kept the legal traditions of Roman government, collecting and organizing many ancient Roman laws.

51. Which of the following is an example of a direct democracy? (Average) (Skill 6.8)

A. Elected representatives

B. Greek city-states

C. The Constitution

D. The Confederate States

52. **The holy book of Islam is:**
(Easy) (Skill 7.1)

A. The Bible

B. The Kaaba

C. The Koran

D. The Torah

53. **The difference between manorialism and feudalism was:**
(Rigorous) (Skill 7.2)

A. Land was owned by the noblemen in manorialism

B. Land was owned by noblemen in both feudalism and manorialism

C. Land was owned by the noblemen in feudalism

D. The king owned all the land in both

54. **The lords of feudal Japan were known as:**
(Easy) (Skill 2.6)

A. Daimyo

B. Samurai

C. Ronin

D. Bushido

55. **The religious orientation of the African kingdom of Mali was:(Average) (Skill 7.4)**

A. Islamic

B. A blend of Islam and ancient African belief

C. Christian

D. A mixture of faiths, with no one faith dominating

56. **Native South American tribes included all of the following except:**
(Easy) (Skill 7.5)

A. Aztec

B. Inca

C. Minoans

D. Maya

57. **In Western Europe, the achievements of the Renaissance were many. All of the following were accomplishments except:**
(Rigorous) (Skill 7.6)

A. Invention of the printing press

B. A rekindling of interest in the learning of classical Greece & Rome

C. Growth in literature, philosophy, and art

D. Better military tactics

58. Who is considered to be the most important figure in the spread of Protestantism across Switzerland?
(Average) (Skill 7.7)

A. Calvin

B. Zwingli

C. Munzer

D. Leyden

59. The Age of Exploration begun in the 1400s was led by:
(Easy) (Skill 8.1)

A. The Portuguese

B. The Spanish

C. The English

D. The Dutch

60. Many governments in Europe today have which of the following type of government:
(Average) (Skill 8.2)

A. Absolute monarchies

B. Constitutional governments

C. Constitutional monarchies

D. Another form of government

61. Studies in astronomy, skills in mapping, and other contributions to geographic knowledge came from:
(Average) (Skill 8.3)

A. Galileo

B. Columbus

C. Eratosthenes

D. Ptolemy

62. Karl Marx believed in:
(Average) (Skill 9.1)

A. Free Enterprise

B. Utopian Socialism

C. Absolute Monarchy

D. Scientific Socialism

63. Which of the following took a scientific view of the world:
(Average) (Skill 9.1)

A. Rousseau

B. Immanuel Kant

C. Montesquieu

D. John Locke

64. The concepts of social contract and natural law were espoused by: (Rigorous)(Skill 9.1)

    A. Locke

    B. Rousseau

    C. Aristotle

    D. Montesquieu

65. One South American country quickly and easily gained independence in the 19th century from European control. This Latin American country is: (Rigorous) (Skill 9.3)

    A. Chile

    B. Argentina

    C. Venezuela

    D. Brazil

66. Which of the following was not a leader for independence in Mexico and South America in the early 19th century? (Average) (Skill 9.3)

    A. Joao of Brazil

    B. Francisco de Miranda

    C. Miguel Hidalgo

    D. Simon Bolivar

67. Which of the following was not a factor contributing to the Agricultural Revolution? (Average) (Skill 9.4)

    A. Steam-powered tractors

    B. Depletion of farmland

    C. Crop rotation

    D. Soil enrichment

68. The Baroque period is characterized by all of the following except: (Rigorous) (Skill 9.5)

    A. Ornamentation

    B. Chiaroscuro

    C. Religiosity

    D. Dramatic flair

69. Colonial expansion by Western European powers in the 18th and 19th centuries was due primarily to: (Average) (Skill 9.6)

    A. Building and opening the Suez Canal

    B. The Industrial Revolution

    C. Marked improvements in transportation

    D. Complete independence of all the Americas and loss of European domination and influence

70. **Nineteenth century imperialism by Western Europe nations had important and far-reaching effects on the colonial peoples they ruled. All four of the following are the results of this. Which one was the most important and had lasting effects on key 20th century events? (Rigorous) (Skill 9.6)**

A. Local wars were ended

B. Living standards were raised

C. Demands for self-government and feelings of nationalism surfaced

D. Economic developments occurred

71. **Of all the major causes of both World Wars I and II, the most significant one is considered to be: (Easy) (Skill 11.1)**

A. Extreme nationalism

B. Military buildup and aggression

C. Political unrest

D. Agreements and alliances

72. **Which of the following forms of warfare introduced during World War I was later banned? (Easy) (Skill 10.1)**

A. Machine guns

B. Flame throwers

C. Poison gas

D. Tanks

73. **Which did not contribute to the 1917 Revolution in Russia? (Easy) (Skill 10.2)**

A. World War I

B. Worker strikes

C. Starving peasants

D. Promise of aid from Germany

74. **Which f the following best describes a fascist regime? (Rigorous) (Skill 10.3)**

A. Anti-communist

B. Rigidly controlling

C. Pro-socialist

D. Concerned with oppressed peoples

75. A well known World War II figure who was the leader of Italy was:
(Easy) (Skill 10.4)

   A. Hitler

   B. Stalin

   C. Tojo

   D. Mussolini

76. Which one of the following would not be considered a result of World War II?
(Rigorous) (Skill 10.4)

   A. Economic depressions and slow resumption of trade and financial aid

   B. Western Europe was no longer the center of world power

   C. The beginnings of new power struggles not only in Europe also Asia

   D. Territorial and boundary changes for many nations, especially in Europe

77. The international organization established to work for world peace at the end of the Second World War is the:
(Average) (Skill 10.4)

   A. League of Nations

   B. United Federation of Nations

   C. United Nations

   D. United World League

78. Which of the following was not an element of the Cold War?
(Rigorous) (Skill 10.5)

   A. Iron Curtain

   B. Glasnost

   C. Arms Race

   D. Economic blockades

79. Nationalism can be defined as the division of land and resources according to which of the following:
(Rigorous) (Skill 10.6)

   A. Religion, race, or political ideology

   B. Religion, race, or gender

   C. Historical boundaries, religion, or race

   D. Race, gender, or political ideology

80. **Globalization in the 21ˢᵗ century means that:**
    (Average) (Skill 10.7)

    A. Few countries or cultures operate in isolation any more

    B. Nationalism has major political, economic, and human ramifications

    C. Neither A or B

    D. Both A and B

81. **The study of past human cultures based on physical artifacts is:**
    (Average) (Skill 11.1)

    A. History

    B. Anthropology

    C. Cultural Geography

    D. Archaeology

82. **The study of the social behavior of minority groups would be in the area of:**
    (Average Rigor) (Skill 11.1)

    A. Anthropology

    B. Psychology

    C. Sociology

    D. Cultural Geography

83. **"Participant observation" is a method of study most closely associated with and used in:**
    (Rigorous) (Skill 11.1)

    A. Anthropology

    B. Archaeology

    C. Sociology

    D. Political science

84. **The study of a people's language and writing would be part of all of the following except:**
    (Rigorous) (Skill 11.1)

    A. Sociology

    B. Archaeology

    C. History

    D. Geography

85. **Divisions of time in history (periodizations) may be determined by all but which of the following:** **(Easy) (Skill 11.2)**

    A. Date

    B. Geography

    C. Cultural advances

    D. Individual historians

86. **Which of the following is not one of the schools of narrative history? (Rigorous) (Skill 11.3)**

    A. Comparative Sociological

    B. Economic

    C. Intellectual

    D. Political-Institutional

87. **In addition to the narrative school, which of the following is also an approach used by historians: (Easy) (Skill 11.3)**

    A. Anecdotal

    B. Biography

    C. Conflict-based

    D. Summative

88. **Which of the following is not part of the scientific method? (Rigorous) (Skill 12.1)**

    A. Identifying sources of material

    B. Formulating a hypothesis

    C. Testing the hypothesis

    D. Stating a research question

89. **Which of the following best describes an argumentative research paper: (Rigorous) (Skill 12.1)**

    A. Understanding various parts of a research topic

    B. Using the research question to investigate a hypothesis

    C. Providing a clear discussion of all pertinent data

    D. Presenting research to prove an interpretation

90. **Which of the following is not a common source of historical data? (Rigorous) (Skill 12.2)**

    A. Autobiographies

    B. Archival materials from labor unions

    C. Technical manuals

    D. Novels

91. **Which of the following is not one of the characteristics of primary sources? (Average) (Skill 12.3)**

    A. Qualitative data

    B. Specific focus and/or detail

    C. Analysis in light of current theories

    D. Quantitative data

92. **Which of the following does NOT describe possible limitations of secondary sources?**
    (Average) (Skill 12.3)

    A. Bias on the part of the author

    B. Eyewitness descriptions of an historical event

    C. Inferences by the author

    D. Personal analysis of an historical event

93. **Which of the following would not be considered a primary source?**
    (Rigorous) (Skill 12.3)

    A. An 1863 newspaper account of the Gettysburg Address

    B. The text of the Gettysburg Address

    C. A historical analysis of the Gettysburg Address

    D. A narrative account of the Gettysburg Address from a spectator in the crowd.

94. **Which of the following is not an example of an historical theme?**
    (Average) (Skill 13.1)

    A. Epochs and eras

    B. Race and ethnicity

    C. Politics

    D. Civil Rights

95. **Which of the following is not a reason that historical themes are a useful form of analysis in historical research and reporting:**
    (Rigorous) (Skill 13.1)

    A. There are multiple recurrences throughout history

    B. They hone in on the most accurate perspective

    C. There are opportunities for comparison

    D. They offer multiple viewpoints

96. In making an argument against a new high school math curriculum under consideration, a speaker praises a recent decision by the superintendent to retain the elementary social studies curriculum implemented last year. This is an example of which type of misleading reasoning? (Rigorous) (Skill 13.2)

A. Red herring

B. Either/or fallacy

C. Appeal to tradition

D. Jumping on the bandwagon

97. Which of the following is not an example of inadequate reasoning? (Rigorous) (Skill 13.2)

A. Faulty analogy

B. Jumping to conclusions

C. False causation

D. False dilemma

98. Historians and social scientists utilize all but which of the following in analyzing data: (Average) (Skill 13.3)

A. Measures of central tendency

B. Bias

C. Demographics

D. Vital statistics

99. Which measure of central tendency describes the observation that is repeated most often? (Rigorous) (Skill 13.3)

A. Median

B. Mean

C. Average

D. Mode

100. Which of the following is most useful in showing differences in variables at a specific point in time? (Average) (Skill 13.4)

A. Histogram

B. Scatter plots

C. Pie chart

D. Bar graph

101. **Which of the following is needed in order to understand the historical significance of a poster?**
(Average) (Skill 13.4)

A. The artist's background

B. The political orientation of the artist

C. The context in which the poster was made

D. How color and shape relate to historical periods

102. **Which of the following is not an example of a visual representation of historical information?**
(Average) (Skill 13.4)

A. Cartoon

B. Poem

C. Map

D. Circle graph

103. **An historian using the lens of the women's movement through which to view the 19th century might get a different perspective on which of the following:**
(Easy) (Skill 13.5)

A. The Civil War

B. The suffrage movement

C. National politics

D. All of the above

104. **A synthesis of historical information requires all of the following except:**
(Rigorous) (Skill 14.1)

A. Understanding the content that is included in the synthesis

B. Documenting the backgrounds of the various historians whose work is included in the synthesis

C. Documenting the source of information included in the synthesis

D. Differentiating the writer's ideas from those of others included in the synthesis

105. **Using graphics can enhance the presentation of social science information because:**
(Average) (Skill 14.2)

A. They can explain complex relationships among various data points

B. Charts and graphs summarize information well

C. Most social science information is boring without visual information

D. Maps can describe geographic distribution of historical information

106. Which of the following is not a potential problem in using graphics to present historical information?
(Average) (Skill 14.2)

A. Use of graphics to summarize key points

B. Copyright infringement

C. Unintended offensive connotations

D. Lack of clarity

107. Which of the following is not an example of a good communication practice?
(Average) (Skill 14.3)

A. Make eye contact when speaking

B. Organize your information in a logical manner

C. Assess your audience before you begin speaking

D. Use repetitive movements to emphasize a point

108. In a written report, try to avoid which of the following?
(Average) (Skill 14.3)

A. Including a formal introduction

B. Making your points explicit

C. Using jargon to express familiarity with a subject

D. Providing a summary of the main points

109. When researchers reach different conclusions using similar data, it is usually because:
(Average) (Skill 14.4)

A. Some researchers aren't as diligent as others

B. Historians have different perspectives and orientations that impact the outcome of their work

C. They have had poor training and education

D. They used bad sources

110. **Which of the following is not an example of a collaborative problem-solving approach? (Easy) (Skill 14.1)**

    A. Repeating your own ideas

    B. Asking another person to explain her perspective

    C. Finding shared values or beliefs with others

    D. Agreeing to disagree

ANSWER KEY

1. B	30. A	59. A	88. A
2. B	31. A	60. C	89. D
3. C	32. C	61. D	90. C
4. A	33. B	62. D	91. C
5. C	34. A	63. B	92. B
6. B	35. C	64. D	93. C
7. D	36. A	65. D	94. A
8. D	37. C	66. A	95. B
9. C	38. B	67. B	96. A
10. C	39. D	68. C	97. D
11. C	40. A	69. B	98. B
12. A	41. B	70. C	99. D
13. A	42. D	71. A	100. D
14. D	43. C	72. C	101. C
15. B	44. A	73. D	102. B
16. A	45. C	74. B	103. D
17. B	46. D	75. D	104. B
18. B	47. B	76. A	105. C
19. D	48. B	77. C	106. A
20. A	49. D	78. B	107. D
21. C	50. C	79. A	108. C
22. B	51. B	80. D	109. B
23. D	52. C	81. D	110. A
24. C	53. A	82. C	
25. C	54. A	83. A	
26. D	55. B	84. A	
27. B	56. C	85. D	
28. D	57. D	86. A	
29. D	58. A	87. B	

Rigor Table

	Easy 16%	Average 50%	Rigorous 34%
Question #	5, 14, 151, 18, 28, 30, 33, 35, 52, 54, 56, 59, 71, 72, 73, 75, 85, 87, 103, 110	1, 2, 3, 6, 7, 11, 13, 16, 17, 19, 22, 23, 25, 27, 29, 31, 32, 34, 36, 37, 40, 41, 43, 44, 47, 48, 51, 55, 58, 60, 61, 62, 63, 66, 67, 69, 77, 80, 81, 82, 91, 92, 94, 98, 100, 101, 102, 105, 106, 107, 108, 109	4, 8, 9, 10, 12, 20, 21, 24, 26, 38, 39, 45, 46, 49, 50, 53, 57, 64, 65, 68, 70, 74, 76, 78, 79, 83, 84, 86, 88, 89, 90, 93, 95, 96, 97, 99, 104

Answer Rationales for Sample Test Questions

1. **Which of the following is not a native North American tribe? (Average) (Skill 1.1)**

   A. Algonquian

   B. Inca

   C. Iroquois

   D. Hopi

Answer: B. Inca

The (A) Algonquian and (C) Iroquois are native to the American Northeast. The (D) Hopi are a Southwestern U.S. tribe. The (B) Incas are native to Peru.

2. **Which one of the following is not a reason why Europeans came to the New World? (Average) (Skill 1.2)**

   A. To find resources in order to increase wealth

   B. To establish trade

   C. To increase a ruler's power and importance

   D. To spread Christianity

Answer: B. To establish trade

The Europeans came to the New World for a number of reasons; often they came to find new natural resources to extract for manufacturing. The Portuguese, Spanish and English were sent over to increase the monarch's power and spread influences such as religion (Christianity) and culture. Therefore, the only reason given that Europeans didn't come to the New World was to establish trade.

3.   **The only colony not founded and settled for religious, political, or business reasons was: (Average) (Skill 1.2)**

    A. Delaware

    B. Virginia

    C. Georgia

    D. New York

Answer: C. Georgia

The Swedish and the Dutch established Delaware and New York as Middle Colonies. They were established with the intention of growth by economic prosperity from farming across the countryside. The English, with the intention of generating a strong farming economy settled Virginia, a Southern Colony. Georgia was the only one of these colonies not settled for religious, political or business reasons as it was started as a place for debtors from English prisons.

4.   **After 1783, the largest "land owner" in the Americas was: (Rigorous) (Skill 1.2)**

    A. Spain

    B. Britain

    C. France

    D. United States

Answer: A. Spain

Despite the emergence of the United States as an independent nation in control of the colonies over the British, and the French control of Canada, Spain remained the largest "land owner" in the Americas controlling much of the southwest as well as much of Central and South America.

5. **The Navigation Acts of 1650 and 1661 reflected Britain's efforts to control which of the following: (Easy) (Skills 1.4)**

   A. The number of colonists who left for America

   B. The number of ships sailing for America

   C. Trade

   D. The way captains ran their ships

Answer: C. Trade

Britain was concerned primarily with economic issues in relation to the colonies. The Navigation Acts were attempts to control which products were shipped in and out of Colonial America.

6. **During the period of Spanish colonialism, which of the following was not fundamental to the goal of exploiting, transforming and including the native people? (Average) (Skill 1.5)**

   A. Missions

   B. Ranchos

   C. Presidios

   D. Pueblos

Answer: B. Ranchos

The goal of Spanish colonialism was to exploit, transform and include the native people of California. The Spanish empire sought to do this first by gathering the native people into communities where they could both be taught Spanish culture and be converted to Roman Catholicism and its value system. The social institutions by which this was accomplished were the encouragement of the Mission System, which established a number of Catholic missions a day's journey apart. Once the native people were brought to the missions, they were incorporated into a mission society and indoctrinated in the teachings of Catholicism. The Presidios were fortresses that were constructed to protect Spanish interests and the communities from invaders. The Pueblos were small civilian communities that attracted settlers with the gift of land, seed, and farming equipment. The function of the Pueblos was to produce food for the missions and for the presidios

7.   **Which of the following was not one of the events leading to the Revolutionary War? (Average) (Skill 1.6)**

   A. Stamp Act

   B. Quartering Act

   C. Sugar Act

   D. Monroe Doctrine

Answer: D Monroe Doctrine

The (A) Stamp Act placed a tax on newspapers and other items. The (B) Quartering Act required the colonists to house British troops in their homes. The (C) Sugar Act placed a tax on molasses. The (D) Monroe Doctrine did not occur until 1823 when the President declared that any attempts at other countries trying to establish colonies in the Americas would be seen as a threat.

8.   **France decided in 1777 to help the American colonies in their war against Britain. This decision was based on: (Rigorous) (Skill 1.6)**

   A. The naval victory of John Paul Jones over the British ship "Serapis"

   B. The survival of the terrible winter at Valley Forge

   C. The success of colonial guerilla fighters in the South

   D. The defeat of the British at Saratoga

Answer: D. The defeat of the British at Saratoga

The defeat of the British at Saratoga was the overwhelming factor in the Franco-American alliance of 1777 that helped the American colonies defeat the British. Some historians believe that without the Franco-American alliance, the American Colonies would not have been able to defeat the British and American would have remained a British colony.

9. **There is no doubt of the vast improvement of the U.S. Constitution over the weak Articles of Confederation. Which one of the four statements below is not a description of the document? (Rigorous) (Skill 1.7)**

   A. The establishment of a strong central government in no way lessened or weakened the individual states

   B. Individual rights were protected and secured

   C. The Constitution demands unquestioned respect and subservience to the federal government by all states and citizens

   D. Its flexibility and adaptation to change gives it a sense of timelessness

Answer: C. The Constitution demands unquestioned respect and subservience to the federal government by all states and citizens

The U.S. Constitution was indeed a vast improvement over the Articles of Confederation and the authors of the document took great care to assure longevity. It clearly stated that the establishment of a strong central government in no way lessened or weakened the individual states. In the Bill of Rights, citizens were assured that individual rights were protected and secured. Possibly the most important feature of the new Constitution was its flexibility and adaptation to change which assured longevity.

Therefore, the only statement made that doesn't describe some facet of the Constitution is "The Constitution demands unquestioned respect and subservience to the federal government by all states and citizens". On the contrary, the Constitution made sure that citizens could critique and make changes to their government and encourages such critiques and changes as necessary for the preservation of democracy.

10.   The Federalists: (Rigorous) (Skill 2.1)

A. Favored state's rights

B. Favored a weak central government

C. Favored a strong federal government

D. Supported the British

Answer: C. Favored a strong federal government

The Federalists were opposed to (A) state's rights and a (B) weak federal government. (D) Most of them opposed the British. (C) The Federalists favored a strong federal government.

11.   Under the brand new Constitution, the most urgent of the many problems facing the new federal government was that of: (Average) (Skill 2.2)

A. Maintaining a strong army and navy

B. Establishing a strong foreign policy

C. Raising money to pay salaries and war debts

D. Setting up courts, passing federal laws, and providing for law enforcement officers

Answer: C. Raising money to pay salaries and war debts

Maintaining strong military forces, establishment of a strong foreign policy, and setting up a justice system were important problems facing the United States under the newly ratified Constitution. However, the most important and pressing issue was how to raise money to pay salaries and war debts from the Revolutionary War. Alexander Hamilton then Secretary of the Treasury proposed increased tariffs and taxes on products such as liquor. This money would be used to pay off war debts and to pay for internal programs. Hamilton also proposed the idea of a National Bank.

12. **Which one of the following was not a reason why the United States went to war with Great Britain in 1812? (Rigorous) (Skill 2.2)**

   A. Resentment by Spain over the sale, exploration, and settlement of the Louisiana Territory

   B. The westward movement of farmers because of the need for more land

   C. Canadian fur traders were agitating the northwestern Indians to fight American expansion

   D. Britain continued to seize American ships on the high seas and force American seamen to serve aboard British ships

Answer: A. Resentment by Spain over the sale, exploration, and settlement of the Louisiana Territory

The United States went to war with Great Britain in 1812 for a number of reasons including the expansion of settlers westward and the need for more land, the agitation of Indians by Canadian fur traders in eastern Canada, and the continued seizures of American ships by the British on the high seas. Therefore, the only statement given that was not a reason for the War of 1812 was the resentment by Spain over the sale, exploration and settlement of the Louisiana Territory. In fact, the Spanish continually held more hostility towards the British than towards the United States.

13. **Which one of the following events did not occur during the period known as the "Era of Good Feeling"?** (Average) (Skill 2.2)

A. President Monroe issued the Monroe Doctrine

B. Spain ceded Florida to the United States

C. The building of the National Road

D. The charter of the second Bank of the United States

Answer: A. President Monroe issued the Monroe Doctrine

The so-called "Era of Good Feeling" describes the period following the War of 1812. This was under President James Madison and focused the nation on internal national improvements such as the building of the second national bank and construction of new roads, as well as the Treaty of Ghent, ending the War of 1812 and forcing Spain to cede Florida to the United States. The Monroe Doctrine (1823), which called for an end to any European occupation and colonization in the Americas, came after the "Era of Good Feeling."

14. **From about 1870 to 1900, the last settlement of America's "last frontier", the West, was completed. One attraction for settlers was free land but it would have been to no avail without:** (Easy) (Skill 2.3)

A. Better farming methods and technology

B. Surveying to set boundaries

C. Immigrants and others to see new lands

D. The railroad to get them there

Answer: D. The railroad to get them there

From about 1870 to 1900, the settlement for America's "last frontier" in the West was made possible by the building of the railroad. Without the railroad, the settlers never could have traveled such distances in an efficient manner.

15,   **The belief that the United States should control all of North America was called: (Easy) (Skill 2.3)**

A. Westward Expansion

B. Manifest Destiny

C. Pan Americanism

D. Nationalism

Answer: B. Manifest Destiny

The belief that the United States should control all of North America was called (B) Manifest Destiny. This idea fueled much of the violence and aggression towards those already occupying the lands such as the Native Americans. Manifest Destiny was certainly driven by sentiments of (D) nationalism and gave rise to (A) westward expansion.

16.   **As a result of the Missouri Compromise:
(Average) (Skill 2.4)**

A. Slavery was not allowed in the Louisiana Purchase

B. The Louisiana Purchase was nullified

C. Louisiana separated from the Union

D. The Embargo Act was repealed

Answer: A. Slavery was not allowed in the Louisiana Purchase

The Missouri Compromise was the agreement that eventually allowed Missouri to enter the Union. It did not nullify (B) the Louisiana Purchase and (D) the Embargo Act and did not (C) separate Louisiana from the Union. (A) As a result of the Missouri Compromise slavery was specifically banned north of the boundary 36° 30'.

17. **Which Supreme Court ruling dealt with the issue of civil rights? (Average) (Skill 2.6)**

    A. Jefferson v. Madison

    B. Lincoln v. Douglas

    C. Dred Scott v. Sanford

    D. Marbury v. Madison

Answer: B. Dred Scott v. Sanford

Marbury v. Madison established the principal of judicial review. The Supreme Court ruled that it held no authority in making the decision (regarding Marbury's commission as Justice of the Peace in District of Columbia) as the Supreme Court's jurisdiction (or lack thereof) in the case, was conflicted with Article III of the Constitution. (D) The Dred Scot case is the well-know civil rights case that had to do with the rights of the slave.

18. **The term "sectionalism" refers to: (Easy) (Skill 2.6)**

    A. Different regions of the continent

    B. Issues between the North and South

    C. Different regions of the country

    D. Different groups of countries

Answer: B. Issues between the North and South

The term "sectionalism" referred to the slavery and related issues before the Civil War. The Southern economy was agricultural and used slave labor. The North was anti-slavery and industrial.

19. The principle of "popular sovereignty," allowing people in any Territory to make their own decision concerning slavery was stated by:
(Average) (Skill 2.7)

A. Henry Clay

B. Daniel Webster

C. John C. Calhoun

D. Stephen A. Douglas

Answer: D. Stephen A. Douglas

(A) Henry Clay (B) Daniel Webster were prominent Whigs whose main concern was keeping the United States one nation and were in favor of promoting what Clay called "the American System." (C) John C. Calhoun was very pro-slavery and a champion of states' rights. The principle of "popular sovereignty", in which people in each territory could make their own decisions concerning slavery, was the doctrine of (D) Stephen A. Douglas.

20. The Radical Republicans who pushed the harsh Reconstruction measures through Congress after Lincoln's death lost public and moderate Republican support when they went too far:
(Rigorous) (Skill 2.8)

A. In their efforts to impeach the President

B. By dividing ten southern states into military-controlled districts

C. By making the ten southern states give freed African-Americans the right to vote

D. Sending carpetbaggers into the South to build up support for Congressional legislation

Answer: A. In their efforts to impeach the President

The moderate Republicans were actually being drawn towards the more radical end of the Republican spectrum during Reconstruction, because many felt Andrew Johnson's policies towards the South were too soft and ran the risk of rebuilding the old system of white power and slavery. However, the radical Republicans were so frustrated that the President would make concessions to the old Southerners that they attempted to impeach him. This turned back the support that they had received from the public and from moderates.

21. **The post-Civil War years were a time of low public morality, a time of greed, graft, and dishonesty. Which one of the reasons listed would not be accurate? (Rigorous) (Skill 2.8)**

    A. The war itself because of the money and materials needed to carry on war

    B. The very rapid growth of industry and big business after the war

    C. The personal example set by President Grant

    D. Unscrupulous heads of large impersonal corporations

Answer: C. The personal example set by President Grant

The Civil War had plunged the country into debt and ultimately into a recession by the 1890s. The rapid growth of industry and big business caused a polarization of rich and poor, workers and owners. The heads of large impersonal corporations were arrogant in treating their workers inhumanely and letting morale drop to a record low. Despite accusations against his Presidency, however, Grant was an honest man who would have been a positive example.

22. **The American labor union movement started gaining new momentum: (Average) (Skill 3.2)**

    A. During the building of the railroads

    B. After 1865 with the growth of cities

    C. With the rise of industrial giants such as Carnegie and Vanderbilt

    D. During the war years of 1861-1865

Answer: B. After 1865 with the growth of cities

The American Labor Union movement had been around since the late eighteenth and early nineteenth centuries. The Labor movement began to first experience persecution by employers in the early 1800s. The American Labor Movement remained relatively ineffective until after the Civil War. In 1866, the National Labor Union was formed, pushing such issues as the eight-hour workday and new policies of immigration. This gave rise to the Knights of Labor and eventually the American Federation of Labor (AFL) in the 1890s and the Industrial Workers of the World (1905). Therefore, it was the period following the Civil War that empowered the labor movement in terms of numbers, militancy, and effectiveness.

23. **In the 1800s, the era of industrialization and growth were characterized by: (Average) (Skill 3.2)**

    A. Small firms

    B. Public ownership

    C. Worker owned enterprises

    D. Monopolies and trusts

Answer: D. Monopolies and trusts

Industrialization and business expansion was characterized by big businesses and monopolies that merged into trusts. There were few (A) small firms and there was no (B) public ownership or (C) worker owned enterprises.

24. **Historians state that the West helped to speed up the Industrial Revolution. Which one of the following statements was not a reason for this? (Rigorous) (Skill 3.3)**

    A. Food supplies for the ever-increasing urban populations came from farms in the West.

    B. A tremendous supply of gold and silver from western mines provided the capital needed to build industries.

    C. Descendants of western settlers, educated as engineers, geologists, and metallurgists in the East, returned to the West to mine the mineral resources needed for industry.

    D. Iron, copper, and other minerals from western mines were important resources in manufacturing products.

Answer: C. Descendants of western settlers, educated as engineers, geologists, and metallurgists in the East, returned to the West to mine the mineral resources needed for industry.

The West helped to speed up the Industrial Revolution in a number of important and significant ways, including providing food, gold and silver and natural resources for mining. The miners themselves, however, were typically working class and not the educated descendants of western settlers.

25. **What event triggered World War I? (Average) (Skill 3.4)**

   A. The fall of the Weimar Republic

   B. The resignation of the Czar

   C. The assassination of Austrian Archduke Ferdinand

   D. The assassination of the Czar

Answer: C. The assassination of Austrian Archduke Ferdinand

There were regional conflicts and feeling of intense nationalism prior to the outbreak of World War I. The precipitating factor was the assassination of Austrian Archduke Ferdinand and his wife while they were in Sarajevo.

26. **The Great Depression resulted from all of the following except: (Rigorous) (Skill 3.6)**

   A. Speculative investments on the stock market

   B. Uneven distribution of wealth

   C. Economic conditions in Europe

   D. Individual spending and saving patterns such as hoarding

Answer: D. Individual spending and saving patterns such as hoarding

Although the hoarding of cash happened after the Stock Market Crash of 1929, factors A, B, and C were major causes of the Great Depression. The economic conditions in Europe meant that the U.S. was lending large amounts of money, thus depleting U.S. funds.

27.   **The New Deal was: (Average) (Skill 3.6)**

A. A trade deal with England

B. A series of programs to provide relief during the Great Depression

C. A new exchange rate regime

D. A plan for tax relief

Answer: B. A series of programs to provide relief during the Great Depression

The New Deal consisted of a myriad of different programs aimed at providing relief during the Great Depression. Many of the programs were public works programs building bridges, roads and other infrastructure.

28.   **Which country was not a part of the Axis in World War II? (Easy) (Skill 3.7)**

A. Germany

B. Italy

C. Japan

D. United States

Answer: D. United States

(A) Germany, (B) Italy and (C) Japan were the member of the Axis in World War II. (D) The United States was a member of the Allies which opposed the Axis.

29.   After World War II, the United States: (Average) (Skill 3.7)

  A. Limited its involvement in European affairs

  B. Shifted foreign policy emphasis from Europe to Asia

  C. Passed significant legislation pertaining to aid to farmers and tariffs on imports

  D. Entered the greatest period of economic growth in its history

Answer: D. Entered the greatest period of economic growth in its history

After World War II, the United States, entered into the Cold War with the Soviet Union at a swift pace and attempted to contain Communism to prevent its spread across Europe. There was no significant legislation pertaining to aid to farmers and tariffs on imports. In fact, since World War II, trade has become more liberal than ever. Free trade has become the economic policy of the United States. Due to this, the United States after World War II entered the greatest period of economic growth in its history and remains a world superpower.

30.   Which country was a Cold War foe? (Easy) (Skill 4.1)

  A. Russia

  B. Brazil

  C. Canada

  D. Argentina

Answer: A. Russia

Russia is the country that was a Cold War superpower and foe of the United States in its determination to fight the spread of Communism.

31.   **Which one of the following was not a post World War II organization? (Average) (Skill 4.2)**

A. Monroe Doctrine

B. Marshall Plan

C. Warsaw Pact

D. North Atlantic Treaty Organization

Answer: A. Monroe Doctrine

(B) The Marshall Plan provided funds for the reconstruction of Europe after World War II. (C) The Warsaw Pact and (D) NATO were both organizations that came into being for defense purpose. The Warsaw Pact was for the defense of Eastern Europe and NATO was for the defense of Western Europe. (A) The Monroe Doctrine was a nineteenth century agreement in which the United States was committed to defend all countries in the hemisphere.

32.   **Which of the following is not a name associated with the Civil Rights movement? (Average) (Skill 4.3)**

A. Rosa Parks

B. Emmett Till

C. Tom Dewey

D. Martin Luther King, Jr.

Answer: C. Tom Dewey

(A) Rosa Parks was the black lady who wouldn't move to the back of the bus. (B) Emmett Till was the civil rights worked who was killed. (C) Martin Luther King, Jr. was a Civil Rights leader. (C) Tom Dewey was never involved in the Civil Rights movement.

33.   **Which of the following women was not a part of the women's rights movement? (Easy) (Skill 4.3)**

  A. Elizabeth Cady Stanton

  B. Lucretia Borgia

  C. Lucretia Mott

  D. Susan B. Anthony

Answer: B. Lucretia Borgia

Although many women worked hard in the early nineteenth century to make gains in medicine, writing, and temperance movements, the names associated with the women's rights movement are (A) Elizabeth Cady Stanton, (C) Lucretia Mott and (D) Susan B. Anthony. (B) Lucretia Borgia is not a name associated with women's rights.

34.   **What conflict brought the United States and the Soviet Union to the brink of war in 1962? (Average) (Skill 4.4)**

  A. Cuban Missile Crisis

  B. Viet Nam war

  C. Crisis in Brazil

  D. Crisis in India

Answer: A. Cuban Missile Crisis

In 1962, the Russian were installing nuclear missiles in Cuba to prevent another U.S. invasion. The missiles were detected by U.S. reconnaissance flights and the U.S. quarantined Russian ships to prevent them from reaching Cuba. The Russian ships turned back and averted further conflict.

35. On the spectrum of American politics the label that most accurately describes voters to the "right of center" is: (Easy) (Skill 4.4)

   A. Moderates

   B. Liberals

   C. Conservatives

   D. Socialists

Answer: C. Conservatives

(A) Moderates are considered voters who teeter on the line of political centrality or drift slightly to the left or right. (B) Liberals are voters who stand on the left of center. (C) Conservative voters are those who are "right of center." (D) Socialists would land far to the left on the political spectrum of America.

36. A major factor that contributed to the technological growth of the last 50 years is: (Average) (Skill 4.5)

   A. The development of the microchip

   B. The accessibility of personal computers

   C. The increased infrastructure of electrical power plants

   D. The global satellite system

Answer: A. The development of the microchip

The development of the microchip has made personal computers and global satellite systems common features in today's environment. Electrical power plant development has been a corollary, not a contributor, to the technological growth of recent years.

37.   **Globalization: (Average) (Skill 4.6)**

   A. Is inherently good for the U.S. economy overall in spite of recent downturns

   B. Has resulted from U.S. technological developments

   C. Refers to the complex interaction and interdependence of nations around the world

   D. Has been negative for the U.S. during the recent 2008-2009 recession

Answer: C. Refers to the complex interaction and interdependence of nations around the world

Although globalization has grown as a result of technological advancements, it is not solely due to developments in the U.S. but rather to those around the world. It is not possible to make broad generalizations about whether globalization is good or bad; it is simply part of the reality of the 20th and 21 centuries, affecting not only economics, but science and medicine, ecology, customs and beliefs, business practices, education and more – in short, all facets of American life.

38.   **Which of the following best characterizes the native people of the state of Washington? (Rigorous) (Skill 5.1)**

   A. They came from two main tribes, divided by the Cascade Mountains

   B. They were primarily fishers living in longhouses in the west, and hunter-gathers who traveled a large territory in the eastern part of the state

   C. They consisted of 35-40 different tribes, all of whom had quite different lifestyles and cultures

   D. They were unique to the state of Washington, sharing little similarity to other tribes in the northwest

Answer: B They were primarily fishers and trappers living in longhouses in the west, but were hunter-gathers who traveled a large territory in the east.

The 35-40 tribes living in what is now the state of Washington had many commonalities with Indians across the northwest U.S. and southwest Canada. They did have different cultures, but with many overlapping features, as seen by the difference in the tribes to the west of the Cascades and those in the eastern plains.

39. **By the 1880s, which of the following statements is most accurate: (Rigorous) (Skill 5.2)**

A. Most Indian tribes were living in peaceful settlements amidst the growing numbers of white and Asian settlers.

B. Chinese and Scandinavian immigrants constituted the largest ethnic groups in the area due to the need for unskilled labor for building railroads.

C. There was very little discrimination in early Washington, as the state was a mix of people from all over, as well as having large numbers of Indians.

D. Most of the Indians land had been taken by white settlers, and most tribes were living on reservations.

Answer: D. Most of the Indians land had been taken by white settlers, and most tribes were living on reservations.

Although Chinese and Scandinavian immigrants did come to Washington in large numbers, they were still outnumbered by the white settlers. The white settlers felt the land was theirs, and often discriminated against the native people, Asian immigrants, Blacks, and others who came to the region.

40. **The Grand Coulee Dam, a New Deal Project, contributed to which of the following industries during and after World War II: (Average) (Skill 5.3)**

A. Agriculture, aluminum processing, and airplane building

B. Agriculture

C. Aluminum processing

D. Airplane building

Answer: A Agriculture, aluminum processing, and airplane building

The dam, built to aid irrigation in the eastern part of the state, also brought cheap electricity to Washington, which in turn spawned the plants that processed bauxite ore intro aluminum. The presence of aluminum plants attracted Boeing to build plants for constructing airplanes. So, all three industries benefited from the Grand Coulee Dam project.

41.   **The Hanford Nuclear Plant: (Average) (Skill 5.4)**

    A. Was originally built to make plutonium during World War II and was never shut down

    B. Closed in 1988, and was found to have leaked hazardous waste

    C. Was built in 1966 as a nuclear power plant to make electricity

    D. Is one of the cleanest nuclear power plants operating today

Answer: B Closed in 1988, and was found to have leaked hazardous waste

Although Hanford was originally built to make plutonium, it was converted to generate electricity in 1966. It was discovered in the late 1980s and early 1990s that there were hazardous waste leaks and contamination exposure to people living downwind from the plant.

42.   **The Fertile Crescent was bounded by all of the following except: (Rigorous) (Skill 6.1)**

    A. Mediterranean Sea

    B. Arabian Desert

    C. Taurus Mountains

    D. Ural Mountains

Answer: D. Ural Mountains

The Mediterranean Sea forms the Western border of the Fertile Crescent, the Arabian Desert is the Southern boundary and the Taurus Mountains form the Northern boundary. The Ural Mountains are further North in Russia and form the border between Russia and Europe.

43.   The end to hunting, gathering, and fishing of prehistoric people was
        due to: (Average) (Skill 6.1)

        A. Domestication of animals

        B. Building crude huts and houses

        C. Development of agriculture

        D. Organized government in villages

Answer: C. Development of agriculture

Although the domestication of animals, the building of huts and houses and the
first organized governments were all very important steps made by early
civilizations, it was the development of agriculture that ended the once dominant
practices of hunting, gathering, and fishing among prehistoric people. The
development of agriculture provided a more efficient use of time and for the first
time a surplus of food. This greatly improved the quality of life and contributed to
early population growth.

44.   Bathtubs, hot and cold running water, and sewage systems with
        flush toilets were developed by the: (Average) (Skill 6.2)

        A. Minoans

        B. Mycenaeans

        C. Phoenicians

        D. Greeks

Answer: A. Minoans

Both the (A) Minoans on Crete and the (B) Mycenaeans on the mainland of
Greece flourished from about 1600 B.C. to about 1400 B.C. However, it was the
Minoans on Crete that are best known for their advanced ancient civilization in
which such advances as bathtubs, hot and cold running water, sewage systems
and flush toilets were developed. The (C) Phoenicians created an alphabet that
has still considerable influence in the world today. The great developments of the
(D) Greeks were primarily in the fields of philosophy, political science, and early
ideas of democracy.

45.   The principle of zero in mathematics is the discovery of the ancient civilization found in: (Rigorous) (Skill 6.2)

   A. Egypt

   B. Persia

   C. India

   D. Babylon

Answer: **C. India**

Although the Egyptians practiced algebra and geometry, the Persians developed an alphabet, and the Babylonians developed Hammurabi's Code, which would come to be considered among the most important contributions of the Mesopotamian civilization, it was the Indians that created the idea of zero in mathematics changing drastically our ideas about numbers.

46.   Development of a solar calendar, invention of the decimal system, and contributions to the development of geometry and astronomy are all the legacy of: (Rigorous) (Skill 6.2)

   A. The Babylonians

   B. The Persians

   C. The Sumerians

   D. The Egyptians

Answer: D. The Egyptians

The (A) Babylonians of ancient Mesopotamia flourished for a time under their great contribution of organized law and code, called Hammurabi's Code (1750 B.C.), after the ruler Hammurabi. The fall of the Babylonians to the Persians in 539 B.C. made way for the warrior-driver Persian Empire that expanded from Pakistan to the Mediterranean Sea until the conquest of Alexander the Great in 331 B.C. The Sumerians of ancient Mesopotamia were most noted for their early advancements as one of the first civilizations and their contributions towards written language known as cuneiform. It was the (D) Egyptians who were the first true developers of a solar calendar, the decimal system, and made significant contributions to the development of geometry and astronomy.

47. The world religion which includes a caste system, is:
     (Average) (Skill 6.3)

     A. Buddhism

     B. Hinduism

     C. Sikhism

     D. Jainism

Answer: B. Hinduism

Buddhism, Sikhism, and Jainism all rose out of protest against Hinduism and its practices of sacrifice and the caste system. The caste system, in which people were born into castes, would determine their class for life including who they could marry, what jobs they could perform, and their overall quality of life.

48. The Roman Empire gave so much to the world, especially the
     Western world. Which of the legacies below has been most
     influential and had the most lasting effect: (Average) (Skill 6.5)

     A. The language of Latin

     B. Roman law, justice, and political system

     C. Engineering and building

     D. The writings of its poets and historians

Answer: B. Roman law, justice, and political system

It is the law, justice, and political systems of the Roman Empire that have been the most effective and influential on our Western world today. The idea of a Senate and different houses came from Rome, and their legal justice system is also the foundation of our own. Although, the Roman language was the basis for many modern languages, Latin itself has died out. Roman engineering and building, their writings and poetry have also been influential but not nearly to the degree that their government and justice systems have been.

49.   The first ancient civilization to introduce and practice monotheism
        was that of the: (Rigorous) (Skill 6.6)

        A. Sumerians

        B. Minoans

        C. Phoenicians

        D. Hebrews

Answer: D. Hebrews

The (A) Sumerians and (C) Phoenicians both practiced religions in which many
gods and goddesses were worshipped. The (B) Minoan culture shared many
religious practices with the Ancient Egyptians. It seems that the king was
somewhat of a god figure and the queen, a goddess. Much of the Minoan art
points to worship of multiple gods. Therefore, only the (D) Hebrews introduced
and fully practiced monotheism, or the belief in one God.

50.   Which one of the following is not an important legacy of the
        Byzantine Empire? (Rigorous) (Skill 6.7)

        A. It protected Western Europe from various attacks from the East by
            such groups as the Persians, Ottoman Turks, and Barbarians

        B. It played a part in preserving the literature, philosophy, and language
            of ancient Greece

        C. Its military organization was the foundation for modern armies

        D. It kept the legal traditions of Roman government, collecting and
            organizing many ancient Roman laws.

Answer: C. Its military organization was the foundation for modern armies

The Byzantine Empire (1353-1453) protected Western Europe from invaders
such as the Persians and Ottomans. It was a Christian incorporation of Greek
philosophy, language, and literature along with Roman government and law.
Therefore, although regarded as having a strong military, the Byzantine Empire is
not particularly considered a foundation for modern armies.

51.   **Which of the following is an example of a direct democracy? (Average) (Skill 6.8)**

   A. Elected representatives

   B. Greek city-states

   C. The Constitution

   D. The Confederate States

Answer: B. Greek city-states

The Greek city-states are an example of a direct democracy as their leaders were elected directly by the citizens and the citizens themselves were given voice in government. (A) Elected representatives in the United States as in the case of the presidential elections are actually elected by an electoral college that is supposed to be representative of the citizens. As we have learned from the elections of 2000, this is a flawed system. The United States Congress, the Senate, and the House of Representatives are also examples of indirect democracy as they represent the citizens in the legislature as opposed to having citizens represent themselves.

52.   **The holy book of Islam is: (Easy) (Skill 7.1)**

   A.   The Bible

   B.   The Kaaba

   C.   The Koran

   D.   The Torah

Answer: C. The Koran

The (A) Bible is the holy book of Christianity; the (D) Torah is the holy book of Judaism. The (B) Kaaba means the Circle and is in Mecca. The holy book of Islam is (C) the Koran.

53. **The difference between manorialism and feudalism was:**
    (Rigorous) (Skill 7.2)

    A. Land was owned by the noblemen in manorialism

    B. Land was owned by noblemen in both feudalism and manorialism

    C. Land was owned by the noblemen in feudalism

    D. The king owned all the land in both.

Answer: A. Land was owned by the noblemen in manorialism

The difference between feudalism and manorialism lay in who owned the land. In feudalism the land was owned by the king. In manorialism the land is owned by the noblemen.

54. **The lords of feudal Japan were known as:** **(Easy) (Skill 2.6)**

    A. Daimyo

    B. Samurai

    C. Ronin

    D. Bushido

Answer: A. Daimyo

The lords of feudal Japan were known as Daimyo (A). They had warriors, known as Samurai (B) who served them. Samurai without masters were referred to as Ronin (C). Bushido (D) was the code of conduct of the Samurai.

55. **The religious orientation of the African kingdom of Mali was: (Average) (Skill 7.4)**

A. Islamic

B. A blend of Islam and ancient African belief

C. Christian

D. A mixture of faiths, with no one faith dominating

Answer: B. A blend of Islam and ancient African belief

Although the Mali leaders converted to Islam and were responsible for spreading Islam throughout Africa, the people did not follow strict Islamic law. They drew on their traditional beliefs in many ways, including how they viewed the king as a divine ruler removed from the people.

56. **Native South American tribes included all of the following except: (Easy) (Skill 7.5)**

A. Aztec

B. Inca

C. Minoans

D. Maya

Answer: C. Minoans

The (A) Aztec were a tribe in Mexico and Central America. (B) The Inca and (D) the Maya were South American tribes. The Minoans were an early civilization but not from the Americas.

57. **In Western Europe, the achievements of the Renaissance were many. All of the following were accomplishments except: (Rigorous) (Skill 7.6)**

  A. Invention of the printing press

  B. A rekindling of interest in the learning of classical Greece & Rome

  C. Growth in literature, philosophy, and art

  D. Better military tactics

Answer: D. Better military tactics

Some of the most important developments during the Renaissance were Gutenberg's invention of the printing press and a reexamination of the ideas and philosophies of classical Greece and Rome. Also important during the Renaissance was the growth in literature, philosophy and art. Therefore, improved military tactics is the only possible answer as it was clearly not a characteristic of the Renaissance in Western Europe.

58. **Who is considered to be the most important figure in the spread of Protestantism across Switzerland? (Average) (Skill 7.7)**

  A. Calvin

  B. Zwingli

  C. Munzer

  D. Leyden

Answer: A. Calvin

While Huldreich Zwingli was the first to spread the Protestant Reformation in Switzerland around 1519, it was John Calvin and his less radical approach to Protestantism who really made the most impact in Switzerland. Calvin's ideas separated from the Lutherans over the "Lord's Supper" debate over the sacrament, and his branch of Protestants became known as Calvinism. Thomas Munzer was a German Protestant reformer whose radical and revolutionary ideas about God's will to overthrow the ruling classes and his siding with the peasantry got him beheaded. Leyden (or Leiden) was a founder of the University of Leyden, a Protestant place for study in the Netherlands.

59.   The Age of Exploration begun in the 1400s was led by:
       (Easy) (Skill 8.1)

       A. The Portuguese

       B. The Spanish

       C. The English

       D. The Dutch

Answer: A. The Portuguese

Although the Age of Exploration had many important players among them, the Dutch, Spanish and English, it was the Portuguese who sent the first explorers to the New World.

60.   Many governments in Europe today have which of the following type of government: (Average) (Skill 8.2)

       A. Absolute monarchies

       B. Constitutional governments

       C. Constitutional monarchies

       D. Another form of government

Answer: C. Constitutional monarchies

Over the centuries absolute monarchies were modified, and constitutional monarchies emerged. This form of government recognizes a monarch as leader, but invests most of the legal authority in a legislative body such as a Parliament.

61. **Studies in astronomy, skills in mapping, and other contributions to geographic knowledge came from:**
(Average) (Skill 8.3)

   A. Galileo

   B. Columbus

   C. Eratosthenes

   D. Ptolemy

Answer: D. Ptolemy

Ptolemy was active in the field of astronomy, but was also important for his contributions to the fields of mapping, mathematics, and geography. Galileo was also important in the field of astronomy but did not make the mapping and geographic contributions of Ptolemy.

62. **Karl Marx believed in:** (Average) (Skill 9.1)

   A. Free Enterprise

   B. Utopian Socialism

   C. Absolute Monarchy

   D. Scientific Socialism

Answer: D. Scientific Socialism

Marx did not believe in (A) Free Enterprise, (B) Utopian Socialism or (C) Absolute Monarchy. He believed that he applied a scientific process in his analysis and he named this Scientific Socialism.

63. **Which of the following took a scientific view of the world: (Average) (Skill 9.1)**

A. Rousseau

B. Immanuel Kant

C. Montesquieu

D. John Locke

Answer: B. Immanuel Kant

Immanuel Kant (1724-1804) was the German metaphysician and philosopher, who was a founding proponent of the idea that world organization was the means for achieving universal peace. Kant's ideas helped to found such world peace organizations as the League of Nations in the wake of World War I. He also took a scientific view of the world.

64. **The concepts of social contract and natural law were espoused by: (Rigorous)(Skill 9.1)**

A. Locke

B. Rousseau

C. Aristotle

D. Montesquieu

Answer: D. Montesquieu

The principle that "men entrusted with power tend to abuse it" is attributed to Montesquieu, the great French philosopher whose ideas based much on Locke's ideas, along with Rousseau, had a strong influence on the French Revolution of 1789. Although it would be reasonable to assume that Locke, Rousseau, and Aristotle would probably agree with the statement, all four of these men had profound impacts on the ideas of the Enlightenment, from humanism to constitutionals.

65. **One South American country quickly and easily gained independence in the 19th century from European control . This Latin American country is: (Rigorous) (Skill 9.3)**

    A. Chile

    B. Argentina

    C. Venezuela

    D. Brazil

Answer: D. Brazil

While Chile, Argentina, and Venezuela all have had histories marred by civil wars, dictatorships, and numerous violent coups during their quests for independence, Brazil experienced a more rapid independence. Independence was gained quickly and more easily than the other countries due to a bloodless revolution in 1820s that officially made Brazil a republic and the economic stability they had in place from a strong coffee and rubber based economy.

66. **Which of the following was not a leader for independence in Mexico and South America in the early 19th century? (Average) (Skill 9.3)**

    A. Joao of Brazil

    B. Francisco de Miranda

    C. Miguel Hidalgo

    D. Simon Bolivar

Answer: A. Joao of Brazil

Joao of Brazil was the son of Queen Maria of Portugal. He was the Prince Regent of Brazil, still a colony of Portugal. His son Pedro rebelled and declared independence for Brazil, establishing himself as the first emperor. Francisco de Miranda, Miguel Hidalgo and Simon Bolivar were all advocates of independence from colonial powers.

67. **Which of the following was not a factor contributing to the Agricultural Revolution? (Average) (Skill 9.4)**

A. Steam-powered tractors

B. Depletion of farmland

C. Crop rotation

D. Soil enrichment

Answer: B. Depletion of farmland

Steam-powered tractors increased crop production, as did the scientific practices of crop rotation and soil enrichment. All three were part of the Agricultural Revolution, along with improved irrigation and harvesting methods.

68. **The Baroque period is characterized by all of the following except: (Rigorous) (Skill 9.5)**

A. Ornamentation

B. Chiaroscuro

C. Religiosity

D. Dramatic flair

Answer: C. Religiosity

Although many pieces of music, especially, were grounded in religious expression and ideas, the Baroque style is not noted for being religious, per se. Dramatic storytelling, sensational shifts from light to dark (chiaroscuro) and from soft to loud), and fancy ornamentation all describe the Baroque style in art, music and architecture.

69. **Colonial expansion by Western European powers in the 18th and 19th centuries was due primarily to: (Average) (Skill 9.6)**

    A. Building and opening the Suez Canal

    B. The Industrial Revolution

    C. Marked improvements in transportation

    D. Complete independence of all the Americas and loss of European domination and influence

Answer: B. The Industrial Revolution

Colonial expansion by Western European powers in the late eighteenth and nineteenth centuries was due primarily to the Industrial Revolution in Great Britain that spread across Europe and needed new natural resources and therefore, new locations from which to extract the raw materials needed to feed the new industries.

70. **Nineteenth century imperialism by Western Europe nations had important and far-reaching effects on the colonial peoples they ruled. All four of the following are the results of this. Which one was the most important and had lasting effects on key 20th century events? (Rigorous) (Skill 9.6)**

    A. Local wars were ended

    B. Living standards were raised

    C. Demands for self-government and feelings of nationalism surfaced

    D. Economic developments occurred

Answer: C. Demands for self-government and feelings of nationalism surfaced

The nineteenth century imperialism by Western European nations had some very serious and far-reaching effects. However, both World War I and World War II were caused to a large degree by the rise of nationalist sentiment across Europe and Asia. Nationalism has also fueled numerous liberation movements and revolutionary movements across the globe from Central and South America to the South Pacific to Africa and Asia.

71.   **Of all the major causes of both World Wars I and II, the most significant one is considered to be: (Easy) (Skill 11.1)**

   A. Extreme nationalism

   B. Military buildup and aggression

   C. Political unrest

   D. Agreements and alliances

Answer: A. Extreme nationalism

Although military buildup and aggression, political unrest, and agreements and alliances were all characteristic of the world climate before and during World War I and World War II, the most significant cause of both wars was extreme nationalism. Nationalism is the idea that the interests and needs of a particular nation are of the utmost and primary importance above all else. The nationalism that sparked WWI included a rejection of German, Austro-Hungarian, and Ottoman imperialism by Serbs, Slavs and others culminating in the assassination of Archduke Ferdinand by a Serb nationalist in 1914. Following WWI and the Treaty of Versailles, many Germans and others in the Central Alliance Nations, malcontent at the concessions and reparations of the treaty started a new form of nationalism. Adolf Hitler and the Nazi regime led this extreme nationalism. Hitler's ideas were an example of extreme, oppressive nationalism combined with political, social and economic scapegoating, all of which combined were the primary cause of WWII.

72.   **Which of the following forms of warfare introduced during World War I was later banned? (Easy) (Skill 10.1)**

   A. Machine guns

   B. Flame throwers

   C. Poison gas

   D. Tanks

Answer: C. Poison gas

Although all these forms of warfare were introduced for the first time during World War I, only poison gas was banned after the war.

73. **Which did not contribute to the 1917 Revolution in Russia? (Easy) (Skill 10.2)**

   A. World War I

   B. Worker strikes

   C. Starving peasants

   D. Promise of aid from Germany

Answer: D. Promise of aid from Germany

At the time of the 1917 Revolution, (A) World War I was in progress taking a heavy toll of the Russians. The (C) peasants were starving and there were (B) many worker strikes. There was no such thing as the (D) promise of aid from Germany.

74. **Which f the following best describes a fascist regime? (Rigorous) (Skill 10.3)**

   A. Anti-communist

   B. Rigidly controlling

   C. Pro-socialist

   D. Concerned with oppressed peoples

Answer: B. Rigidly controlling

Fascism, though at times it has grown out of socialist movements, crushes all political parties on both the right and left, and seeks to regulate both labor and capital. It is interested only in maintaining governmental control, using class conflict and nationalism as vehicles to achieving and retaining power.

75. **A well known World War II figure who was the leader of Italy was: (Easy) (Skill 10.4)**

    A. Hitler

    B. Stalin

    C. Tojo

    D. Mussolini

Answer: D. Mussolini

(A) Adolf Hitler, the Nazi leader of Germany, and (C) Hideki Tojo, the Japanese General and Prime Minister, were well known World War II figures who led Axis forces into war on a quest of spreading fascism. (B) Joseph Stalin was the Communist Russian head of state during World War II. Although all three were repressive in their actions, it was (D) Benito Mussolini, the Fascist and widely-considered incompetent leader of Italy during World War II, who once said "democracy was like a rotting corpse that had to be replaced by a superior way of life and more efficient government".

76. **Which one of the following would not be considered a result of World War II? (Rigorous) (Skill 10.4)**

    A. Economic depressions and slow resumption of trade and financial aid

    B. Western Europe was no longer the center of world power

    C. The beginnings of new power struggles not only in Europe also Asia

    D. Territorial and boundary changes for many nations, especially in Europe

Answer: A. Economic depressions and slow resumption of trade and financial aid

Following World War II, the economy was vibrant and flourished from the stimulant of war and an increased dependence of the world on United States industries. Therefore, World War II didn't result in economic depressions and slow resumption of trade and financial aid. Western Europe was no longer the center of world power. New power struggles arose in Europe and Asia and many European nations underwent changing territories and boundaries.

77. **The international organization established to work for world peace at the end of the Second World War is the: (Average) (Skill 10.4)**

   A. League of Nations

   B. United Federation of Nations

   C. United Nations

   D. United World League

Answer: C.   United Nations

The international organization established to work for world peace at the end of the Second World War was the United Nations. From the ashes of the failed League of Nations, established following World War I, the United Nations continues to be a major player in world affairs today.

78. **Which of the following was not an element of the Cold War? (Rigorous) (Skill 10.5)**

   A. Iron Curtain

   B. Glasnost

   C. Arms Race

   D. Economic blockades

Answer: B. Glasnost

The Iron Curtain (an ideological, symbolic and physical division between West and East in Europe), the buildup of nuclear and conventional arms by both the U.S. and the Soviet Union, and economic blockades between Communist and non-Communist countries were all part of the Cold War which existed between 1947 to 1991, when the Soviet Union collapsed. Glasnost was the term Soviet leader Gorbachev gave to the new openness and sense of freedom, including freedom of information, in the Soviet Union toward the end of its regime in the mid 1980s. Although it occurred while the Cold War was still in effect, it was actually one of the elements that ended the Cold War.

79. **Nationalism can be defined as the division of land and resources according to which of the following: (Rigorous) (Skill 10.6)**

    A. Religion, race, or political ideology

    B. Religion, race, or gender

    C. Historical boundaries, religion, or race

    D. Race, gender, or political ideology

Answer: A. Religion, race, or political ideology

Religion, race and political ideology are some of the characteristics which determine a national entity. Tribal membership, language, ethnic affiliation, and even treaty demarcations can dictate national boundaries. Historical boundaries may contribute to conflicts among peoples, but they are generally secondary to a another affiliation. To date, gender has not been a determining factor, although the treatment of women, for example, may be a contributing factor to some nationalistic conflicts.

80. **Globalization in the 21st century means that: (Average) (Skill 10.7)**

    A. Few countries or cultures operate in isolation any more

    B. Nationalism has major political, economic, and human ramifications

    C. Neither A or B

    D. Both A and B

Answer: D. Both A and B

Nearly all cultures are impacted by other civilizations today. Nationalism is a challenge, as many people struggle to maintain pride and encourage the health and wealth of their countries while still competing on the global market and cooperating with other countries on many cultural, educational, scientific and human rights endeavors.

81. **The study of past human cultures based on physical artifacts is: (Average) (Skill 11.1)**

    A. History

    B. Anthropology

    C. Cultural Geography

    D. Archaeology

Answer: D. Archaeology

Archaeology is the study of past human cultures based on physical artifacts such as fossils, carvings, paintings, and engraved writings.

82. **The study of the social behavior of minority groups would be in the area of: (Average Rigor) (Skill 11.1)**

    A. Anthropology

    B. Psychology

    C. Sociology

    D. Cultural Geography

Answer: C. Sociology

The study of social behavior in minority groups would be primarily in the area of Sociology, as it is the discipline most concerned with social interaction and being. However, it could be argued that Anthropology, Psychology, and Cultural Geography could have some interest in the study as well.

83. **"Participant observation" is a method of study most closely associated with and used in: (Rigorous) (Skill 11.1)**

    A. Anthropology

    B. Archaeology

    C. Sociology

    D. Political science

Answer: A. Anthropology

"Participant observation" is a method of study most closely associated with and used in (A) anthropology or the study of current human cultures. (B) Archaeologists typically the study of the remains of people, animals or other physical things. (C) Sociology is the study of human society and usually consists of surveys, controlled experiments, and field studies. (D) Political science is the study of political life including justice, freedom, power and equality in a variety of methods.

84. **The study of a people's language and writing would be part of all of the following except: (Rigorous) (Skill 11.1)**

    A. Sociology

    B. Archaeology

    C. History

    D. Geography

Answer: A. Sociology

The study of a people's language and writing would be a part of studies in the disciplines of sociology (study of social interaction and organization), archaeology, (study of ancient artifacts including written works), and history (the study of the past). Language and writing would be less important to geography that tends to focus more on locations and spatial relations than on the people in those regions and their languages or writings.

85. **Divisions of time in history (periodizations) may be determined by all but which of the following: (Easy) (Skill 11.2)**

    A. Date

    B. Geography

    C. Cultural advances

    D. Individual historians

Answer: D. Individual historians

While there are obvious examples for the first three answers (1500's, Roman Era, Renaissance), historians themselves, no matter how much they may contribute to our understanding of an era, did not generally live in it nor are representative of it. Consequently, though some eras are named for individuals (Victorian Era), these are not historians.

86. **Which of the following is not one of the schools of narrative history? (Rigorous) (Skill 11.3)**

    A. Comparative Sociological

    B. Economic

    C. Intellectual

    D. Political-Institutional

Answer: A. Comparative Sociological

The narrative history approach attempts to provide a general account of the most important things people have said, done, written, etc. in the past. Some scholars feel that what happened in economic terms (B), or the ideas (C) or the politics and laws (D) of a period are most important. Sociology is generally concerned with contemporary society and in any event would be more interested in people's interactions than trying to form a narrative from past sources.

87.   **In addition to the narrative school, which of the following is also an approach used by historians: (Easy) (Skill 11.3)**

    A. Anecdotal

    B. Biography

    C. Conflict-based

    D. Summative

Answer: B. Biography

Some historians use biography (the study of a person's life) as a way of understanding history. Biography may or may not utilize a psychological orientation.

88.   **Which of the following is not part of the scientific method? (Rigorous) (Skill 12.1)**

    A. Identifying sources of material

    B. Formulating a hypothesis

    C. Testing the hypothesis

    D. Stating a research question

Answer: A. Identifying sources of material

Although identifying data sources is part of the process of scientific inquiry, it is not a fundamental element of the scientific method.

89.   **Which of the following best describes an argumentative research paper: (Rigorous) (Skill 12.1)**

A. Understanding various parts of a research topic

B. Using the research question to investigate a hypothesis

C. Providing a clear discussion of all pertinent data

D. Presenting research to prove an interpretation

Answer: D. Presenting research to prove an interpretation

A, B, and C are all elements of analytic research papers. Only option D is consistent with an argumentative paper.

90.   **Which of the following is not a common source of historical data? (Rigorous) (Skill 12.2)**

A. Autobiographies

B. Archival materials from labor unions

C. Technical manuals

D. Novels

Answer: C. Technical manuals

Technical manuals may offer some historical data, but they are less likely than the other sources listed to provide historical data. When utilizing novels as a source of historical information, care must be taken to do further research to determine what is based on actual fact and what is fiction.

91. **Which of the following is not one of the characteristics of primary sources? (Average) (Skill 12.3)**

   A. Qualitative data

   B. Specific focus and/or detail

   C. Analysis in light of current theories

   D. Quantitative data

Answer: C. Analysis in light of current theories

Primary sources generally offer a specific focus and varying degrees of detail. The data can be qualitative or quantitative, depending on the nature of the document. However, primary source data do not contain analyses utilizing current theories related to the topic.

92. **Which of the following does NOT describe possible limitations of secondary sources? (Average) (Skill 12.3)**

   A. Bias on the part of the author

   B. Eyewitness descriptions of an historical event

   C. Inferences by the author

   D. Personal analysis of an historical event

Answer: B. Eyewitness descriptions of an historical event

An eyewitness account is not a secondary source, therefore would not be a limitation related to secondary sources. Bias, inference and analysis can all be possible limitations in using some secondary sources.

93. **Which of the following would not be considered a primary source? (Rigorous) (Skill 12.3)**

   A. An 1863 newspaper account of the Gettysburg Address

   B. The text of the Gettysburg Address

   C. A historical analysis of the Gettysburg Address

   D. A narrative account of the Gettysburg Address from a spectator in the crowd.

Answer: C. A historical analysis of the Gettysburg Address

All of the other answers are considered first-hand accounts of Lincoln's speech, or the speech itself. Therefore only (C), the second-hand analysis, is not a primary source.

94. **Which of the following is not an example of an historical theme? (Average) (Skill 13.1)**

   A. Epochs and eras

   B. Race and ethnicity

   C. Politics

   D. Civil Rights

Answer: A. Epochs and eras

Epochs and area are examples of periodization, where history is divided into time periods. They are not historical themes.

95. **Which of the following is not a reason that historical themes are a useful form of analysis in historical research and reporting: (Rigorous) (Skill 13.1)**

    A. There are multiple recurrences throughout history

    B. They hone in on the most accurate perspective

    C. There are opportunities for comparison

    D. They offer multiple viewpoints

Answer: B. They hone in on the most accurate perspective

The value of using historical themes as a tool for analysis in the study of history is that it looks at events and people in a large context, thereby providing multiple perspectives and enhanced understanding. The goal is not to hone in on the "most accurate" perspective or in isolation, but rather the opposite: to view events in a multi-layered fashion.

96. **In making an argument against a new high school math curriculum under consideration, a speaker praises a recent decision by the superintendent to retain the elementary social studies curriculum implemented last year. This is an example of which type of misleading reasoning? (Rigorous) (Skill 13.2)**

    A. Red herring

    B. Either/or fallacy

    C. Appeal to tradition

    D. Jumping on the bandwagon

Answer: A. Red herring

Although all of the options are forms of misleading reasoning, the primary use here is the "red herring," which distracts the listeners away from the topic at hand. The speaker might then move to an appeal to tradition or jumping on the bandwagon – "let's keep everything the same." But at this point, mentioning the decision about the social studies curriculum merely serves to distract from the issue, which is the new math curriculum.

97. **Which of the following is not an example of inadequate reasoning? (Rigorous) (Skill 13.2)**

    A. Faulty analogy

    B. Jumping to conclusions

    C. False causation

    D. False dilemma

Answer: D. False dilemma

A false dilemma creates a sense that there are only two options. This is an example of misleading reasoning, not inadequate reasoning. Inadequate reasoning involves coming to false conclusions, using faulty data or analogies, and not having enough information to reach a conclusion. Inadequate reasoning is not intended to mislead, though it can have that effect.

98. **Historians and social scientists utilize all but which of the following in analyzing data: (Average) (Skill 13.3)**

    A. Measures of central tendency

    B. Bias

    C. Demographics

    D. Vital statistics

Answer: B. Bias

Bias is not utilized to analyze data but can be a confounding factor in analyzing data. It can occur in sample selection, choices of measures used, how the methods are implemented and how the data are analyzed.

99.   **Which measure of central tendency describes the observation that is repeated most often? (Rigorous) (Skill 13.3)**

A. Median

B. Mean

C. Average

D. Mode

Answer: D. Mode

The median is the middle score of all observations. The mean (or average) is found by adding all observations and dividing by the number of observations. The mode is the one that occurs most often.

100.   **Which of the following is most useful in showing differences in variables at a specific point in time? (Average) (Skill 13.4)**

A. Histogram

B. Scatter plots

C. Pie chart

D. Bar graph

Answer: D. Bar graph

Bar graphs are simple and basic, showing a difference in variables at a specific point in time. Histograms are good for summarizing large sets of data into intervals. Pie charts show proportions well and scatter plots demonstrate correlations, or relationships between variables.

101. **Which of the following is needed in order to understand the historical significance of a poster? (Average) (Skill 13.4)**

   A. The artist's background

   B. The political orientation of the artist

   C. The context in which the poster was made

   D. How color and shape relate to historical periods

Answer: C. The context in which the poster was made

Understanding the context of a poster – the events surrounding it, what prompted the particular words and graphics, the social and political implications of the words and graphics, key historical events of the period – is often necessary to grasp the meaning of the poster.

102. **Which of the following is not an example of a visual representation of historical information? (Average) (Skill 13.4)**

   A. Cartoon

   B. Poem

   C. Map

   D. Circle graph

Answer: B. Poem

Although in rare cases, poems may offer graphical information, largely they consist of written words. Visual forms of historical information come in many forms, including newspaper ads, graphs and charts, political cartoons, illustrations and photographs and more.

103. **An historian using the lens of the women's movement through which to view the 19th century might get a different perspective on which of the following: (Easy) (Skill 13.5)**

   A. The Civil War

   B. The suffrage movement

   C. National politics

   D. All of the above

Answer: D. All of the above

Social movements, like other phenomena with a specific set of values and beliefs, can impact the way history is viewed. This perspective is not limited to the issues that may seem most obvious to the particular movement, but are relevant to the entire period of history.

104. **A synthesis of historical information requires all of the following except: (Rigorous) (Skill 14.1)**

   A. Understanding the content that is included in the synthesis

   B. Documenting the backgrounds of the various historians whose work is included in the synthesis

   C. Documenting the source of information included in the synthesis

   D. Differentiating the writer's ideas from those of others included in the synthesis

Answer: B. Documenting the backgrounds of the historians whose work is included in the synthesis

There may be circumstances in which the background of the historians has relevance to the synthesis. However, most of the time, the other options are more important in writing and effective and accurate synthesis of historical research.

105. **Using graphics can enhance the presentation of social science information because: (Average) (Skill 14.2)**

    A. They can explain complex relationships among various data points

    B. Charts and graphs summarize information well

    C. Most social science information is boring without visual information

    D. Maps can describe geographic distribution of historical information

Answer: C. Most social science information is boring without visual information

Social science reporting can be interesting and exciting without graphics, however, visual presentations can aid in bringing the data to life.

106. **Which of the following is not a potential problem in using graphics to present historical information? (Average) (Skill 14.2)**

    A. Use of graphics to summarize key points

    B. Copyright infringement

    C. Unintended offensive connotations

    D. Lack of clarity

Answer: A. Use of graphics to summarize key points

Graphics can be a great way to summarize information. Problems can occur if images or other elements are copyrighted and permission is not received for use, there is a lack of clarity in the graphic, or there are unintended connotations or suggestions.

107. **Which of the following is not an example of a good communication practice? (Average) (Skill 14.3)**

   A. Make eye contact when speaking

   B. Organize your information in a logical manner

   C. Assess your audience before you begin speaking

   D. Use repetitive movements to emphasize a point

Answer: D. Use repetitive movements to emphasize a point

Repetitive movements tend to be a distraction. Avoid them whenever possible.

108. **In a written report, try to avoid which of the following? (Average) (Skill 14.3)**

   A. Including a formal introduction

   B. Making your points explicit

   C. Using jargon to express familiarity with a subject

   D. Providing a summary of the main points

Answer: C. Using jargon to express familiarity with a subject

Jargon rarely serves a useful purpose. Avoid it whenever possible, and when it is used, explain any special terms in plain English so the reader can easily follow your points.

109. **When researchers reach different conclusions using similar data, it is usually because:** (Average) (Skill 14.4)

    A. Some researchers aren't as diligent as others

    B. Historians have different perspectives and orientations that impact the outcome of their work

    C. They had poor training and education

    D. They used bad sources

Answer: B. Historians have different perspectives and orientations that impact the outcome of their work

Although poor training, inadequate research methods, bad sources and a lack of diligence can contribute to bad research results, outcome differences among researchers are generally related to different perspectives and different starting points. .

110. **Which of the following is not an example of a collaborative problem-solving approach?** (Easy) (Skill 14.1)

    A. Repeating your own ideas

    B. Asking another person to explain her perspective

    C. Finding shared values or beliefs with others

    D. Agreeing to disagree

Answer: A. Repeating your own ideas

In general, repeating your own ideas will not invite others to engage in useful dialogue with you about a disputed topic. It sends a message that you think your ideas are the best or the only viable approach, or that your ideas haven't been heard. It is more effective to be inviting and curious, and listen to others. Sometimes, later in the discussion it will become clear if there is a need to reiterate something you said earlier.

XAMonline, INC. 25 First St. Suite 106 Cambridge MA 02141

Toll Free number 800-509-4128

TO ORDER Fax 781-662-9268 OR www.XAMonline.com

WEST SERIES

P0#   Store/School:

Address 1:

Address 2 (Ship to other):

City, State Zip

Credit card number_____-_____-_____-_____   expiration_____

EMAIL _____

PHONE   **FAX**

ISBN	TITLE	Qty	Retail	Total
978-1-58197-638-0	WEST-B Basic Skills		$27.95	
978-1-58197-609-0	WEST-E Biology 0235		$59.95	
978-1-58197-693-9	WEST-E Chemistry 0245		$59.95	
978-1-58197-566-6	WEST-E Designated World Language: French Sample Test 0173		$15.00	
978-1-58197-557-4	WEST-E Designated World Language: Spanish 0191		$59.95	
978-1-58197-614-4	WEST-E Elementary Education 0014		$28.95	
978-1-58197-636-6	WEST-E English Language Arts 0041		$59.95	
978-1-58197-634-2	WEST-E General Science 0435		$59.95	
978-1-58197-637-3	WEST-E Health & Fitness 0856		$59.95	
978-1-58197-635-9	WEST-E Library Media 0310		$59.95	
978-1-58197-674-8	WEST-E Mathematics 0061		$59.95	
978-1-58197-556-7	WEST-E Middle Level Humanities 0049, 0089		$59.95	
978-1-58197-043-2	WEST-E Physics 0265		$59.95	
978-1-58197-563-5	WEST-E Reading/Literacy 0300		$59.95	
978-1-58197-552-9	WEST-E Social Studies 0081		$59.95	
978-1-58197-639-7	WEST-E Special Education 0353		$73.50	
978-1-58197-633-5	WEST-E Visual Arts Sample Test 0133		$15.00	
978-1-60787-141-5	WEST-E History 027		$59.95	
	SUBTOTAL			
	1 book $8.25, 2 books, $11.00, 3+ books $15.00		**SHIP**	
	FOR PRODUCT PRICES VISIT WWW.XAMONLINE.COM		**TOTAL**	

CPSIA information can be obtained at www.ICGtesting.com
Printed in the USA
270572BV00003B/39/P